OHIO PRIDE

A Guide to Ohio Roadside History

by JEFF TRAYLOR
Author of *Life in the Slow Lane*

Backroad
Chronicles

Copyright 1990 by Jeff Traylor

Published and distributed by:

Backroad Chronicles
P.O. Box 292066
Columbus, Ohio 43229

Printed in New Washington, Ohio, U.S.A.
by Herald Printing Co., Inc.

ISBN 0-941467-04-X

To my beautiful wife, Nadean

PREFACE

As a boy growing up in the small town of Westerville, Ohio, I remember feeling proud when we would drive into town and pass our historical marker that proclaimed our town as "Home of Benjamin R. Hanby, Who Wrote Darling Nelly Gray." Admittedly, I knew very little about Benjamin R. Hanby, and I knew even less about his song. I also must admit to some feelings of jealousy when we would pass through other towns whose markers read "Colonel Crawford Fought His Last Indian Battle Near Here," or "Home of the Fighting McCooks of Civil War Fame." I didn't know much about those things either, but they just sounded more exciting than "Darling Nelly Gray."

Years later, while traveling the backroads of Ohio writing the *Life in the Slow Lane* books, I again became fascinated by the historical markers that greeted me at the edge of towns. Some were relatively self-explanatory, like "Geographical Center of Ohio," others less so (at least to an out-of-towner), such as "First Woman's Rights Convention Held Here in 1850" or "Birthplace of Paul Siple, Polar Explorer." Still others intrigued with words like "Home and Resting Place of Captain M.V. Bates' Family, Famed Ohio Giants" or "Mingo Indian Village Site Where George Washington Camped, 1770." Presidents, scientists, artists, educators, colleges, forts, religious sects, Indians, prehistoric mounds, underground streams, canals, and railroads are but a few of the subjects found on the hundreds of town markers throughout Ohio. Each marker was an invitation to explore a place and a time, and was like a trailhead leading into Ohio's past, often intersecting other trails and forming a mosaic that is the story of Ohio. This book, bringing together the inscriptions found on all 256 Ohio-shaped town historical markers with the stories behind them, weaves a tapestry of "Ohio Pride." And as for Benjamin R. Hanby, I am pleased to report that **three** Ohio towns boast of an association with him. I'm sorry I ever doubted you, Ben.

Jeff Traylor
Columbus, Ohio

INTRODUCTION

As part of Ohio's statehood sesquicentennial celebration in 1953, the Ohio legislature passed a bill authorizing the placement of historical markers at the corporation limits of towns along state highways. Communities that wished to participate in the program were invited to submit an application to the Ohio Historical Society for these "historic corporate limit markers," which were cast in the shape of the outline of the state of Ohio. Each qualifying community could submit up to sixteen words of text for the marker, describing an event, person, or other historical fact related to their town. Since the program's inception, communities from Aberdeen to Zoar have responded, and more than 250 Ohio towns have now received historic corporate limit markers.

Each community selected its own inscription to be displayed on their town's marker. Care was taken by the communities to provide accurate texts based on sound historical research, and this writer, in compiling the narratives that expand on the markers' texts, has likewise attempted to be as accurate as possible. The kind and generous assistance provided by historical societies, libraries, museums, and others is greatly appreciated, yet the author remains responsible for any errors.

A work such as this would not be possible without the help of many people. I would especially like to thank Ed Hoffman of Hoffman's Book Shop in Columbus for his careful reading of the manuscript and for allowing me access to the excellent collection of Ohio books in his store; to Tom Kuhn at the Ohio Historical Society and Charlotte Douthitt of Sewah Studios in Marietta for helping me compile the list of markers; and to my colleagues in the Ohio Authors Group for their support.

Finally, the reader is invited to use this book as an armchair guide to Ohio's past, or as a beginning point for exploring the Buckeye state in person. 1-800-BUCKEYE stands ready to provide the traveler with information concerning sites, museums, and other attractions associated with Ohio history.

CONTENTS

ILLUSTRATIONS*

*Unless otherwise noted, illustrations are from Henry Howe's *Historical Collections of Ohio*, 1889.

Aberdeen

**OHIO RIVER TERMINUS
OF ZANE'S TRACE**

First Continuous Road
Through Ohio,
1798

ABERDEEN (Brown County)

Ebenezer Zane knew as well as anyone the dangers of travel on the Ohio River. Although it was the best transportation route available from his town at Wheeling down to Kentucky, the river, with its snags and wintertime ice floes, was a fickle friend to many travelers familiar only with small streams and creeks. Zane, an experienced trail blazer and town founder, saw the need for an overland route from Wheeling to Limestone, Kentucky, the gateway to the Bluegrass Country. He knew that an old twisting Indian path snaked through the Ohio Country to a place on the Ohio River opposite Limestone, and he determined to make a "road" of the old Indian trail.

Zane sought federal help for building the road, and in May, 1796, received authorization from Congress to build a road from Wheeling to Limestone (now Maysville). This road, however, was little more than a forest pathway, intended to be passable for men on horseback. Zane, along with his brother and son-in-law, experienced woodsmen all, cleared the trail, lopping limbs off of trees with double-bladed hand axes; widening of the road would be left to future wagoneers trying to make their way through the forest. In exchange for his services, Zane asked that Congress grant him land at each of three places where his road had to cross a river. He was an astute businessman, for in the ensuing years, the towns of Zanesville, Lancaster, and Chillicothe sprung up where the road crossed the Muskingum, Hocking, and Scioto Rivers.

Today, the Ohio River town of Aberdeen marks the southern end of the first continuous road through Ohio, the famous Zane's Trace.

1

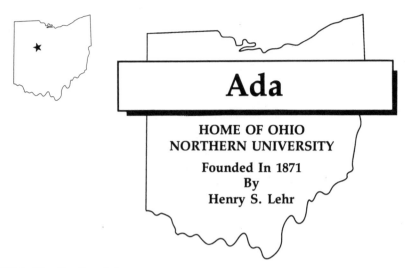

Ada

HOME OF OHIO NORTHERN UNIVERSITY
Founded In 1871
By
Henry S. Lehr

ADA (Hardin County)

Following his discharge from the Union Army after the Civil War, schoolteacher Henry Solomon Lehr came to Ada in 1866 to teach in the village schools. Distressed at the poor quality of teacher education he had found upon his discharge, he entered into a unique arrangement in Ada to remedy the problem. Receiving permission to use the empty school buildings during vacation, he secured an agreement whereby if he was able to attract a sufficient number of students wishing to be trained as teachers, the community would erect a permanent building where Lehr could continue such training. He attracted 120 students, and in 1871 the Northwestern Ohio Normal School opened in Ada. As a "normal school," it was dedicated to "training teachers in the science of education."

Mr. Lehr believed that financial considerations should not bar young people of moderate means from pursuing higher education, so he opened his doors to students who were unable to find educational opportunities elsewhere. In 1885 the school was chartered as Ohio Normal University, and was taken over by the Methodist Episcopal Church in 1898. In 1904, the school was renamed Ohio Northern University.

Today, Ohio Northern University is a four year liberal arts college with an enrollment of about 2,500 students. The university offers degrees to the doctorate level, and boasts among its graduates two U.S. senators, Frank B. Willis and Simeon D. Fess.

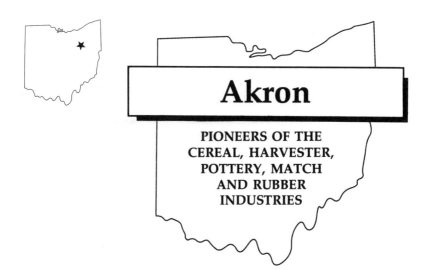

Akron

**PIONEERS OF THE
CEREAL, HARVESTER,
POTTERY, MATCH
AND RUBBER
INDUSTRIES**

AKRON (Summit County)

About the only boast Akron leaves off its town marker is "pioneer of the canal industry," yet it was the Ohio & Erie Canal that gave birth to Akron, the summit of the little "silver ribbon." The water power supplied by the canal attracted the early grist mills, which led to the creation of Akron's flouring industry. In 1863, Ferdinand Schumacher built the Empire Barley Mill, the first of Akron's great cereal mills, supplying the Union Army and founding the American breakfast cereal industry. His string of mills eventually became the Quaker Oats Company. An inventive genius, Schumacher invented the machine that cracked the hulls of cereal grains to make rolled oats, and developed a system of "pneumatic levitation" to blow his cereal through miles of pipes from one mill location to another.

A few years after Schumacher built his first mill, Dr. Benjamin Franklin Goodrich of Melrose, New York read a promotional pamphlet about Akron, Ohio, and decided to move there. Arriving in 1870, he managed to sell nineteen Akronites on the idea of investing $1,000 each to start a factory to make fire hoses and other rubber products. In the gay nineties, bicycle and buggy owners began clamoring for the pneumatic tires that were used on a sulky to break speed records in Detroit, and shortly thereafter the rubber industry was off to the races. Although also noted for the manufacture of farm machinery, fine kitchen crockery, and matches (see Barberton), for the next 100 years the words rubber and Akron would be synonymous.

3

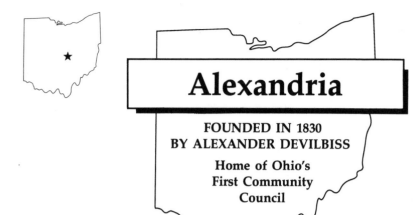

Alexandria

FOUNDED IN 1830
BY ALEXANDER DEVILBISS

Home of Ohio's
First Community
Council

ALEXANDRIA *(Licking County)*

Alexander Devilbiss was born in Maryland in 1780 into a slaveholding family. The Devilbisses had extensive land holdings, and operated a mill on their plantation. When the elder Devilbiss died in 1813, his son Alexander inherited the mills and slaves. Eventually, the practice of slaveholding clashed with Alexander's religious beliefs, and in 1819 he liberated his slaves, sold his property, and headed west to Ohio. The Devilbiss family crossed the Alleghenies in a covered wagon, and forty days later reached Licking County, Ohio, where he purchased land in the Raccoon bottoms. He built a mill, just as his forefathers had done in Maryland, and soon his enterprise had become a community center. In 1830, Alexander Devilbiss laid out the village of Alexandria on his own land, but he was to die only one year later. He was buried according to his wishes on land that overlooked his mill in the Raccoon Valley. Today, there is nothing left of the old graveyard, as it has been obliterated over the years.

Alexandria continued to grow following its founder's death, and in 1930, as an outgrowth of planning the community's centennial, the Alexandria Community Council was born as "a device whereby representatives of as many forces as possible may be brought together for a cooperative discussion of community welfare," the first such organization in Ohio. Fittingly enough, one of the first improvements initiated by the group was the erection of a monument to Alexander Devilbiss one hundred years after he laid out the village of Alexandria.

4

Alliance

THE "CARNATION CITY"

Home of
Ohio State Flower
The Scarlet
Carnation

ALLIANCE *(Stark County)*

Ohio has a number of "official" emblems, including a state bird, the cardinal; a state tree, the buckeye; a state fossil, the trilobite; and a state flower, the carnation. Often in the wake of tragedy, a mourning people memorializes a fallen leader by naming a holiday, building, or boulevard in his honor, and that is how the scarlet carnation came to be Ohio's state flower.

William McKinley, born in Niles, made his home in Canton, from where he launched a successful front porch campaign for the presidency. He was a gentle man, and generally exhibited the qualities of patience and kindness in keeping with his deep religious faith. His good luck piece was a scarlet carnation, developed by Levi Lamborn of Alliance, and it became a McKinley trademark.

In 1901, just a few months into his second term, President McKinley was visiting the Pan American Exposition at Buffalo. In the line of well-wishers greeting the president was a man with a small concealed handgun who fired twice, mortally wounding McKinley. In an outpouring of rage, the assassin, Leo Czolgosz, was tried, executed and his remains were dissolved in sulfuric acid in a New York prison yard. And in an outpouring of affection and mourning, the Ohio General Assembly made McKinley's beloved scarlet carnation the official state flower "as a token of love and reverence for the memory of William McKinley."

Amelia

**HOME OF
CHARLES CYRUS KEARNS
Congressman,
1915-1931**

AMELIA *(Clermont County)*

Amelia, located just south of Batavia, the county seat, was the home of eight-term Congressman Charles Cyrus Kearns. Kearns was born on a farm in Tonica, LaSalle County, Illinois on February 11, 1869, and at the age of five moved to Ohio with his parents. Raised in the Brown County community of Georgetown, Kearns attended public school before going on to Ohio Northern University in Ada and the Lebanon College at Lebanon, Ohio. He graduated from the Cincinnati Law School and was admitted to the bar in 1894, and began the practice of law at Batavia.

Mr. Kearns practiced law for a few years, then headed to Las Vegas, New Mexico to serve as the managing editor of the *Las Vegas (N.M.) Daily Record* in 1900-01. Another two year stint as editor of the *Hot Springs (Ark.) Daily Record* followed, and in 1903 Kearns returned to Batavia to resume his law practice. He made a successful bid for the office of county prosecutor in 1906, and won reelection in 1908. In 1914, Charles Kearns was elected as the sixth district's representative to the Sixty-fourth Congress of the United States.

Kearns proved to be a popular choice among not only his fellow Republicans, but also enjoyed the good will of Democrats. Elected to Congress eight times, Kearns served as a friend and advisor to President Harding and was a member of the Ways and Means Committee. After finally being defeated in 1930 after sixteen years in Congress, Kearns returned to his home in Amelia and practiced law in Cincinnati. On December 17, 1931, Mr. Kearns died following a sudden illness, and was interred in Mount Moriah Cemetery in Tobasco, Ohio.

6

Amesville

**SALE OF PELTS FINANCED
THE FOUNDING OF THE
FAMED COONSKIN
LIBRARY HERE,
1804**

AMESVILLE *(Athens County)*

Frontier life is generally thought of as being rough and coarse, with the struggle for survival leaving little time for the "finer things" in life. But in Ames Township in Athens County in 1804, a group of settlers came together at a public meeting to address another pressing issue - the lack of books in their community, and the lack of funds with which to purchase books for a library.

In pioneer Ohio, money was virtually unknown to many settlers, and business was conducted on a barter basis. It was therefore decided that barter would be the best way to secure books. The resources of Amesville included the hunting skills of its citizens and the game that abounded in the woods, so when Samuel Brown left on a business trip to the east, he took with him the wolf and coonskins collected by Amesville's people. When he reached Boston, Mr. Brown sold his furs to agents of fur trader and financier John Jacob Astor, and with the assistance of Rev. Manasseh Cutler, used the money to secure books for the settlers back home. Fifty-one cherished volumes comprised that first little library, which was given the formal name of the Western Library Association. But to the people of Amesville, it was simply called the Coonskin Library. Today, the Coonskin Library reposes at the Ohio Historical Center in Columbus.

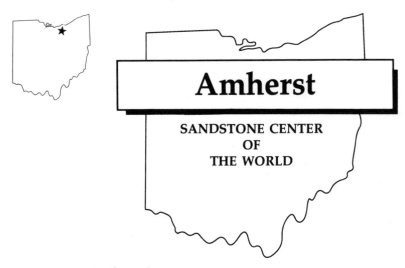

Amherst

**SANDSTONE CENTER
OF
THE WORLD**

AMHERST (*Lorain County*)

Sandstone has played an important role in northern Ohio for centuries, dating back long before the arrival of the white man. In prehistoric times, the sandstone which overlaid soft shale formed projecting ledges, creating grottos which sheltered man and beast. Excavations into the floors of these domiciles have unearthed charcoal, ashes, and the bones of bear, deer, wolf, and birds. The sandstone was not always protective, however, as excavators also found in one of these caves the skeletons of three prehistoric Indians crushed thousands of years earlier by a falling sandstone slab.

In the early nineteenth century settlers found other uses for the beautiful stone of the region, and Amherst grew up with the quarrying industry. The stone was considered to be of an exceptional quality and nearly inexhaustible. The layers had a good bed-seam that allowed them to be quarried separately, depending on their purpose. The best layers were reserved for the making of grindstones, which required a smooth, even surface, while other layers were used for building purposes. The latter material was called Amherst building stone, and was known as the best stone in the world for that purpose.

Hundreds of men toiled in the pits, assisted by the power of steam, swinging huge slabs of stone on derricks up from the floor of the quarry onto rail cars or into the saw-mill for cutting. The massive blocks were sent forth to all parts of the country and Canada, and the beautiful Amherst building stone was used in the building of the Canadian Parliament at Ottawa, the Michigan State Capitol at Lansing, and the old Post Office in Columbus.

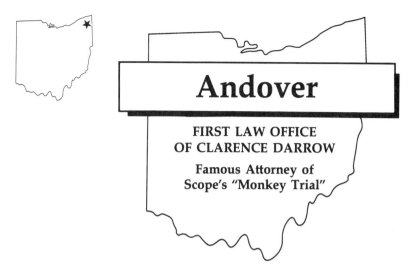

Andover

**FIRST LAW OFFICE
OF CLARENCE DARROW**

Famous Attorney of
Scope's "Monkey Trial"

ANDOVER (Ashtabula County)

"You can only protect your liberties in this world by protecting the other man's freedom. You can only be free if I am free." These words belong to one of America's greatest lawyers, Clarence Darrow, born in an octagon house in Kinsman, Ohio, and later practicing attorney in Andover and Ashtabula. In one of the most celebrated cases in American jurisprudence, Darrow served as attorney for John T. Scopes, the defendant in "The Scopes Monkey Trial."

The year was 1925, and in the sweltering heat of Dayton, Tennessee, Darrow squared off against William Jennings Bryan to defend the right of a school teacher to teach evolution in public school. The fundamentalist-dominated state legislature in Tennessee had passed a law forbidding the teaching of any "theory that denies the Divine Creation as taught in the Bible, and to teach instead that man has descended from a lower order of animals." Scopes, dedicated to personal and religious freedom as guaranteed by the Constitution, volunteered to test the law.

The trial took place in a circus-like atmosphere, with the attention of the nation drawn to the courtroom. The tone was set when the trial opened, over Darrow's objections, with a prayer. At the trial's end, a decidedly unpopular Darrow rose to give his summation, saying, in part, that "if you make it a crime to teach evolution in the public school... at the next session you may ban books and newspapers. Soon you may set Catholic against Protestant and Protestant against Protestant, and try to foist your own religion upon the minds of men." The jury, described by newspaperman H.L. Mencken as "unanimously hot for Genesis," returned the expected guilty verdict. Darrow had lost the battle, but as it turned out, won the war. The law was not again enforced, and was officially repealed in 1967.

Clarence Darrow died in 1938.

Antwerp

HOME OF
OTTO E. EHRHART,
NATURALIST

ANTWERP (Paulding County)

August 19, 1965 is a special day in Antwerp history, for on that day the governor of Ohio was present to formally dedicate a museum in this small Paulding County village. The governor's appearance marked only the second time that a chief executive of the state had visited Antwerp, the first being Gov. Foraker in 1889 in connection with a local insurrection that involved the destruction of canal lands. This second visit, by Gov. James Rhodes, was to honor the memory of Antwerp naturalist Otto E. Ehrhart.

Otto E. Ehrhart was born in Germany in 1884. As a schoolboy, young Otto was impressed by a schoolteacher who lectured on wildlife while displaying mounted specimens of birds, and when he came to America as a young boy, he carried this love of nature with him. Otto worked alongside his father planting onions and potatoes on their Paulding County farm, learning the lessons of man's interdependence with the soil and the animals. Insects, butterflies, birds, and reptiles all held a great fascination for Otto, and he began collecting specimens of the various species.

In 1906, Otto married and bought a portrait studio, but this did little to interfere with his first love. To the Ehrhart home in Antwerp came a number of distinguished naturalists to view Otto's expanding collection, including such notables as Professor Mosely of Bowling Green University and Robert Conant, the renowned reptile authority who recognized Ehrhart in his *Reptiles of Ohio*. Ehrhart's collection eventually reached upwards of 500 mounted birds, 7,000 insects, 1,200 bird eggs, and a large number of snakes and mammals, becoming Ohio's largest natural history collection collected by an individual.

Otto E. Ehrhart died on May 15, 1963, leaving his celebrated collection to his townspeople. Today, visitors to Antwerp continue to be fascinated by the Otto E. Ehrhart Museum in the Antwerp City Hall.

Ashland

**HOME OF
ASHLAND COLLEGE
Founded
1878**

ASHLAND (Ashland County)

The area where Ashland now stands was largely wilderness in the early 1800's, frequented by Indians and a wiry, bearded eccentric who roamed barefooted, preaching and planting apple orchards. Into this land came Daniel Carter in 1811, and his log cabin became the first dwelling in this part of the forest. Four years later a town was laid out and named Uniontown, nestled along the stage line that brought settlers from New England. Uniontown was renamed Ashland in 1822 in honor of Henry Clay's Ashland estate in Kentucky.

Johnny Appleseed, whose real name was John Chapman, was perhaps the first to introduce what was considered to be "peculiar" religious doctrine here, but he was not the last. While Chapman was spreading the gospel according to Emmanuel Swendenborg, a group of German Baptists, officially known as the Church of the Brethren, was spreading west from Pennsylvania with their New Testament message and rituals. The Brethren practiced foot washing and the love feast, and their ritual of baptism which involved dunking the initiate three times face first earned them the name "Dunkards." Emphasizing the simple life, abstinence from worldly pleasures, and pacifism, the Church of the Brethren gained a foothold in Ashland County, and in 1878 they chartered Ashland College.

The college had as its major objective the training of ministers for the Brethren Church, but after only three years a split in the church put the school into jeopardy. The progressive branch of the denomination rescued the school and chartered it as Ashland University in 1888. The college "was hindered by adverse sentiment" in its early days, but went on to establish "collegiate, preparatory, normal, commercial, and musical departments," and by 1905 fourteen faculty members served two hundred students.

Today, Ashland College, still affiliated with the Church of the Brethren, is a four year coeducational liberal arts school offering degrees up to the Masters level. It has an enrollment of about 4,000 students.

11

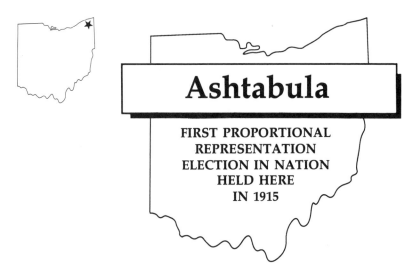

Ashtabula

**FIRST PROPORTIONAL
REPRESENTATION
ELECTION IN NATION
HELD HERE
IN 1915**

ASHTABULA (Ashtabula County)

Political machines and bosses had dominated the scene in the closing decades of the nineteenth century, but the dawning of the twentieth century brought with it a progressive era characterized by political reform. In Ohio, the "Home Rule" amendment gave the people the right to form and adopt charters prescribing the rules for their city government. This amendment, coupled with a desire for wider political participation, set the stage for a new system called proportional representation, or "P.R."

Mr. C. G. Hoag, a Philadelphia Quaker and member of the P.R. League, brought the P.R. message to Ashtabula in 1913. He argued that the old "winner take all" system was unfair to minority parties and perpetuated machine politics. He urged the adoption of a system that would allow representation on council of all views, with the number of seats apportioned mathematically among parties according to the number of votes their candidates polled. For example, in a district electing five members, the party that polled three-fifths of the vote would get three seats, a party drawing one-fifth would get one seat, etc.

In 1915, the issue was on the ballot in Ashtabula, and in a light voter turnout, it carried by a vote of 558-440, making the city the first in the country to adopt P.R. The drys and wets, the Protestants and Catholics, the business, professional, and laboring men, the English, Swedes and Italians - all were represented after the first P.R. election. The system was adopted by twenty more U.S. cities in the early 20th century, but it was not without opposition. "Unworkable, disorderly, and irresponsible," "a glorified opinion poll," "a census, not a consensus," decried its critics. By 1950, P.R. was largely abandoned as a political system in the United States.

Athens

**HOME OF
OHIO UNIVERSITY**

First University
In The
Northwest Territory

ATHENS (Athens County)

"The Ohio University, the oldest college in Ohio, is situated here, but has temporarily suspended its operations, for the purpose of recovering from pecuniary embarrassment. It was first chartered by the territorial government, and afterwards, in 1804, by the state legislature. It was early endowed by Congress with the two townships of Athens and Alexander, containing 46,000 acres of land, which, with the connecting resources, yield an annual income of about $5,000. The buildings are substantial and neat, and stand in a pleasant green. This institution has exerted a most beneficial influence upon the morals and intelligence of this region. Among its graduates are many who do it honor, and it will, doubtless, when again in successful operation - as it soon will be - continue its good work."
- Henry Howe, *Historical Collections of Ohio,* 1847.

Ohio University has lived up to Howe's prophecy, and today over 900 faculty members serve more than 15,000 students on the Athens campus. Degrees up to the doctorate level are awarded by Ohio University.

Bainbridge

**HOME OF
FIRST DENTAL SCHOOL
IN THE
UNITED STATES**

BAINBRIDGE *(Ross County)*

In the early years of the nineteenth century, aspiring dentists often learned their skills from itinerant dentists passing through the area. One such aspirant was Dr. John Harris, who lived in Madison and learned his skills from dentists traveling to nearby Cincinnati.

In 1825, Dr. Harris opened a dental and medical practice in Bainbridge, and shortly thereafter announced the opening of a school for teaching dentistry. The little one-story brick building where the class was held became the nation's first dental school, and earned for Bainbridge the sobriquet "Cradle of American Dentistry." The little school sent forth such notables as Chapin A. Harris, editor of the first issue of the *American Journal of Dental Science* and the founder in 1840 of one of the world's first dental colleges at Baltimore; James Taylor, who established the Ohio College of Dental Surgery at Cincinnati in 1845; and Wesley Sampler, who pulled the first tooth Abraham Lincoln ever had extracted by a dentist.

The building on Main Street that housed that first dental school has been restored as a museum, a fitting memorial to these early pioneers of dentistry.

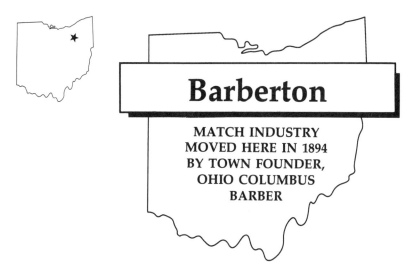

Barberton

MATCH INDUSTRY
MOVED HERE IN 1894
BY TOWN FOUNDER,
OHIO COLUMBUS
BARBER

BARBERTON *(Summit County)*

Ohio Columbus Barber was destined for extravagance from the moment he was named, and the flamboyance of his name was indeed matched by the colorfulness of his life. Born the son of an itinerant matchmaker who peddled his own matches, O.C. Barber grew to become the "Match King," the owner of Diamond Match Company, and the founder of the town to which he gave his name.

Barber organized the Diamond Match Company in 1880, and eleven years later, from his extensive land options, laid out the town he called Barberton. He successfully promoted his new town by making generous offers of land to industries, and the ensuing demand for labor in the factories, including his own, attracted residents. In its heyday, Diamond Match Company produced a quarter billion matches a day. Barber retired as president of his company in 1913, and embarked on a venture known locally as "Barber's Folly." Spending extravagantly on his Anna Dean Farm, he poured hundreds of thousands of dollars into a manor house with marble floors and rich tapestries, barns where cattle and horses lived in luxury, and the feeding of laboratory-tested food to 75,000 Pekin ducks who dined at the Barberton Reservoir.

Ohio Columbus Barber died in 1920, and shortly thereafter came the collapse of his empire.

Barnesville

BARNESVILLE *(Belmont County)*

Warren, the township in which Barnesville is situated, was first settled in 1800 by George Shannon, the father of Wilson Shannon, Ohio governor from 1838-40. Other settlers, mostly Quakers from Pennsylvania, North Carolina, and Maryland, soon followed, and in 1808 James Barnes, a Quaker from Maryland, founded Barnesville. Barnesville prospered as a tobacco producer in the 1800's, but it was its strawberry production that put it on the agricultural map in the last quarter of the century. Shipping its "Sharpless" variety to distant cities, the fame of the Barnesville strawberries was purported to have spread "so far as Russia."

As in any town with a prosperous economy, the banks also flourished. While Barnesville still boasts of a large number of historic homes and mansions built during the last years of the preceding century, none surpasses the "Gay '90's Mansion" built by the Bradfield family, owners of the First National Bank at the turn of the century. Now the home of the Belmont County Museum, the Bradfield home was a stunning showpiece of elegance with twenty-six rooms encompassing 11,400 square feet. Described as both Romanesque and Queen Anne in style and sporting a striking turret, the building took five years to build, commencing in 1888 and costing an estimated $60,000. The mansion became the center of social life in Barnesville, with guests congregating around fireplaces adorned with hand carved butternut mantels. A solid oak staircase led the visitors to the third floor, where parties and dances were held in the ballroom. The trim, ranging from the decorative door hinges to the leather wainscot crowned by copper and oak, was typical of the Bradfields' taste for elaborate homes.

Over the years, the mansion fell into disrepair, and when the Historical Society purchased it in 1966, it was in a severe stage of neglect. Now handsomely restored to its original appearance, the mansion again hosts visitors who wish to glimpse the elegance of days gone by.

16

Batavia

HEADQUARTERS OF
THE BATAVIA
GOLD MINING
COMPANY,
1868

BATAVIA *(Clermont County)*

While Batavia stakes a claim to the Batavia Gold Mining Company, established in 1868, it could also boast of a second gold mine, but, alas, the Batavia Gold Mining Company was the bigger loser of the two failed ventures, and so earned a place on the town's historical marker.

It was just a few years after the Civil War that glittering flecks of gold were discovered in "them thar hills" of Batavia. No matter that they turned out to be traces of gold in pieces of mica, and could never be profitably mined, would-be golddiggers descended upon this isolated region, creating an "Eldorado panic." Five speculators, including a state senator, set out to raise $5,000 by selling $100 shares of stock. They expended $3,000 before the venture collapsed (the other company spent a paltry $100, so is destined for obscurity).

In more recent years, a dam on Elk Lick has flooded the banks where the gold mine stood, staking the final claim on Batavia's golden past.

Bedford

**BIRTHPLACE OF
ARCHIBALD M. WILLARD,
1836-1918,**

Painter of
"The Spirit of '76"

BEDFORD *(Cuyahoga County)*

(Please see Wellington, Ohio.)

18

BELLAIRE *(Belmont County)*

Jacob Heatherington was born in England in 1814, and when but a child of seven years was put to work in a coal mine, having never spent a day in school. In 1837, twenty-three years old, illiterate, and living in America, he rented a coal-bank from Capt. Mike Fink, the famed riverboat man, and purchased eight acres of land on credit.

Jake began wheeling out his coal with a wheelbarrow at first, and eventually took in a four-legged partner named Jack, his faithful mule. Jack was a small mule, only three and a half feet high, and utterly devoted to Jake. The steady efforts of Jake and Jack led to a great increase in Jake's fortune, and his eight acres became eight hundred. He owned steamboats and shares in glass works, and in 1870 he built the famed Jacob Heatherington Mansion, which he dedicated to the memory of Jack. "The House that Jack Built," he called it, saying that without the tireless efforts of his faithful mule he could never have achieved his dreams. Over the doorway projected a likeness of Jack. When the mansion was completed, Jake took his now retired old friend through the house, gratefully showing him its splendor and talking to him as if to another man. Jack died shortly thereafter at the age of forty years, and Jake, whose grief was indescribable, buried the little mule, now white with age, near the house beneath an apple tree.

Today, Jake's beautiful mansion is gone, having been razed in recent years to make room for an addition to the Shady Belle Motel.

19

Bellefontaine

FIRST
CONCRETE STREET
IN AMERICA
BUILT HERE
1891

BELLEFONTAINE *(Logan County)*

As the 1800's drew to a close, there were about two million miles of poorly kept roads in America. Almost all of these roads were unsurfaced and unsuitable for traffic, which was, with the exception of a few new-fangled automobiles, mostly horse-drawn buggies and bicycles. The bicycling craze was just getting underway, propelled in large part by the introduction of the "safety bike," a bike with a chain-driven rear wheel, brakes, and rubber tires. The safety bike replaced the dangerous "ordinary" that had a huge front wheel and tiny rear wheel. Bicycle clubs, chief among them the League of American Wheelmen, sprang up throughout the country, and these organizations, in addition to providing group rides for social purposes, pressed for better roads.

Into this arena stepped the enterprising Buckeye Cement Company that operated a limestone pit north of Bellefontaine. In 1891, they laid an eight foot strip of concrete along Main Street where horses were hitched, and two years later paved around the court house as a demonstration of the usefulness of concrete in road building. The road attracted engineers from across the country, and in 1893 a block from the street was exhibited at the World's Fair in Chicago, earning a gold medal. When Bellefontaine held a Golden Jubilee celebration fifty years after the street was laid, the Postmaster General authorized a special commemorative cachet for use on letters mailed from Bellefontaine on June 13, 1941, and a marker was unveiled that proclaimed, "Here started the better roads movement." Today, parts of that original concrete street are still uncovered and have been in continual use for a century.

Bellevue

**BUILT OVER
SUBTERRANEAN
STREAMS**

BELLEVUE *(Huron/Sandusky Counties)*

Bellevue is located at the junction of four counties, Huron, Sandusky, Erie and Seneca, and it also straddles the western border of the Western Reserve. Noted as a former rail center, it was the terminus of two grand divisions of the "Nickel-plate railway" that ran between Buffalo and Chicago, and as such was the home of roundhouses and repair shops. Today, the town's rail history can be seen in the local train museum, and occasional excursions powered by the old steam engines still depart from Bellevue. But it is not Bellevue's rail history that is mentioned on its marker - it is the town's location above underground streams that informs the traveler passing through town.

In selecting the inscription for Bellevue's historical marker, much debate ensued as to whether the description was geologically correct. While the term "stream" is not totally accurate, neither was the alternative term "fissure." For the sake of simplicity it was finally decided to use the term "subterranean streams" to describe the water-bearing rock strata below.

Before the installation of modern sewer systems, the town disposed of its sewage through sinkholes that honeycombed the area, leading to the underground streams. However, during times of heavy rain, the streams would back up, creating geysers and flooding the low-lying parts of the city. At those times, "rain, rain, go away" was an especially plaintive plea from the citizenry of Bellevue.

Belpre

SETTLED 1789.

First Library
In Ohio Country
Established Here,
1796

BELPRE *(Washington County)*

For many years the famed Coonskin Library of Athens County was believed to be the first library in the Northwest Territory. And while the history of that library is quite colorful, it had to surrender its claim as the first library in the Ohio Country to the Belpre Library of Washington County. The circulating collection of books in Belpre dates back to the late 1790's, and has borne the names "Belpre Library," "Belpre Farmers' Library," and the "Putnam Library." The latter name is in honor of Gen. Israel Putnam, from whose family library the first books came.

When Gen. Putnam passed away in 1790, the family library was split among his heirs, including Col. Israel Putnam, who brought his books to Belpre in 1795. Among the volumes in the Belpre Library were Locke's *Essays on Human Understanding*, Johnson's *Lives of the English Poets,* and Goldsmith's *Animated Nature.* The books were divided among the shareholders upon the dissolution of the library in 1815-16.

Berlin

**BIRTHPLACE OF
ATLEE POMERENE**

United States
Senator
1911-23

BERLIN *(Holmes County)*

Atlee Pomerene was born in Berlin, Ohio on December 6, 1863. He attended Vermillion Institute in Hayesville, and went on to graduate from Princeton in 1884. Two years later, he graduated from the Cincinnati Law School and was admitted to the bar.

Atlee Pomerene's ability and integrity gained the notice of Cleveland's famed reform mayor Tom Johnson, who persuaded him to enter politics. In 1910 he was elected lieutenant governor, and shortly thereafter the general assembly elected him to the U.S. Senate. In 1916, he was reelected by popular vote.

Pomerene's integrity and honesty again attracted the confidence of others, and in 1924 President Coolidge appointed him as special counsel to investigate the corruption in the Harding administration. In one of the government's most famous cases, Pomerene was able to have oil leases that had been turned over improperly to the oil companies cancelled. The leases in question were the Elk Hills Reserve and the Teapot Dome Reserve, the latter giving its name to one of the country's biggest scandals. Albert Fall, Harding's secretary of the interior, was convicted as a result of this litigation, and was fined and sentenced to a year and a day in the penitentiary.

Pomerene was considered one of the best constitutional lawyers of his time, possessing a keenness of mind and a devotion to moral principles. He died in Cleveland on Nov. 12, 1937.

Bethel

HOME OF U.S. SENATOR
THOMAS MORRIS

Advocate of
Human Liberty
1776-1844

BETHEL *(Clermont County)*

The 1830's in Ohio saw the proliferation of antislavery societies throughout the state, especially local chapters of the American Antislavery Society and its state affiliate, the Ohio Antislavery Society. By the end of the decade more than 200 antislavery societies flourished within the state. These local chapters were active not only on a local basis, but were also effective on a national level. After 1836, one of their most successful tactics was to have petitions opposing slavery introduced by Congressmen sympathetic to their cause. One of the first legislators in Washington to introduce such a petition was Sen. Thomas Morris, a Democrat from Brown County and ardent antislavery man, who believed that slavery "was wrong, in principle, in practice, in every country and under every condition of things," and was a libel upon America's republican institutions.

The reading of antislavery petitions in the Senate caused a firestorm of protest from slave-state senators, who attempted to stifle such expression. Ultimately, the petitions were presented and then tabled. Over in the House, a veritable gag rule was imposed against such expression, where anitslavery petitions were tabled without so much as a reading until 1844. Sen. Morris's early opposition to the pro-slavery sentiments of John C. Calhoun and Henry Clay cost him his political career when the Ohio legislature chose someone else for his office in December, 1838.

Sen. Thomas Morris died December 7, 1844, and was buried in the historic Early Settlers Burying Ground in Bethel. He reposes beneath a marble monument that reads "Thomas Morris, Late U.S. Senator, Unawed by power and uninfluenced by flattery, he was through life the fearless advocate of human Liberty."

Bexley

**HOME OF
CAPITAL UNIVERSITY
SINCE 1876**

BEXLEY *(Franklin County)*

The first quarter of the nineteenth century was marked by the rapid influx of settlers into the West, drawn by the promise of new lands opening up in Ohio. With the Indian Wars and the War of 1812 past, the business of settlement was proceeding in earnest. One of the major groups to immigrate to Ohio was the Germans, and the Evangelical Lutheran Synod of Ohio quite early saw the need to train pastors to minister to these new arrivals. In 1828, Rev. William Schmidt began instructing six students in his home at Canton, thereby beginning the German Evangelical Lutheran Seminary, the forerunner of Capital University. At the time, there were only two other such seminaries in the entire country. In 1831, the seminary was moved to Columbus, and within two years its new building on the south side of town was opened to students.

The seminary stayed on its fourteen acre campus until 1850, when it moved near Goodale Park on the city's north side. Capital University had just been incorporated, and the seminary became part of the university. Capital University thus began as a literary and theological institution under the auspices of the Lutheran Church. The university remained near Goodale Park until 1876, when it moved to its present location in Bexley, three miles east of the state capitol.

Today, Capital University is a four year private liberal arts college with an enrollment of about 3,000 students. The school offers degree programs up to the doctorate level.

Bloomingburg

FOUNDED 1815
BY SOLOMON BOWERS

Site of One of
Ohio's First
Academies

BLOOMINGBURG *(Fayette County)*

When George Coil built his cabin in 1803 at what is now Paint Township, the land was unbroken forest, inhabited only by Indians. In spite of the fears that drove other early settlers away, Coil stayed on, and a dozen years later Solomon Bowers platted a village here which would grow into Bloomingburg. The village in its earliest days was called New Lexington, then later New Purchase. Mathew Gillespie, a local storekeeper, was responsible for the name being changed to Bloomingburg, the name of his hometown in New York. Gillespie pressed into service a commonly used frontier device for getting all kinds of goals accomplished, from clearing trees to erecting cabins - he bought everyone a drink if they would do it! And so the men of the village agreed to his request to change the name of their town, and on Feb. 5, 1847, the Ohio legislature officially named the village Bloomingburg.

The Bloomingburg Academy Association was formed in 1863, the result of the will of Col. James Stewart, a veteran of the War of 1812. In his will he left $2,000 for the building of an academy, if an equal amount of money could be raised from other sources. After raising the money, the plans for the academy were delayed by the Civil War, but at the war's close the doors to the Bloomingburg Academy were proudly thrown open. The academy, like other academies of the day, was more like a high school and drew most of its students from the immediate vicinity. It lasted only about ten years, and in 1877 it was transformed into a normal school for the training of teachers. A few years later it became a three year high school. In 1909, the building was condemned and torn down, eventually to be replaced by the Bloomingburg School.

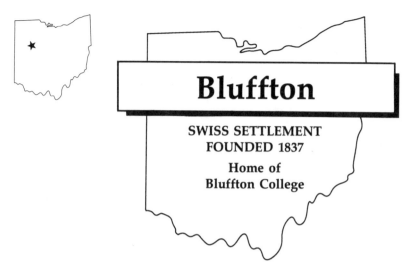

Bluffton

SWISS SETTLEMENT
FOUNDED 1837

Home of
Bluffton College

BLUFFTON *(Allen County)*

Bluffton, a progressive community of 3,000 situated in a prosperous agricultural area, was founded in 1837 as Shannon. With many of its residents of Swiss Mennonite descent, it changed its name to Bluffton after a Mennonite community of that name in Indiana. Today, Bluffton is home of Bluffton College, the only college in Ohio under the direction of the Mennonite Church.

Bluffton College was begun in 1899 as Central Mennonite College to educate the young people of the Middle District of the General Conference Mennonite Church. Several Mennonite groups in the United States and Canada joined in the support of the school, with a purpose "to provide a Christian higher education in harmony with the principles of faith and the way of life as conceived by Mennonites since the Reformation." The school grew from what was basically an academy in its earliest days to a college, and in 1914 it reorganized as Bluffton College. One year later it awarded its first baccalaureate degree.

Today, Bluffton College is a private four year liberal arts college with an undergraduate student enrollment of about 600. It is open to all students without regard to religious affiliation, and about 20% of the students are Mennonite. College Hall, erected in 1900, is still in use, and the library houses Swiss Mennonite material that draws scholars from across the country. The college takes its motto from the words of Christ: "The truth makes free."

Bolivar

NAMED FOR
SIMON BOLIVAR,
SOUTH AMERICAN LIBERATOR.

Site of Ohio's Only
American Revolutionary
Fort 1778

BOLIVAR *(Tuscarawas County)*

In the summer of 1986, an archaeologist and several volunteers unearthed the bones of twelve soldiers who had been hurriedly buried in a mass grave on March 28, 1799. They had been killed in an Indian attack almost a month before their burial, but fear of further Indian depredations kept the other soldiers safely within the confines of Fort Laurens. The skull of at least one of the soldiers bore tomahawk marks, but the expected skeletons of wolves, who according to legend had fed on the bodies and were then killed and tossed into the grave, were not found.

Fort Laurens was built in November 1778 by 1200 troops under the command of Gen. Lachlan McIntosh. The soldiers came from companies of the 8th Pennsylvania Regiment, the 13th/9th Virginia Infantry Regiment, and the North Carolina Dragoons. It was called "Fort Nonsense" by the men, as it was built as a base for attacks on a British fort at Detroit, an attack that was never mounted. The fort was besieged by British and Indians, and the 150 men garrisoned at the fort under the command of Col. John Gibson nearly starved.

With the fort's intended purpose never realized, it was abandoned August 10, 1779. Although it saw only limited action, it actually helped win the Ohio Country for the United States following the end of the war. Fort Laurens, Ohio's only Revolutionary fort, strengthened America's claim to the land north and west of the Ohio River. Today, the ground where Fort Laurens stood is a state historical site and home to America's only "Tomb of the Unknown Revolutionary War Soldier."

Bowersville

BIRTHPLACE OF
THE REV.
NORMAN VINCENT PEALE,
MINISTER AND AUTHOR

BOWERSVILLE *(Greene County)*

Rev. Norman Vincent Peale, called by many the most influential Protestant clergyman in the United States, was born on May 31, 1898 in the rural community of Bowersville, Ohio. Because his father was a Methodist circuit minister whose post was frequently rotated, young Norman spent his childhood in several Ohio towns, including Highland, Cincinnati, and Greenville before graduating from Bellefontaine High School in 1916. After high school, Peale attended Ohio Wesleyan University in Delaware, and received his B.A. in 1920. He was soon ordained a minister in the Methodist Episcopal Church, but several years later he changed his denominational affiliation to the Dutch Reformed Church to accept the pastorate at Marble Collegiate College in New York City.

Motivated by "this obsession of mine to reach as many people as I could with the message of Jesus Christ," Rev. Peale was one of the first religious leaders to use the mass media, reaching 5,000,000 people on 125 radio stations by the mid-1950's. His religious magazine *Guideposts* reaches over 2,000,000 subscribers, and his books have sold in the millions. His popularity can be attributed to the blend of religion and psychology that he uses in his approach to helping people, a philosophy summed up in the title of his book *The Power of Positive Thinking*, published in 1952. The book is based on the Biblical passage "As a man thinketh, so he is," and has sold well over 3,000,000 copies, staying on the New York Times best-seller list for a record-breaking three years.

Rev. Peale continues to maintain a positive attitude into his nineties, and lives in New York City with his wife Ruth.

Bowling Green

HOME OF
BOWLING GREEN
STATE UNIVERSITY

BOWLING GREEN (Wood County)

Private academies and seminaries flourished from the founding of the state up until the end of the Civil War, but by 1880 public high schools were well on their way to replacing the earlier private schools. Growing cities were erecting new up-to-date buildings with electric lighting, sanitary facilities, and other modern amenities, and a new emphasis was being placed on education. The curriculum of the public high school was no longer just the three R's: standard fare included algebra, geometry, history, philosophy, and science, and these courses were sometimes augmented by Latin, Greek, chemistry, and rhetoric. An early form of technical training included manual training courses for the boys and home economics for the girls.

The increasingly complex curriculum of the public schools required more than many early school mar'ms were able to provide, and the demand grew for more training for teachers. A number of private normal schools existed for this purpose in Ohio, and after the turn of the century Ohio University and Miami University offered state-subsidized teacher training programs. With a still growing demand, the legislature authorized additional normal schools throughout the state, including one at Bowling Green in 1910.

Bowling Green opened as a state normal school in 1914, but it was not until a year later that its first two buildings were ready. Its student enrollment reached 304 that first year, served by a faculty of 21, and the school awarded its first bachelor's degrees in 1917. By 1929, the curriculum was expanded to include four-year degrees in the College of Education and the College of Liberal Arts. Bowling Green achieved full university status in 1935.

Today, Bowling Green State University has about 16,000 undergraduate students and 2,000 graduate students on its campus, and its first two buildings, although late to open, still stand as University Hall and Williams Hall.

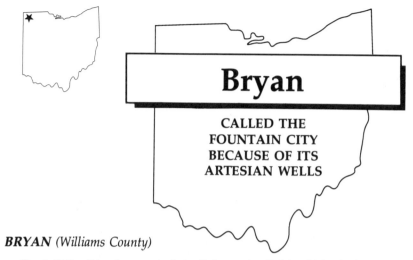

Bryan

CALLED THE
FOUNTAIN CITY
BECAUSE OF ITS
ARTESIAN WELLS

BRYAN *(Williams County)*

Daniel Wyatt had run out of daylight, so he finished his day's work and retired. He had spent the day digging a well behind his log cabin, one of the first dwellings in Bryan in that year of 1841, and had stopped when he reached hard pan. When he came out of his cabin the next morning, water was flowing freely out of the hole he had dug. Thus was Wyatt's the first fountain in what was to become the Fountain City.

The fountains of Bryan became an attraction for settlement. The *Williams County Gazette* reported in 1858 that, "Boring is easy until the hard pan is reached, which requires a drill to go through, when the auger suddenly drops three to four feet, and water gushes up with great force. Fine white sand is thrown up for several days, after which the water flows as clear as crystal. Almost every family has a fountain playing in its dooryard."

The early fountains in Bryan were little more than a hole dug in the ground with a wooden tube driven in a few feet, yet these simple fountains were the cause of legal action in 1887. A Col. Greene of New York had sent to the several hundred fountain owners in Bryan a notice of infringement on his driven well patent, and was attempting to collect $10 from each owner. In Bryan, this became known as the "Great Swindle." "Owners of all kinds of wells- sunk, bored, drilled, or driven- were served with notices, and a few persons who have no wells on their places were not overlooked," reads a newspaper of the day. "Wells were bored and penstocks driven into them nearly twenty years before Col. Greene claims to have made his discovery. Farmers who own bored fountains would do well to hesitate a long time before paying money upon a claim for patent infringement."

The free flowing fountains of Bryan eventually dried up, but not before law suits had been brought by persons suffering flooded land. By 1890, most citizens were using wells, and when houses were individually metered, the waste of water dropped dramatically. One local historian notes that the last fountain in town, located appropriately enough at Fountain Grove Cemetery, stopped flowing in 1971.

Bucyrus

COLONEL CRAWFORD
FOUGHT HIS LAST
INDIAN BATTLE
NEAR HERE
1782

BUCYRUS (Crawford County)

The simple words of Bucyrus's historical marker give no hint of the horror of the last encounter Col. William Crawford had with the Delaware and Wyandot Indians in 1782. Crawford, a friend of George Washington, had reluctantly accepted the task of quieting Indian uprisings in the Ohio Country. He led a force of 480 militia intent on destroying the Sandusky River towns of the Delawares and Wyandots, but the Indians were well prepared for Crawford's force. The Indians prevailed and captured Col. Crawford and Dr. Knight. Seeking a terrible revenge for the earlier brutal massacre of Moravian Christian Indians (see Gnadenhutten), the Delawares selected Crawford to receive the torture planned for Col. David Williamson, who had led the barbaric slaughter of the peaceful Moravians. Ironically, Williamson was a member of the only party able to retreat successfully from the Delawares.

Preparations had been made for Crawford's execution by setting a post about fifteen feet high in the ground, and making a large circle of hickory poles about six yards from it. After being stripped and beaten, he was tied on a tether to the pole, where he was able to walk once or twice around it. The hickory poles were set afire, and Crawford died a most horrible and prolonged death. Dr. Knight, who awaited a similar fate, managed to escape and spread the story of the Crawford torture.

Later Ohioans remembered Crawford by naming this county in his honor.

CRAWFORD'S MONUMENT.

Burton

HERE LIVED
SEABURY FORD
Governor of Ohio
1849-1850

BURTON *(Geauga County)*

"Burton...has had some noted characters, especially [among them] Gov. Seabury Ford, born in Cheshire, Connecticut, in 1801. Mr. Ford came here when a child. He was educated for the law, was long in political life, serving as speaker of both branches of the State Legislature, and was governor of the state in 1849-51, and died soon after from paralysis. He was an ardent Whig and greatly instrumental in carrying the State for Henry Clay.

In 1820, with a companion, Mr. D. Witter, he travelled through an almost unbroken wilderness to New Haven, Conn., for a four year's absence to obtain an education at Yale College. They both graduated, and were the very first to do so from the young State of Ohio. While there he was elected the college 'bully'. This was an office for which the physically strongest man was generally chosen, to preside at class meetings and to lead in fights against the 'town boys', so called, the rougher elements of the city, with whom there were sometimes conflicts. The office of 'college bully' has long since become obsolete from the absence of a low-down class of people to cherish enmity against students.

Seabury Ford was one of the most efficient men known to the legislative history of the State. He gave an excellent piece of advice, so characteristic of the man and so likely to be of use to some reader, that I know nothing more fitting for a close here than its quotation: 'Avoid politics and public life until, by a careful and industrious attention to a legitimate and honorable calling, you have accumulated a fortune sufficiently large to entitle you to the respect and confidence of your fellow-men as a business man and a man of integrity, and sufficiently large to render you thoroughly and entirely independent of any official salary.'"

-Henry Howe, *Historical Collections of Ohio,* 1889.

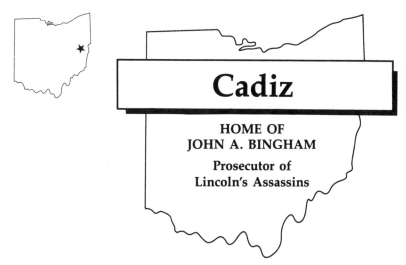

Cadiz

**HOME OF
JOHN A. BINGHAM**

Prosecutor of
Lincoln's Assassins

CADIZ (Harrison County)

The small town of Cadiz boasts more famous sons than any other small community in the entire country, according to the results of a poll conducted in Hollywood in 1938. The town's impressive roster includes, among others, Clark Gable; Edwin Stanton, Lincoln's secretary of war; Bishop Simpson, a noted abolitionist whom Lincoln called the greatest orator he had ever heard; and John A. Bingham, "prosecutor of Lincoln's assassins."

John Bingham was born in Mercer, Pennsylvania on January 21, 1815, and spent four of his childhood years in Ohio. In 1840, he moved to the Buckeye State to practice law and became involved in the extraordinary presidential contest of that year, serving in William Henry Harrison's campaign as a Whig orator. His antislavery sentiments were expressed at the National Whig Convention in 1848 when he proposed a resolution calling for "no more slave states, no more slave territories." He was first elected to Congress in 1854, and served sixteen years. While in Congress, he was appointed special judge-advocate for the trial of Lincoln's assassins, and played an active role in the impeachment proceedings against President Andrew Johnson in 1868. From 1873 to 1885 Mr. Bingham served as Minister to Japan.

Following his tenure as ambassador to Japan, John Bingham returned to his beloved Cadiz. "The hills and primeval forest which girdle this village make a picture of quiet beauty which, I think, is scarcely surpassed in any part of our country which I have seen, or in Japan, the Land of the Morning," he would tell visitors to his home. John Bingham died in 1900, and his memory was honored by the placing of the John A. Bingham Statue in front of the courthouse in Cadiz.

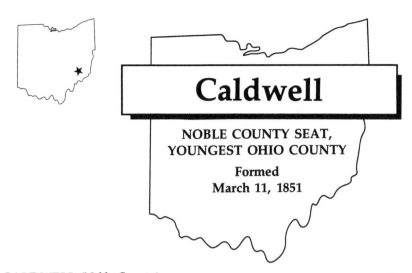

Caldwell

**NOBLE COUNTY SEAT,
YOUNGEST OHIO COUNTY**

Formed
March 11, 1851

CALDWELL (Noble County)

Noble County is both the youngest, and crookedest, of all of Ohio's counties, having no less than thirty corners in its borders. Formed in 1851 from Guernsey, Monroe, Morgan, and Washington counties, the new county was named for James Noble, one of the area's earliest settlers.

Although Noble County is the baby of the family, she claims several distinctions in her relatively short number of years. In 1875, Gen. Rutherford B. Hayes and John Bingham stopped to measure the girth of a "monster tree" near Sarahsville, finding that the giant white oak measured thirty-four and a half feet in circumference. A skeptical Gen. James A. Garfield later confirmed the measurement while passing through the area.

The first oil well in Ohio was inadvertently drilled in what was to become Noble County by a Mr. Thorley in 1814. Unfortunately, he was drilling for salt brine, and the pesky black substance proved to be quite a nuisance. Too smoky and noxious to be used in lamps, some enterprising peddlers named it "Seneca oil," calling it a "cure for what ails you." They would gather the oil by soaking blankets in it, then travel the countryside on horseback selling it to farmers' wives as a treatment for rheumatism, sprains, and bruises.

Noble County also boasts a "last" - John Gray, the last surviving soldier of the American Revolution. Serving in the war at the age of sixteen, he had taken up a musket that had dropped from his father's hands when he fell at White Plains. Two years later, he was present at Yorktown when the British surrendered, and following his mustering out, he worked for George Washington at Mount Vernon. In 1803, he moved to what is now Noble County, Ohio. John Gray died at Hiramsburg, Ohio, on March 29, 1868, at the age of 104. Inscribed on his tombstone beneath his name and date of death were the words "The Last of Washington's Companions."

35

Caledonia

**BOYHOOD HOME,
1872-1881, OF
WARREN G. HARDING
29TH PRESIDENT**

CALEDONIA *(Marion County)*

(Please see Marion, Ohio.)

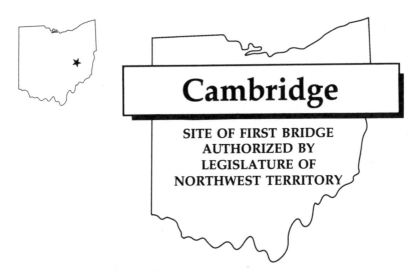

Cambridge

**SITE OF FIRST BRIDGE
AUTHORIZED BY
LEGISLATURE OF
NORTHWEST TERRITORY**

CAMBRIDGE *(Guernsey County)*

The first continuous road through Ohio was the famous Zane's Trace (see Aberdeen), and it is therefore not surprising that the first bridge authorized by the legislature of the Northwest Territory was a span along the trace. Wills Creek was the first stream of importance encountered by travelers along the road from Wheeling, and in 1798 an enterprising gentleman named Ezra Graham built a cabin on the north bank of the stream and began a profitable ferry business. Graham, at that time perhaps the only white man living in what would become Guernsey County, operated the ferry alone for two years, then went into partnership with two other men. Soon, the business expanded, with Graham's cabin becoming a tavern for the refreshment of road-weary travelers.

While the ferry was a blessing for the earliest travelers along Zane's Trace, it was no competition for a bridge. In 1801, the territorial legislature authorized the construction of a bridge over Wills Creek, the first authorized bridge in the Northwest Territory. Within a few years, Wills Creek was spanned by a log bridge that featured a puncheon floor, and, of course, a toll.

When the National Road finally reached Ohio in 1828, it followed in part Zane's Trace through eastern Ohio. The log toll bridge that carried the road over Wills Creek was replaced by a covered bridge that came to be known as the "Old National Bridge." This covered bridge was a beautiful single-span "double-barrelled" bridge with a walkway along one side. Interestingly, the bridge was built on dry land near the stream, and the stream was then rerouted beneath it. The Great Flood of 1913 damaged this bridge, and it was eventually replaced by the viaduct built in 1925.

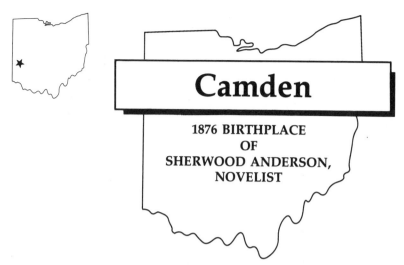

Camden

1876 BIRTHPLACE
OF
SHERWOOD ANDERSON,
NOVELIST

CAMDEN *(Preble County)*

Sherwood Anderson was born in 1876 in Camden, where he spent part of his boyhood before moving to Clyde, Ohio. His experiences growing up in small Midwestern towns gave him the opportunity to observe what he considered to be the isolated, ingrown lives of many small town Americans in the Midwest. While managing a paint factory in Elyria, legend has it that he suddenly walked out in the middle of dictation, leaving his wife and job. From Elyria he made his way to Chicago, where he became immersed in that city's literary scene. There he produced the American classic *Winesburg, Ohio,* based largely on his boyhood home of Clyde (and not to be confused with the real Winesburg, Ohio). His other works include *Tar - A Midwest Childhood, Windy McPherson's Son, Poor White, Horses and Men,* and *Dark Laughter.*

In 1941, while on a ship bound for South America, Anderson died of peritonitis. The Clyde newspaper noted the event under the headline, "Sherwood Anderson, Former Elyria Manufacturer, Dies." Today, Clyde seems to be forgiving Anderson for his portrayal of its residents, and even conducts a Winesburg tour through the town. And Camden, the author's birthplace and boyhood home, proudly boasts of Sherwood Anderson on its historical marker.

Canal Winchester

BIRTHPLACE OF
OLEY SPEAKS,
1874-1948

Musician and Composer

CANAL WINCHESTER (Franklin County)

Noted Ohio composer Oley Speaks was born in Canal Winchester on June 28, 1874. Oley's father was a grain merchant, and his brother John went on to become a U.S. Congressman. After attending school in Canal Winchester, Oley and his family moved up the road to Columbus, where Oley was a member of a quartet that sang for the congregation of the famed churchman Washington Gladden.

Oley Speaks later moved to New York City and was selected in intense competition as the soloist at St. Thomas Protestant Episcopal Church, considered one of the most prestigious positions in New York City. While in the east, he wrote about the New York music scene for Ohio newspapers and turned his attention to music composition. During his career, Oley Speaks wrote more than 200 songs. *On the Road to Mandalay,* a 1907 composition inspired by the Rudyard Kipling poem, is his most famous song, selling more than 1,000,000 copies. Speaks also set to music Paul Laurence Dunbar's *Who Knows,* and John Hay's *When the Boys Come Marching Home*, one of World War I's most popular patriotic ballads. Among his many sacred songs are *The Lord is My Light* (1913) and *It Came Upon a Midnight Clear* (1917).

Speaks was active in the development of the American Society of Composers, Authors, and Publishers, and served as one of the organization's first directors. He died in New York City on August 27, 1948, and the following year, the Oley Speaks Music Library of Canal Winchester High School, to which he had donated his manuscripts, was dedicated.

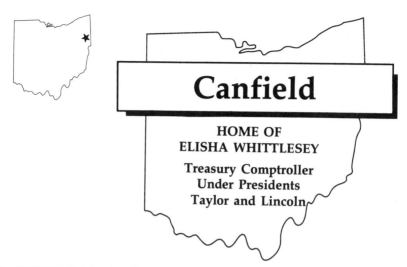

Canfield

**HOME OF
ELISHA WHITTLESEY**

Treasury Comptroller
Under Presidents
Taylor and Lincoln

CANFIELD (Mahoning County)

Elisha Whittlesey was born in Connecticut in 1783 and raised on a farm. He studied law and was admitted to the bar in 1805. In 1807, he arrived in the Western Reserve, a poor but determined man, and soon built up a successful practice. Whittlesey had had the advantage of being educated in the East, where law schools were well established. With no such schools in pioneer Ohio, justice in the West had a different look. Travelers through Ohio at the time characterized judges as "rustic, dirty-looking fellows," lawyers as "dressed in plain box-coats, sitting with their feet higher than their noses." Men prepared for the law simply by reading in the office of a practicing attorney, and then passing a simple examination. Fortunate were those young men who traipsed to the little box-like building in Canfield to read with Whittlesey, among them Joshua Giddings of Jefferson, who went on to become the author of the Republican Party's first platform.

In 1815, Whittlesey ventured over to the Firelands (Huron County) on law business, and while there selected a site for a town. With Platt Benedict and Frederic Fallig, he laid out the town of Norwalk, which would become one of the most beautiful in the entire Reserve. Whittlesey went on to serve in the Ohio legislature and the Congress, and in 1849 was appointed by President Taylor as the first comptroller of the U.S. Treasury. After being removed from the position by President Buchanan, he was reappointed to the post by Abraham Lincoln in 1861 and served until his death in 1863.

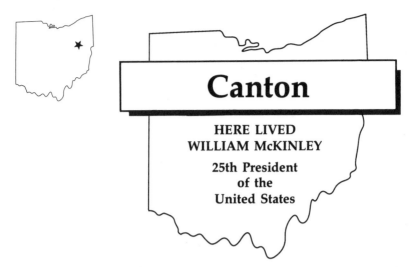

Canton

HERE LIVED
WILLIAM McKINLEY
25th President
of the
United States

CANTON (Stark County)

William McKinley was born in Niles, Ohio on January 29, 1843. He volunteered as a private in the Civil War after attending college for one term, and rose to the rank of major. Following the war, "the major", as he would forever be called by his friends, moved to Canton from Poland, Ohio and opened a law office. Active in politics, he was first elected to Congress in 1876, where he served for fourteen years. In 1890, he was elected to his first of two gubernatorial terms.

Under the guidance of industrialist Marcus Hanna, McKinley won the 1896 Republican nomination for president. His opponent in the presidential contest was the fiery barnstormer, William Jennings Bryan, who traveled the country like an evangelical preacher. In contrast to the Bryan whirlwind, McKinley stayed home in Canton and conducted the original "front porch campaign." Specially chartered trains would bring groups, accompanied by bands and banners, to his lawn to await his appearance on the porch. McKinley's approach proved successful, and he was elected the 25th president of the United States.

Under President McKinley, the United States defeated Spain in the Spanish-American War, and acquired far flung possessions including the Philippines, Guam, Hawaii, and Puerto Rico. Throughout his presidency, McKinley devoted much time and patience to his sickly wife, Ida, who never recovered from the deaths of their two young daughters. In 1900, he was reelected, but an assassin's bullets cut him down just months into his second term.

William McKinley's body was returned to Canton, and through funds donated by more than a million Americans, a beautiful tomb was built where he, his wife and two infant daughters now rest.

Carey

HOME OF
THE 1875 SHRINE
OF OUR LADY
OF CONSOLATION

CAREY (Wyandot County)

When the Germans, Irish and Italians crossed the Atlantic and made their way to the Midwest, they often brought with them a strong devotion to their church. Along with the log houses of the frontier went up the log churches, and as the communities grew, the churches were also updated and improved. Eventually, the cross-tipped spires of northwest Ohio gave to the area the sobriquet "land of the cross-tipped churches." Catholic immigrants in America felt at home with their God and their saints, and wanted them in their midst. It was in this spirit that a number of shrines came into being, including Our Lady of Consolation in Carey.

The Parish of Our Lady of Consolation was formed in 1868 as St. Edwards, but was changed to its present name at the request of Rev. Joseph P. Gloden. Bishop Adames of Luxembourg, home of the mother shrine, sent a replica of the image of Our Lady, along with relics taken from the wood and cloth of the statue of the mother shrine. Its arrival at Father Gloden's home in Berwick, Ohio on May 24, 1875 was welcomed by a thousand people, who carried it on a portable platform seven miles to the church in Carey, singing hymns and chanting prayers along the way.

As the devotion to the shrine grew, the walls of the little church bulged with pilgrims. On Christmas Eve, 1918, the revered image was carried from the little church to its present home, a red brick cruciform structure capable of seating 2,600 people. It has a triple-arched entrance beneath a large round stained glass window, and at the front corner stands a soaring bell tower that rises high above the tiled roof of the main building. Tens of thousands of Catholics make pilgrimages to Carey each year, where "on a summer afternoon the scene, in movement and religious fervor, can resemble one of those thronged tapestries of the Middle Ages."

Carrollton

HOME OF
THE FIGHTING McCOOKS
OF CIVIL WAR FAME

CARROLLTON *(Carroll County)*

Carrollton's famed Fighting McCooks were comprised of two families, the family of Maj. Daniel McCook and the family of his brother, Dr. John McCook, known as the "Tribe of Dan" and the "Tribe of John." The McCook clans sent fifteen of their members to the battlefield, with the following results:

Tribe of Dan

Maj. Daniel, killed at Buffington Island during Morgan's Raid; Maj. Latimer, surgeon, twice wounded; Brig. Gen. George, regimental commander, later Ohio attorney-general; Midshipman John, died at sea prior to Civil War; Brig. Gen. Robert, murdered by guerillas as he lay wounded in an ambulance; Maj. Gen. Alexander, commander at Bull Run; Brig. Gen. Daniel Jr., law partner of Sherman and Thomas Ewing, killed leading charge at Kennesaw Mt.; Maj. Gen. Edwin, thrice wounded, made Sherman's march to the sea, later assassinated while acting governor of Dakota; Pvt. Charles, killed at Bull Run while fighting alongside his father; and Col. John, severely wounded in Virginia.

Tribe of John

Maj. Gen. Edward, captured Confederate soldiers behind the lines in advance of Sherman's march, later appointed governor of Colorado Territory; Brig. Gen. Anson, in many battles, including Bull Run, later Congressman; Rev. Henry, chaplain; Marine Lt. Roderick, received the surrender of a Confederate regiment of infantry; and Lt. John, served at Kelleysville, one of the earliest engagements of the war.

The 1837 Dan McCook House is now a county historical site on the square in Carrollton.

THE FIGHTING McCOOKS.

MAJOR DANIEL McCOOK.

Head of the "Tribe of Dan."

DR. JOHN McCOOK.

Head of the "Tribe of John."

Castalia

**COLD CREEK
RISES HERE**

**A Stream
That Never Freezes**

CASTALIA (Erie County)

Cold Creek is born of five artesian springs that rise from a large pond called Duck Pond. It was known to Indians long before the first white man set eyes upon it in 1761, and, like many other springs that bubbled up in Ohio, it was believed to have special healing properties. The temperature of the water is a fairly constant 46-51 degrees, and thus never freezes. This constantly flowing stream, with a fall of 57 feet in its three mile descent to Sandusky Bay, attracted one of the first mills in the Firelands in 1810, and soon the stream's channel was virtually a millrace, powering several grist mills. The mineral composition of the water, which rises from a limestone aquifer, did not go unnoticed by the early millers, who noted that the water wheels of the mills on Cold Creek were "imperishable from decay in consequence of their being incrusted by petrifaction."

In 1870, Mr. John Hoyt procured a few thousand eggs of the brook trout, constructed a number of hatching troughs along Cold Creek, and began raising trout. The well stocked stream was then leased to "two clubs of gentlemen for sporting purposes," and became a popular spot for anglers.

Cold Creek is noted not just for its own virtues, but also has one of the most famous offspring in the world. In 1812, a miller built a dam on Cold Creek to supply water to turn his water wheel. The milldam caused a change in the underground water flow, and in 1820 the famous Castalia Blue Hole erupted to the surface. The Blue Hole, a crystal clear spring about 75 feet across, bubbles up at a rate of about 11 million gallons a day. This natural phenomenon continues to be an attraction for the curious, drawing visitors from all over the world.

Cedarville

**BIRTHPLACE OF
U.S. SENATOR
JAMES. H. KYLE
"Father" of
Labor Day**

CEDARVILLE (Greene County)

James H. Kyle was born in Cedarville on Feb. 24, 1854, and as a child moved to Illinois. He returned to his native state to attend Oberlin College, from which he graduated in 1878. Kyle went on to the ministry in South Dakota, but the ministry led him into politics. After giving the invocation at a political rally, he was asked to continue speaking while the desperate organizers and impatient crowd waited for a tardy politician. Kyle captured the crowd with his eloquence, and soon he was elected to the state senate. Only a year later, the state senate sent him to Washington as a U.S. senator.

Prior to Kyle's election to the Senate, the Knights of Labor had been organizing workers around the country. In 1882, 10,000 workers paraded up Fifth Avenue in New York City, in spite of the threats of many of their employers. This first march inaugurated what would become Labor Day, and in 1887 Oregon became the first state in the Union to make Labor Day a legal holiday. In the Senate, Kyle had achieved a reputation as a champion of the workingman, and in 1894 he introduced the bill in the Senate that would ultimately make Labor Day a national holiday. On June 28, 1894, President Grover Cleveland signed the bill into law. Kyle's energy and devotion to his work led to a loss of health, and in 1901 he died at home in Aberdeen, S.D.

Cedarville's connection with Labor Day went unnoticed for many years. A schoolmate of Kyle's in Cedarville, Andrew "Doc" Creswell, took the podium at the Cedarville Labor Day rally in 1944, half a century after Kyle's bill became law. "Doc" was now in his nineties, and when he asked the crowd, "Do you fellows have any idea who founded Labor Day?", no one could answer. "Well, it was Jimmy Kyle - Senator James Henderson Kyle - and he was a Cedarville boy!" Today, Cedarville's historical marker proudly proclaims the town as "Birthplace of the Father of Labor Day."

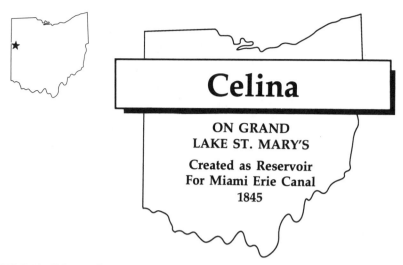

Celina

ON GRAND
LAKE ST. MARY'S

Created as Reservoir
For Miami Erie Canal
1845

CELINA (Mercer County)

The Miami & Erie Canal, stretching through western Ohio from the Ohio River to Lake Erie, needed a reliable and plentiful source of water to maintain the flow in its channel. At the canal's summit near Celina, Grand Lake St. Mary's was dug as a reservoir to fill this need. At the time of its construction, it was the largest man-made lake in the world, created by 1,700 men who were paid 30 cents a day plus a jigger of whiskey. The west embankment was completed in 1843, and the completion of the entire reservoir followed two years later.

After the laborers had created two walls of earth, from ten to twenty-five feet high, two and four miles long, the area was transformed into a basin into which the water began to collect. Trouble followed immediately, as growing crops of wheat were submerged along with entire farms for which the state had not yet paid. A newspaper of the day reported that on May 15, 1843, at seven o'clock in the morning, more than one-hundred citizens armed with shovels, spades, and wheelbarrows began to cut the bank. The following day at noon, the cutting was complete, and the reservoir was held back by only a flimsy breastwork. The tools were removed, and Samuel Ruckman said, "Who will start the water?" "I", answered John Sunday and Henry Linzee, and in a moment the water was pouring through the bank, a flow that took six weeks to subside. A grand jury could not be found in Mercer County that would indict the men, and the state had to pick up a $17,000 repair bill.

Today, Grand Lake St. Mary's is the centerpiece of a popular state park.

Centerburg

GEOGRAPHICAL
CENTER
OF
OHIO

CENTERBURG (Knox County)

The Knox County community of Centerburg is named for its location at the center of the state. The determination of the geographical center of Ohio played a major role in the location of the state capital, for the state assembly in 1810 mandated that the capital be located within a forty mile radius of the common center of the state. With the legislature sitting at the temporary capital at Zanesville at the time, this act necessitated a move to a new location, which ultimately proved to be Columbus.

Centerburg's location at the center of the state places it not only in the center of the plane of Ohio, but also amid five natural zones that make up the Buckeye State. These areas were created in large part by the movement of glaciers over most of the state thousands of years ago. In northwestern Ohio are found the Lake Plains, an extremely flat area that slopes only slightly toward Lake Erie. Once the bottom of a larger lake, this poorly drained area was home to the Great Black Swamp until it was drained by farmers in the nineteenth century. To the south of the Lake Plains and east of a line running roughly through Centerburg is the Till Plains region, a rich farming area named for the "till", or glacial deposits of soil and rock, left behind when the glacier retreated. Southeast Ohio, home of rugged hills, caves, and waterfalls, lies in the Unglaciated Appalachian Plateau, a region not touched by the smoothing influence of the ice masses from the north, while the Glaciated Plateau, covering northeast Ohio and snaking down through the center of the state, is less wild and more suitable for agriculture than its unglaciated counterpart. Finally, a small area in Adams County in the southern tip of Ohio is part of the Bluegrass Region that gives neighboring Kentucky its name.

Ohio's marvelously diverse topography, ranging from the flat land of the northwest to the rugged features of the southeast, gives the state a diversity that makes it one of the more interesting geographical areas in the country.

Chardon

**THE CENTER
OF THE
MAPLE SUGAR
INDUSTRY**

CHARDON *(Geauga County)*

March in northeast Ohio is a special time. The warming days coupled with the still cool nights spell maple sugaring time, and sugar maple trees throughout Geauga County are festooned with steely-gray buckets hanging from spiles, those taps driven into the trees to draw the sweet sap. As the sun shines on the tree bark, the pace of the dripping from the spiles picks up, and at night, sugary sweet icicles hang from the now quiet tap, awaiting another day in the all-too-short season.

Maple sugaring the old-fashioned way involved tapping the trees, then inserting a spile a couple of inches into the tree. The sap would enter an opening in the end of the spile and run out into a bucket that hung from a notch on the tap. The slow but steady dripping would fill the buckets before the day was out, and then the collector would gather the sap and deliver it to the sugar kettle. Here a fire would be kept going day and night under the large kettle, boiling down the sap to a syrupy consistency. It was a long process, as only about one gallon of syrup was obtained from fifty gallons of sap.

Today, the smoke still rises from the small sugar houses in Geauga County. In some of the larger operations, plastic tubing carries the sap from the trees directly to the stainless steel evaporators that have replaced the old iron kettles. As it has done for over a century, Geauga County leads the state in the production of maple syrup, and is one of the nation's leading producers.

OLD-TIME WAY OF MAKING MAPLE SUGAR.

Chillicothe

**FIRST CAPITAL
OF OHIO
1803-1810
1812-1816**

CHILLICOTHE (Ross County)

As Philadelphia is the cradle of the United States, so Chillicothe is the cradle of the state of Ohio. It is more than the state's first capital, for it was here that the battles for statehood raged, and here where the state's first constitution was formed. Thomas Jefferson was in the White House, and the wealthy and aristocratic Virginians of Chillicothe, led by Thomas Worthington (see Worthington), swamped the President with letters and appeals for statehood. The Virginians in Chillicothe were a young and ambitious group of Republicans, aligned against the old Federalist Arthur St. Clair, whose time was passing. The territorial capital had been moved to Chillicothe from St. Clair's Cincinnati in 1800, and the winds of statehood were blowing ever stronger. When Ohio was admitted to the Union as the seventeenth state in 1803, Chillicothe became the first capital of Ohio.

The territorial legislature in 1802 met in a small two-story log house, but the state capitol, one of the first public stone edifices in the Northwest Territory, was completed in time for the state assembly in 1803. Edward Tiffin was elected Ohio's first governor, and on March 1, 1803, Nathaniel Massie was chosen as speaker by the senators, and Michael Baldwin as speaker by the representatives. John Smith and Thomas Worthington would become the state's first U.S. senators. The old state house stood until 1852, but it did not long serve as the seat of government. Zanesville interrupted Chillicothe's reign from 1810-1812 and in 1816 the capital of Ohio was permanently moved to Columbus.

Today, Thomas Worthington's home, Adena, is a state historical site, and the graves of Worthington, Massie, and Tiffin are found in Chillicothe.

Cincinnati

**BIRTHPLACE OF
WILLIAM HOWARD TAFT
27th President
of the
United States**

CINCINNATI (Hamilton County)

William Howard Taft was born in Cincinnati in 1857, and was admitted to the Ohio bar after graduating from the University of Cincinnati Law School in 1880. His entry into politics came when he worked on the campaign of the Republican candidate for county prosecutor, and was awarded the post of assistant prosecutor. He soon resigned from the job rather than fire members of his staff for political reasons, and this distaste for politics endured throughout his life. "Politics, when I am in it, makes me sick," he would later write to his wife.

Taft's great love was the judiciary. He first was appointed to the Ohio Superior Court in 1887, and won reelection the next year. He served as U.S. solicitor and sat on the bench of the U.S. Circuit Court before becoming the first civil governor of the Philippines.

President Theodore Roosevelt appointed Taft secretary of war, and he became the administration's troubleshooter. Roosevelt, perhaps referring to Taft's 300 pounds, said everything was alright when Taft was "sitting on the lid." Taft was the cabinet member made responsible for the construction of the Panama Canal, and in 1908, with Roosevelt not running, he encouraged Taft to seek the presidency. Taft, under great pressure from his wife and Roosevelt, agreed to run, and defeated perennial candidate William Jennings Bryan, marking the third time Bryan had lost to an Ohio candidate. Taft's single term was stormy, though, and he lost the 1912 election to Woodrow Wilson, having split the Republican vote with "Bull Moose" candidate Theodore Roosevelt.

In 1921, President Warren G. Harding appointed Taft chief justice of the Supreme Court, a post he much preferred to the presidency. Taft died on March 8, 1930, the only man in history to serve as both president and chief justice.

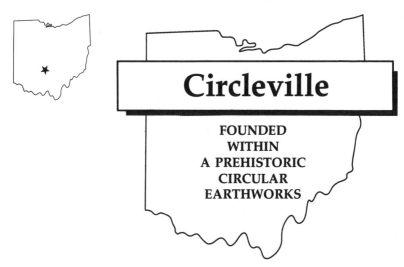

Circleville

FOUNDED
WITHIN
A PREHISTORIC
CIRCULAR
EARTHWORKS

CIRCLEVILLE (Pickaway County)

The town of Circleville, laid out in 1810, draws its name from the prehistoric earthworks, or "fortifications," that were located where Circleville now stands. The mounds are long gone, but an 1836 birds-eye sketch of the community reveals a striking pattern of development, with a circular mound at the town's center, and streets radiating outward from the mound's circumference like spokes in a wheel. Standing in the center of the circular mound was an octagonal courthouse, dubbed by an early wag "The Temple of Justice," due to its location. Today, the old courthouse is gone, victim of a fire in 1841.

In 1820, Caleb Atwater, early Ohio historian and Circleville resident, described the mounds from first hand knowledge: "There are two forts, one being an exact circle, the other being an exact square. The former is surrounded by two walls, with a deep ditch between them; the latter is encompassed by one wall without any ditch. The former was sixty-nine feet in diameter; the latter is exactly fifty-five rods square. The walls of the circular fort were at least twenty feet in height before the town of Circleville was built. There were eight openings into the square fort, one into the circular fort. Before each of these openings was a mound of earth, perhaps four feet high, intended for the defence of these openings. These fortifications will entirely disappear in a few years; I have used the only means within my power to perpetuate their memory, by this brief description."

Clarksburg

**FOUNDED IN 1817
ON THE
URBANA ROAD
BY COLONEL
WILLIAM CLARK**

CLARKSBURG (Ross County)

Settlement of Deerfield Township and the village of Clarksburg began with the coming of White Brown and his slaves from Delaware in 1801. Brown released his bondsmen after relocating in Ross County, Ohio, an action that was consistent with the prohibition on slavery in the Northwest Territory, and with the help of his sons managed to raise a crop of corn that first year. The rest of the family came in 1802, camping for three weeks while a log house, the first in the township, was being raised. Shortly thereafter, a log barn went up on the farm, serving on Sundays as a rude sanctuary for the pioneer Methodist Episcopal Church for several years. Also on Brown's farm was the first cemetery and the first mill, the latter supplied with water by the felling of a tree across a stream and the piling of brush on it to create a milldam.

While the Brown family was busy erecting these first buildings, John Clark, a Scottish immigrant, moved into the township in 1800 and also began claiming a farm from the forest. John's oldest son, William, helped in this arduous work, and after his marriage he settled on a farm adjoining his father's, operating a tannery in addition to farming. When the War of 1812 broke out, William served as a colonel in the Ohio Militia and equipped his troops from his own pocket, money that he never recovered from the government. When the war was over, Clark returned to Deerfield Township, and in 1817 he laid out the village of Clarksburg on his own farm.

Col. Clark, like his father before him, died at a young age, leaving behind a widow and a seven year old son named Milton. This young son would go on to serve in the state legislature, and as a delegate to the 1860 Republican convention cast a vote for Abraham Lincoln. Milton Lee Clark distinguished himself as chief justice of the Ohio Supreme Court from 1894 until his death in 1897.

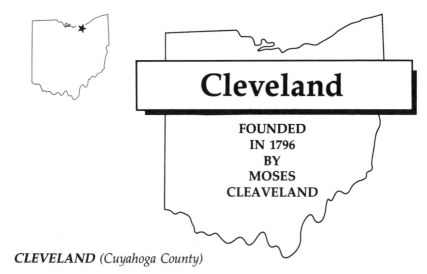

Cleveland

**FOUNDED
IN 1796
BY
MOSES
CLEAVELAND**

CLEVELAND (Cuyahoga County)

The saga of Moses Cleaveland in Ohio began not in Cleveland, but to the east along the shore of Lake Erie at Conneaut (see Conneaut). After landing at Conneaut Creek, Moses Cleaveland and his surveying party established a storehouse for their provisions, and set about surveying the area of the Western Reserve.

Over the next two months, the party worked their way westward as they surveyed, seeking a good spot for a town as they went. The town was envisioned to be a capital town for the Reserve. When they arrived at the mouth of the Cuyahoga River, located mid-point along the Lake Erie shore of the Reserve, they knew they had found their site. Cleaveland laid out the town on the high ground above the river, using the New England design that featured a public square. The associates named the town Cleaveland to honor the party's leader.

It had been an arduous journey for the party of surveyors, and they looked forward to returning to the comforts of New England. Within a few months, virtually the entire party returned home to Connecticut. Moses Cleaveland died in 1806 in his native Wyndham, never seeing the prosperity that was coming to his town.

While the party of surveyors had no real intentions of settling in the Reserve, Lorenzo Carter and his wife were determined to make a go of it. The swampy mouth of the Cuyahoga had repelled many settlers to the surrounding ridgetops, but the rugged Carter held on, keeping the settlement together. His home was the social center and inn, and he assisted new arrivals and improvised "law." In 1800, the population reached seven, but the real boost came a few decades later when the Ohio and Erie Canal emptied into Lake Erie at Cleveland.

As for the spelling of "Cleveland," one story has it that in 1830 a newspaper editor found that he could not quite fit "Cleaveland Advertiser" on the paper's masthead, and so dropped the first "a", forever altering the name of the future metropolis.

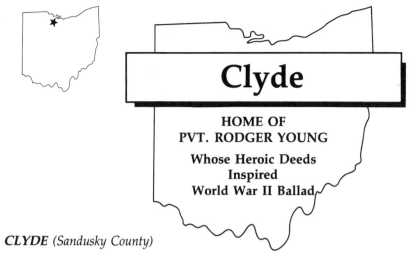

Clyde

**HOME OF
PVT. RODGER YOUNG**

**Whose Heroic Deeds
Inspired
World War II Ballad**

CLYDE (Sandusky County)

Songwriter Frank Loesser, intent on writing a song of American heroism, had asked the War Department to provide him with the single most gallant act of a soldier during World War II. When the War Department finally decided on an appropriate act of heroism, Loesser agreed with their decision and penned the famous ballad *Rodger Young.*

Rodger Young grew up in Clyde and became a combat infantryman. Sent to the South Pacific, Young's outfit was preparing for the invasion of New Georgia Island. The young, thin, bespectacled staff sergeant approached his company commander, asking to be demoted to the rank of private. "My ears are growing bad. I can't hear very well, and I don't want any of my men killed in New Georgia because of me," said Young. If his request meant going home, he would withdraw it rather than be left behind, and if the commander harbored any thought that Young's request was a ruse, it was soon laid to rest by the events of New Georgia Island.

Three weeks later, the troops landed on New Georgia. While out on a patrol, Young's company was pinned down by Japanese machine-gun fire. The situation was dire, as the Japanese would move in at darkness to finish off the troops if they did not extricate themselves from this position. Rodger Young began inching his way toward the machine gun nest and drew fire immediately. Against the shouted orders of his commander, he managed to reach a position within five yards of the gunners. By now severely wounded, he shouted back to the commander, "Sorry, you know I don't hear very well!" He then rose up, pulled the pin and tossed a hand grenade into the nest, wiping it out. He was shot dead in the act.

"Oh, they've got no time for glory in the Infantry, They've got no use for praises loudly sung; But in every soldier's heart in all the Infantry, Shines the name, shines the name of Rodger Young" went the popular ballad about Clyde's local hero. Rodger Young received the Congressional Medal of Honor, and his hometown people honored him with a monument in McPherson Cemetery.

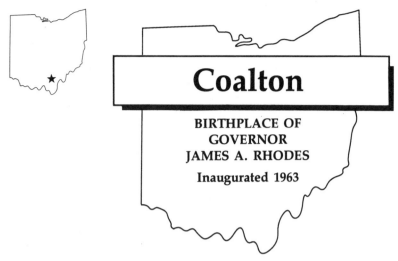

Coalton

BIRTHPLACE OF
GOVERNOR
JAMES A. RHODES

Inaugurated 1963

COALTON (Jackson County)

James A. Rhodes was born in Coalton, Ohio on September 13, 1909, the son of a coal miner who died when James was still a young child. After attending high school in Springfield, Rhodes went to the Ohio State University, but withdrew prior to graduation in order to support his mother and sisters. It was in Columbus that he entered politics, serving on the Columbus Board of Education from 1937-39. This was the first of many rungs on Rhodes' political ladder, with the offices of auditor and mayor of Columbus and auditor of the state of Ohio serving as stepping stones on his way to the governor's office. But even the final steps to that office were many, as he was defeated for the Republican party's nomination in 1950, and after gaining the nomination in 1954 he lost to Frank Lausche in the governor's race. Rhodes' perseverance paid off in 1962 when he defeated the incumbent Michael V. DiSalle to become Ohio's sixty-first governor, and he easily won reelection in 1966.

Forbidden by Ohio law from serving more than two consecutive terms, Rhodes retired from political life for four years, but returned to face the incumbent John J. Gilligan in 1974. With the television networks projecting Gilligan as the winner on election night, many Ohioans went to bed, only to be surprised in the morning when the final tally showed Rhodes with 1,493,679 votes to Gilligan's 1,482,191 votes. Rhodes won reelection over incumbent Lt. Gov. Richard Celeste in 1978, the last time that an incumbent governor and lieutenant governor would face each other in an Ohio election.

After his second set of two terms, Rhodes was again forced to leave the governor's office, but in 1986, at the age of seventy-seven, he again won the Republican Party's nomination for governor. This time he was soundly defeated by Gov. Richard F. Celeste, bringing to an apparent end the political career of James A. Rhodes.

55

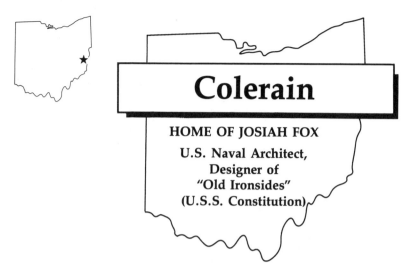

Colerain

HOME OF JOSIAH FOX

U.S. Naval Architect, Designer of "Old Ironsides" (U.S.S. Constitution)

COLERAIN *(Belmont County)*

Old Ironsides is perhaps the most important, and famous, ship in early U.S. Naval history. Built in 1797 and launched from Boston as the *U.S.S. Constitution,* she earned the nickname "Old Ironsides" when enemy cannonballs would bounce off her heavily timbered hull. She saw her first action in the Barbary Wars in 1804, and in the War of 1812 provided a much needed morale boost when she defeated the British frigate "Guerriere" after the Americans had lost Detroit in a shameful surrender.

In 1830, inactivity and idleness was doing to the *Constitution* what no enemy ship had been able to do. Rotting away and scheduled for dismantling, the ship was saved when a poem by Oliver Wendell Holmes called *Old Ironsides* rallied the public to the decaying ship's cause. In recognition of "Old Ironsides" service to the country, the nation saw to it that she was rebuilt, and now she is on permanent exhibit in the Navy Yard in Charlestown, Massachusetts.

Columbiana

BIRTHPLACE
OF
HARVEY S.
FIRESTONE

COLUMBIANA (Columbiana County)

Harvey S. Firestone, industrialist and tire magnate, was born in Columbiana in 1868 into a farm family. As a schoolboy, Harvey was proficient at buying and selling cattle, and set his course toward business rather than farming. After graduating from a business college in Cleveland, he worked for several companies, including the Columbus Buggy Company in the state capital. While in Detroit, he drove the first rubber-tired buggy, and struck on the idea of manufacturing rubber tires for carriages.

Firestone and two friends started the Firestone-Victor Rubber Company in Chicago with $3,000. After buying out one competitor and merging with another, he was the leader of the buggy tire industry. He sold that business, created the Firestone Tire and Rubber Company, and moved back to Ohio, locating his new company at the future rubber capital of the world, Akron.

Firestone's first carriage tires had a single wire running through the heart of the tire, and later he would add more wires to support heavier loads. Another innovation was the making of tires in continuous lengths, like hose, rather than individually molding each tire to a particular wheel, as was the practice of the day. When Henry Ford purchased 2,000 sets of Firestone's tires for his Model T's, a close business and personal relationship was formed that lasted throughout the men's lives. Other innovations of Harvey Firestone included his "One Stop Master Service Stores," created in 1928 to provide auto products and services to the motoring public.

Firestone's success, born of the better roads movement of the late 1890's, gave impetus to a new better roads movement in the 1920's and helped revolutionize the way Americans traveled. In Firestone's later years, he often traveled and camped with his close friends, Henry Ford and Thomas Edison, and continued to own and operate his ancestral farm in Ohio. Harvey S. Firestone died in 1938.

Columbus

CAPITAL OF OHIO
HOME OF
OHIO STATE UNIVERSITY

COLUMBUS (Franklin County)

For the first twelve years of Ohio statehood, the capital had wandered from Chillicothe to Zanesville, then back to Chillicothe. Weary of this instability, the state legislators in 1810 decreed that the permanent site of the capital would be within a forty mile radius of the "common" center of the state. Several communities, chief among them Worthington, Dublin, and Delaware, sought the prize, only to lose out to a town that did not even exist - Columbus.

Lyle Starling, James Johnston, Alexander McLaughlin, and John Kerr, four residents of Franklinton (now Columbus' west side), proposed to the legislature that the capital be located "on the high bank of the Scioto River, across from Franklinton." In exchange, the four men agreed to lay out a town and give to the state two parcels of land, ten acres each, and to build upon them a state house and penitentiary. With the acceptance of this proposal, the four men went to work, laying out the town on the site of an old Wyandot Indian village in virtually unbroken forest. Lots went on sale in June of 1812, and soon houses and shops were erected. Several more years would pass, though, before the stumps, logs and brush would finally be removed from Broad and High Streets. A penitentiary was built in 1813, and, finally, in 1816, the state legislature met in the new brick capitol. At long last, the seat of Ohio government had a permanent home where it could begin "that continuous and monotonous grind of passing laws one winter and repealing them the next." Fire destroyed the original capitol in 1852, and the present capitol was completed in 1861. With its Doric columns and truncated dome, this impressive structure was considered the greatest state capitol in the country.

Columbus' marker also proclaims it the home of the largest college campus in the country, The Ohio State University. Founded as the Ohio Agricultural and Mechanical College, it received its first students in 1873, and from that initial enrollment of seventeen has grown to a burgeoning community of more than 53,000 students.

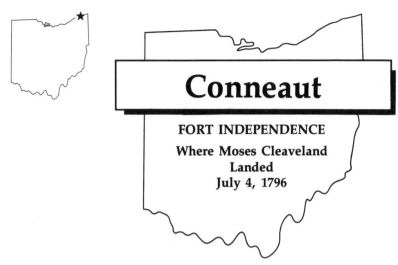

Conneaut

FORT INDEPENDENCE

**Where Moses Cleaveland Landed
July 4, 1796**

CONNEAUT (Ashtabula County)

Conneaut has been called the "Plymouth of the Reserve," for it was here that Moses Cleaveland first set foot in the northeast section of Ohio called "The Western Reserve." Ten years earlier, Connecticut, which claimed all land lying within her extended borders from sea to shining sea, relinquished her claims to these western lands, with the exception of lands reserved for her citizens who suffered fire losses during the war (see Norwalk), and the land stretching east from this tract to the Pennsylvania border. This latter tract was sold to a group of Connecticut citizens who formed the Connecticut Land Company, and on April 28, 1796, a large surveying party under the leadership of Gen. Moses Cleaveland left Connecticut to chart the wilderness of "New Connecticut."

Cleaveland and his men literally stumbled upon the northwest cornerstone of Pennsylvania on July 4, 1796, and only hours later reached the mouth of Conneaut Creek in the Reserve. With the vast expanse of Lake Erie stretching before them, unbroken wilderness behind, the party was overcome with joy and patriotism on this Independence Day. Firing their rifles in a salute to the nation and to New Connecticut, the party "gave three cheers and christened the place Port Independence." The normally staid Cleaveland went on to note that the celebration continued for six toasts, and then "closed with three cheers. Drank several pails of grog, supped and retired in remarkable good order."

The following day, the group set up camp, stored their provisions, and readied for the task for which they had come - to survey, not to settle, the land. Turning their backs on Conneaut, the party headed west.

The reader is invited to continue this adventure by referring to the section on Cleveland.

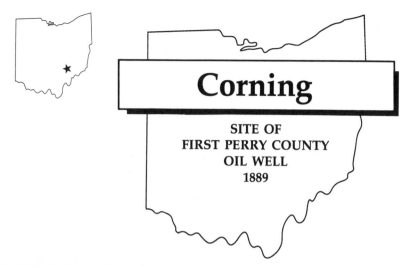

Corning

SITE OF
FIRST PERRY COUNTY
OIL WELL
1889

CORNING *(Perry County)*

The first oil well in Perry County was drilled in 1889, but the history of petroleum in the county predates that event by several decades. Oil was found in the area in the first half of the nineteenth century, primarily on the surface of streams, the result of seepage from nearby oil veins. This oil would be skimmed from the surface much the same as one would skim the cream from the milk jar. Oil not used for lighting the cabin would be sold, but this method never proved to be very profitable.

The real oil boom in the area began with the arrival of the Toledo and Ohio Central Railroad. One of the railroad's financiers was a man named Erastus Corning from New York, for whom the village may have been named. Because the town of Corning was the terminal point for this and another railroad, it was essential that a roundhouse be located here to resupply the steam engines with water. While drilling for water at the roundhouse, salt water was struck, a useless commodity in a boiler. After sealing off the casing, the drillers departed, and upon their return the next day found the casing filled with oil. It was determined that this oil was the same grade as that produced in the Pennsylvania fields that was bringing such prosperity to that state, and soon oil men began arriving at Corning. The first oil well was drilled in 1889.

Within a few short years, oil derricks could be seen on virtually every hill in the area. It was an especially fortuitous turn of events, for the Great Panic of 1893 was about to occur. With oil flowing at Corning, the town missed the hard times that struck elsewhere. In the year of the Panic, an oil pipeline from Corning to Marietta commenced operation, carrying 500 barrels of oil a day 34 miles to the Ohio River.

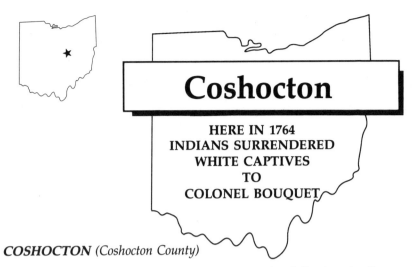

Coshocton

**HERE IN 1764
INDIANS SURRENDERED
WHITE CAPTIVES
TO
COLONEL BOUQUET**

COSHOCTON (Coshocton County)

An uneasy peace returned to colonial America following the Peace of Paris in 1763, which ended the French and Indian War and ostensibly gave control of the Ohio Country to the British. In point of fact, however, it was the Indians who controlled this territory which lay too distant from the eastern colonies for protection. Upset with the defeat of their French allies and the cutting off of presents from the English, the Indians attacked western British posts, including a trading post near Sandusky. The Indians did not contain themselves to the Ohio Country, however, and conducted raids into western Pennsylvania and Virginia, taking hundreds of prisoners back with them across the Ohio River. While some of the prisoners were killed, others were adopted into Indian families and raised as Indians.

In response to the Indian raids, the British sought to remove some of the provocations that led to the attacks. The colonials were forbidden to cross the Appalachians by a Royal Proclamation, an ineffective attempt to hold in check the Americans' westward drive. To retrieve the prisoners, Col. Henry Bouquet marched into the Ohio Country with 1,500 men and, along the banks of the Muskingum at present-day Coshocton, demanded that the Indians, without exception, turn over all of their white captives. In exchange for the more than 200 captives, the Indians could live in peace north of the Ohio River.

While the response of the Indians was generally cooperative, the response of many of the captives was not what the whites had hoped for. Recent captives were happy enough to be released, but many others, among them children who had been taken when quite young, were distressed at being removed from the homes, parents, and culture in which they had grown up. To give up the children was a heart-wrenching experience for many strong Indian men and women, who had demonstrated great kindness and affection for the captives. Tears of joy mixed with tears of sorrow on that November day in 1764 when the Indians turned over their prisoners along the banks of the Muskingum.

61

Crestline

**AN OHIO
RAILROAD CENTER
SINCE 1850**

CRESTLINE *(Crawford County)*

Rensselaer Livingston learned the bitter lesson that while a line may be the shortest distance between two points, it is not always the shortest path to riches. It is that lesson that gave birth to Crestline in 1850, and spelled the end of another town just a half mile away.

Livingston saw the approach of the Ohio and Indiana rail line from the west, the Pennsylvania and Ohio line from the east, and he knew that the north-south 3 C line was already completed as far north as Vernon Station. He figured that the natural place for the east-west lines to meet and intersect the north-south line would be at Vernon, so he bought the land around the station and laid out the town of Livingston. However, the engineer in charge of constructing the Pennsylvania line purchased land a half mile south of Livingston for his own town. He steered the railroad to his land, and named his town Crestline. It became the rail crossroads of the nation, while the town of Livingston died an abrupt death.

Crestline flourished as the terminal for both east-west lines. Repair shops were built for the engines and cars, and hotels catered to the railroad employees. Huge buildings for storing the wood and water that fed the steam engines were constructed, and the engine house employed an average of 90 men a day. Every train through town stopped at the Crestline yards, where up to 1,760 cars would be redirected to their destinations, and every steam engine had to go through the Crestline roundhouse to have its flue cleaned and repairs made. Even livestock had to stop at Crestline while railroad workers cleaned out the cattle cars.

Steam power was good for Crestline, but the advent of the diesel engine, which required less service, was its undoing in the 1950's. Finally, in 1989 it was announced that the last Amtrak line through town was to be eliminated, sounding the death knell for Crestline's rail passenger service.

Crooksville

ESTABLISHED 1874.

The "Clay City"
of
Perry County

CROOKSVILLE (Perry County)

Eleven different kinds of rock comprise the bedrock of Ohio, and each is found in layers that were formed from sediment deposited in the ancient seas, marshes, and swamps that covered Ohio up to a half-billion years ago. Among these layers is clay, which is made of extremely small grains of mica, quartz, and clay minerals. Beneath the soils of Perry County can be found a dozen strata of clays. For the pioneers of the pottery industry, these clays were divided into three main types: fire clay, potters clay, and brick clay. With seams so thick they were described as inexhaustible, it was a natural place for the pottery industry to thrive.

Up until 1882, small "blue bird" potteries filled the need for pottery in the area, but between 1882 and 1885 the demand for stoneware of all kinds, including milk pans, large jars, jugs, churns, fruit cans, and covered fruit jars outstripped what the small potteries could produce. In 1885, the Burley, Winter, and Brown steam pottery stepped into the breech, producing more stoneware of a higher quality and at lower cost than a dozen small potteries combined. After the railroad came through in 1890, Crooksville became the center of the pottery industry.

Pottery after pottery was organized in Crooksville to produce stoneware, including the Crooksville Pottery Co., the Star Stoneware Co., and the Diamond Stoneware Co. In 1902, the Crooksville Art Pottery Co. was formed to produce a new line of vases, flower pots, and novelties, but before production began the company changed its name to the Crooksville China Co. and went into competition with East Liverpool for the dinnerware market. Soon, several more companies joined the dinnerware fray, and Crooksville became the "Clay City" of Perry County.

Dayton

HOME OF
ORVILLE AND WILBUR
WRIGHT

Fathers of
Aviation

DAYTON *(Montgomery County)*

Orville Wright, born in Dayton, Ohio in 1871, and his brother, Wilbur, born in Indiana in 1867, were inventive geniuses from an early age. At their bicycle shop in Dayton, they did not merely repair bicycles, but they sold bikes of their own design. After experimenting with gliders and box kites at Kill Devil Hill in North Carolina, they built a twin engine biplane powered by a homemade gasoline engine.

The Wright Brothers were ready to fly on the morning of December 17, 1903 at Kitty Hawk. A toss of the coin gave the honor of the first flight to Orville, and he took off on a flight of 12 seconds, covering 120 feet. After some fine tuning, Wilbur managed a flight of 59 seconds, covering 852 feet. The aviation age was launched, but no one, including newspaper editors and publishers, believed it until Orville demonstrated the machine for government officials several years later.

President Taft, Vice-President Sherman, and every member of the Supreme Court, the cabinet, and Congress who were in Washington and able to attend were present on July 30, 1909 for the first officially observed flight. The word was given and Orville took off, soaring to a height of 300 feet. After circling a distant balloon that marked his turn, Orville disappeared below some hills on the horizon. As time passed, the suspense grew, and sweat broke out on the face of Wilbur Wright. Finally, Orville rose above the horizon and rushed to the finish, covering ten miles in about fourteen minutes. The government bought the Wright machine for $30,000, which included a $5,000 bonus.

The Wrights had to spend much time in the ensuing years protecting their patents. Wilbur, worn out from these battles, died of typhoid in 1912, but Orville lived in Dayton until 1948. And James Cox, Dayton newspaper publisher, lamented for years "missing the greatest news to ever come out of Dayton."

Defiance

**SITE OF
FORT DEFIANCE
1794**

**Home of
Defiance College**

DEFIANCE *(Defiance County)*

It was July 28, 1794, and Anthony Wayne's troops, intent on securing the Ohio Country for settlement, were on the move again, marching out of Fort Recovery to Fort Loramie, then down the Auglaize River to the Maumee. Indian villages along these rivers were being deserted as the army advanced, and when the troops reached the confluence of the two rivers, Wayne built another in his string of forts. He built it well, mindful that two generals before him had met disastrous defeats at the hands of the Indians and their British friends. "I defy the English, Indians, and all the Devils in Hell to take it!", he exclaimed. And so it was called Fort Defiance. From Fort Defiance, Wayne marched on to the Battle of Fallen Timbers (see Maumee). The victorious troops returned to Fort Defiance after Fallen Timbers, and strengthened it against artillery fire. However, the fort was never used again. When Gen. William Henry Harrison arrived here in 1813, it was in ruins, forcing him to build Fort Winchester nearby. Today, the site of Fort Defiance is a city park.

Wayne's victory had opened Ohio for settlement, and in 1836, Fort Defiance became Defiance, Ohio, now the home of Defiance College. The college began as the Defiance Female Seminary in 1850, and in 1875 nine acres of land north of town were acquired for the campus. Notwithstanding its name, the school graduated its first class of four men and five women in 1888. Defiance College is a four year private liberal arts college, affiliated with the United Church of Christ, with a full time undergraduate enrollment of about 1,000 students.

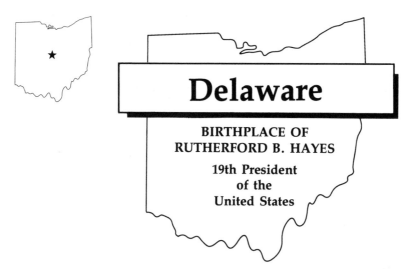

Delaware

**BIRTHPLACE OF
RUTHERFORD B. HAYES**

**19th President
of the
United States**

DELAWARE *(Delaware County)*

Rutherford Birchard Hayes was born in Delaware, Ohio in 1822, the same year that marked the death of his father. Mrs. Hayes' brother, Sardis Birchard, himself only sixteen, took over the care of his sister, her new baby, Rutherford, and two other children, working whatever jobs he could find. After struggling along in Delaware for five years, Sardis moved the family to Fremont.

Sardis gave his nephew "Rud" every advantage he could afford him, and Rutherford went on to graduate from Kenyon College and Harvard Law School. His marriage to Lucy Ware in 1852 had a profound impact on him, and her ardent antislavery and temperance views were instrumental in Hayes, a former Whig, founding the Ohio Republican party. When the Civil War broke out, he became a member of the remarkable 23rd Ohio Regiment, which also gave the country President McKinley. Hayes was elected to Congress in 1864, but he resigned shortly to serve three terms as Ohio governor.

In 1876, with his reputation for honesty and integrity established, he was induced to run for President. An old friend of his, upon hearing the news, stated firmly that he would never vote for Rutherford "because he was too good a man." Hayes actually lost the popular vote in the election, but the electoral commission elected him after he promised to bring Reconstruction to an end. Lucy Ware Hayes earned her nickname "Lemonade Lucy" during Hayes term in office, for she enforced temperance in the White House.

Hayes resigned after one term, returning to his home in Fremont to work on causes ranging from public education to prison reform. He died there in 1893, and today the Hayes house and library are open to the public as a state historical site. In Delaware, a small marker stands at the site of Hayes' birthplace on Williams Street.

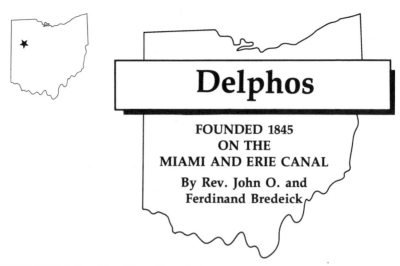

Delphos

**FOUNDED 1845
ON THE
MIAMI AND ERIE CANAL**

By Rev. John O. and
Ferdinand Bredeick

DELPHOS (Allen/Van Wert Counties)

Canals, culverts, and Catholicism dominate this region of northwest Ohio, and nowhere is this more apparent than in Delphos. In 1844, Rev. John Otto Bredeick, a Catholic priest, came from Germany to northwest Ohio, intent on establishing a parish. He was following his brother, Ferdinand, who had earlier made the first plat of the land where Delphos would be. At that time, construction was under way on the Miami & Erie Canal, a forty foot wide ditch of water that would connect the wilderness of western Ohio with the markets of New Orleans and the Atlantic seaboard. Land along the route was being offered to settlers at $1 per acre, and Rev. Bredeick bought the land opposite his brother's and laid out a town in 1845. Until 1850 it was called Section 10, named for that section of the canal on which it was located, but was later given the name Delphos.

Under Rev. Bredeick's able guidance, both spiritual and otherwise, settlers came and the land was cleared. It was a job that required deep faith. It has been said that Delphos, founded in the Great Black Swamp region, could not have been settled without quinine, for the "air was so poisoned with malarial effluvia from swamps and marshes, that not only the pioneers but also the very dogs of the settlement suffered intensely from fever and ague." In spite of the hardships, the industrious German pioneers set about draining the swamp with a system of ditches, and eventually transformed one of the least desirable areas of Ohio into its garden spot.

Delphos had been founded on faith, and in December of 1845, thirty-six townsmen met in a cabin to plan the building of Delphos' first church. It was described as an "ungainly structure," but served the needs of the parish under Rev. Bredeick. In 1880, a magnificat new church was built, one of many in this "land of the cross-tipped churches." Rev. John O. Bredeick died on August 19, 1858, and was buried in the Catholic Cemetery in Delphos.

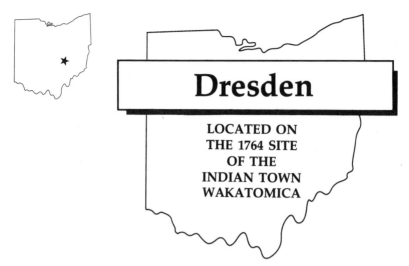

Dresden

**LOCATED ON
THE 1764 SITE
OF THE
INDIAN TOWN
WAKATOMICA**

DRESDEN (Muskingum County)

The town of Dresden is located on the site of the early Shawnee Indian village of Wakatomica, a village that was the target of colonial troops in the year 1774. Col. Angus McDonald, under orders of the Virginia governor, led a force of 400 men against Wakatomica. About six miles from the town the troops were ambushed by the Indians, and suffered the loss of one dead and several wounded. The Wakatomica towns were taken soon afterward, burned, and the corn crop destroyed. Ironically, it was recorded that "the army were out of provisions before they left the towns, and had to subsist on weeds and one ear of corn each day."

In 1799, Maj. Jonathon Cass came to the territory, locating on 4,000 acres of land. An extensive graveyard was said to have been found here by the first settlers, as well as the remains of cabins that had been inhabited by the Indians. George Wilson erected the first mill in Dresden in 1801, and two years later the first road was laid out from Zanesville to Coshocton, passing through the village. In the election of 1805, the township officers elected were: "Trustees, Seth Carhart, Valentine Johnson, and Isaac Cordray; overseers of the poor, John Walmsley, James Sprague; fence viewers, James Wilcox, William Elben; supervisors of highways, Henry Northrup, James Tanner."

Dresden was incorporated March 8, 1839, and a mile long branch canal that connected it with the Ohio & Erie Canal brought commerce to the town. An early history book describes Dresden as "a place of residence that offers beautiful building sites, healthful surroundings and a cultivated, intelligent, progressive class of citizens." Maj. Jonathon Cass, the pioneer settler, died in 1830 and was buried in the Dresden Cemetery. On his monument were recorded these words: "He was a soldier at the Battle of Bunker Hill; an officer of the Revolution, and of the army which, under Gen. Wayne, gave peace to the frontier."

Dublin

LEADING CONTENDER
AS SITE OF
STATE CAPITAL,
1810-1812

Surveyed 1818

DUBLIN *(Franklin County)*

In February of 1810, the Ohio legislature, after passing a resolution moving the state capital from Chillicothe to Zanesville, appointed a five member commission to examine and select the most eligible site for the establishment of the permanent seat of government for the State. The commissioners were to meet at Franklinton and select a site "within forty miles of the 'common' center of the state." When James Findlay, W. Silliman, Joseph Darlinton, Reisin Beall, and William McFarland returned to Zanesville on December 11, 1810, their report to the legislature stated that "they have diligently examined a number of different places within the circle prescribed, and the majority of commissioners are of opinion that a tract of land, owned by John and Peter Sells, situated on the west bank of the Scioto River, four miles and three quarters west of the town of Worthington, in the county of Franklin, and on which said Sells now resides, appears to them the most eligible."

And so it seemed that Dublin was to be the new capital of Ohio. The dream of Dublin was short-lived, however, for the commission's recommendation was never acted upon. In February, 1812, the legislature passed a law establishing the capital twelve miles downstream from Dublin in a forest newly named "Columbus." John Sells proceeded to lay out the town of Dublin in 1818, and his descendants would go on to establish the famed Sells Brothers Circus.

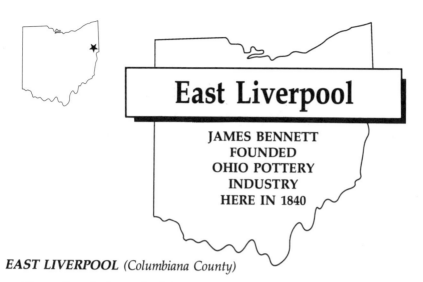

East Liverpool

**JAMES BENNETT
FOUNDED
OHIO POTTERY
INDUSTRY
HERE IN 1840**

EAST LIVERPOOL *(Columbiana County)*

The pottery industry in Columbiana County owes its existence to the discovery of the clay used in the making of "yellow ware," the old-fashioned pottery made by the pioneer potters. As early as 1806, kilns were being fired for the bricks of the Friend's Meeting House in Salem, and rude kilns could be found outside the cabins of the earliest settlers in the first days of the nineteenth century. Up until 1840, however, there was no attempt to utilize the clays in a commercial venture, but that would soon change with the arrival of James Bennett, a potter from England. Bennett, hearing about the clay of the Ohio Valley after arriving in America, walked into East Liverpool on foot, examined the clay, and decided it would make excellent yellow ware. Garnering financial support from two other residents, he opened the first pottery in the winter of 1839-40, its first burn consisting of mugs that were peddled downstream to other communities. That year saw a total net profit of $250, but the next year his business prospered to such an extent that he summoned his brothers from England. Other English potters also came, and in 1845 the Bennetts sold out and left East Liverpool.

Although the Bennetts were gone, East Liverpool potteries flourished, and the district was recognized as the leading producer of general ware pottery. The potter's wheel was replaced here for the first time by machinery, heralding in a new era of commercial production. By the end of the century, 647 kilns were producing in the entire nation, with East Liverpool accounting for 239 of them. Oddly enough, when yellow ware was replaced by higher quality white granites and porcelains, the town continued to thrive, even though the materials had to be imported from elsewhere.

The old Bennett works burned down in 1853, and the ground on which the first pottery stood has long since been claimed by the Ohio River, but in the old post office the past can still be seen in the Museum of Ceramics.

Eaton

SITE OF
FORT ST. CLAIR
Erected 1791-92

EATON (Preble County)

On a windy morning on the outskirts of Eaton, Ohio, if the breezes are just right and one listens very carefully, the tale of a mighty struggle that took place here two centuries ago can be heard. So intense was the struggle between the American forces and the Indian warriors that, according to legend, it echoes through time to this day, told and retold by a witness who was there to see it - the majestic Whispering Oak of Fort St. Clair.

Anthony Wayne had been sent by President Washington to crush the Indian uprisings in Ohio, and was following in the footsteps of defeated Generals Harmar and St. Clair. Fort St. Clair, one in a string of forts stretching from Fort Washington on the Ohio to Fort Wayne at the head of the Maumee, was constructed by Col. Wilkinson in 1791 to protect the army supply lines of Gen. Anthony Wayne as he marched to victory at Fallen Timbers. Fort St. Clair filled the gap between Fort Hamilton to the south (see Hamilton) and Fort Jefferson to the north (see Fort Jefferson).

On the morning of November 6, 1792, Chief Little Turtle and a band of warriors swept in on the camp of a small garrison outside the fort. A fierce battle ensued, with first one side, then the other, gaining the upper hand. When the fray was over, the pack horses of the army were gone, along with the Indians, and six American soldiers lay dead.

Today, the site of Fort St. Clair is an 89 acre state historical site, administered by the Ohio Historical Society. The 200 year old Whispering Oak still stands guard over six small graves that lie beneath its outstretched branches, and the rustling leaves of the tree whisper the names Williams, Jett, Clinton, Bowling, English, and Hale.

Edison

NAMED IN 1882
TO HONOR
THOMAS ALVA EDISON
1847-1931

Inventor - Scientist

EDISON *(Morrow County)*

(Please see Milan.)

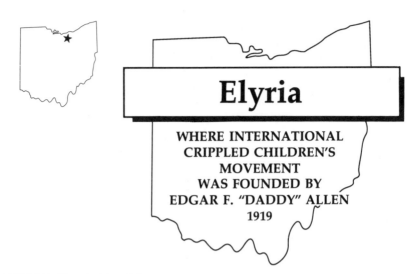

Elyria

WHERE INTERNATIONAL
CRIPPLED CHILDREN'S
MOVEMENT
WAS FOUNDED BY
EDGAR F. "DADDY" ALLEN
1919

ELYRIA (Lorain County)

Edgar Fiske Allen was born in Newton, Massachusetts on May 8, 1862, and following his education in the Newton public schools, took his first job in a hardware store in Cleveland, Ohio. In 1889, he joined in creating the Cleveland Cedar Company, which bought and resold cedar poles and telegraph ties. Telephone and telegraph service was rapidly growing throughout the country at this time, as was railroad construction, and in this expanding market Allen decided to buy stands of cedar in Michigan and Canada instead of just reselling the products made by others. By 1905, the available cedar tracts had been cut, and the company liquidated its $1,000,000 worth of assets.

Allen moved to Elyria where he became involved in several business enterprises, but a tragedy in 1907 changed the direction of his life. A street car accident claimed the lives of nine Elyria residents, including his son. "Daddy" Allen then dedicated his life to helping children, particularly those afflicted with polio. In 1908, he built what became the Gates Memorial Hospital, a nationally recognized facility for the treatment of handicapped children. He founded the Ohio Crippled Children's Society in 1915, and went on to form the International Society for Crippled Children in 1919. His concern for the welfare of handicapped children earned him world wide recognition, and he was presented a medal from the people of the Netherlands. Allen also served as chairman of the Lorain County Red Cross during the first World War.

Edgar Allen died in Elyria on September 21, 1937. With the coming of the Salk and Sabin polio vaccines, the need for a separate hospital for handicapped children diminished, and the former Gates Hospital was absorbed by Elyria Memorial Hospital.

73

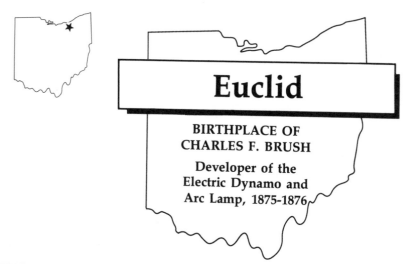

Euclid

BIRTHPLACE OF
CHARLES F. BRUSH

Developer of the
Electric Dynamo and
Arc Lamp, 1875-1876

EUCLID (Cuyahoga County)

Ohio is famous for its many inventors, and is especially noted for its inventors in the field of electricity. Thomas Edison, inventor of the incandescent light, Charles Kettering, inventor of the automobile self-starter and the Delco portable lighting plant, and Charles Brush, developer of the electric arc lamp and dynamo, are all natives of the Buckeye State.

Charles Brush was born in Euclid in 1840, the son of a farmer. His scientific bent manifested itself at an early age, and by the time he was fifteen he was building microscopes and telescopes for himself and his friends. At that time, the streets were illuminated by gas lamps, and he devised a plan for turning on the gas in the lamps, lighting it, then extinguishing it. Soon, this budding scientist was off to the University of Michigan for his education.

In 1875, Brush, now in Cleveland, was presented with the problem of producing a dynamo machine that could provide the proper amount and kind of electric current to power several lamps simultaneously. Within two months, he had developed such a machine. He was then faced with the task of developing a lamp that would work successfully on a circuit with a large number of other lamps so that all would burn uniformly. Within a few weeks, he produced his first electric arc lamp, made of lampblack rods, coke and syrup, baked in a kitchen oven.

The following year, his twin inventions were presented to the public, and on April 29, 1879, he lighted up Cleveland's Monumental Park with a dozen of his arc lamps. In 1881, a central power station was built and lamps installed throughout the city, making Cleveland the first city in the world to be lighted electrically. His Brush Electric Light Company later was merged with Thompson and Edison to become General Electric.

74

Fairport Harbor

SURVEYED IN 1812
AS GRANDON ON AN ERIE
INDIAN VILLAGE SITE.
Lighthouse Built In 1825
By Jonathon Goldsmith

FAIRPORT HARBOR (Lake County)

Jonathon Goldsmith emigrated to the Western Reserve from New England in 1811 at the age of 28, and lived in Painesville until his death in 1847. Known as "the architect-builder of the Western Reserve," he built many of the structures that are so pleasing to view in the "New Connecticut" towns of northeast Ohio, including buildings at Lake Erie College (see Painesville) and the now vanished lighthouse in Fairport Harbor.

Fairport, or Grandon, had a population of about 300 people in 1825, with new settlers arriving at a steady pace. Situated at the mouth of the Grand River on Lake Erie, it was an enviable location with superb growth possibilities. However, a lighthouse was needed to improve the harbor's safety and serve as a beacon to the incoming settlers. On March 26, 1825, the *Painesville Telegraph* published a proposal for such a lighthouse: "Will be received at the office of Collector of Customs at Cleaveland for building a lighthouse at the mouth of the Grand River. The lighthouse to be built of stone or hard brick, the form round. The height of the tower to be thirty feet from the surface of the ground..The outside to be whitewashed twice over.. A sufficient number of circular stairs to lead to within six feet of the lantern..On the top of the tower to be an iron lantern of octagon form...to contain eighteen lights, eleven by nine glass glazed with the best double glass from the Boston manufactory."

Jonathon Goldsmith and Hiram Wood were awarded the contract in 1825 and built the first lighthouse at Fairport Harbor for the sum of $2,900. Records from 1847 reveal that the lighthouse served its purpose, for nearly 3,000 vessels entered the harbor that year. The original lighthouse stood until 1871, when it was replaced by the present tower, which was decommissioned in 1925 and became a maritime museum.

For information on the Erie Indians who occupied this site, please see Vermilion.

Fayetteville

**FOUNDED 1818 BY
CORNELIUS McGROARTY,
AN IRISH IMMIGRANT.**

Incorporated 1868

FAYETTEVILLE (Brown County)

Fayetteville, a Brown County community located on the south bank of the East Fork of the Little Miami River, was founded by Cornelius McGroarty in 1818. However, McGroarty was not the first man to set up housekeeping at the present site of Fayetteville. In 1811, Erastus Atkins built a double log house here, and later in the same year a Thomas McCarthy established a farm just to the south of Atkins. Nathan Bishop, a salt-manufacturer from Virginia, bought a nearby farm in 1811 and ran a huckster wagon between Fayetteville and Cincinnati. He became justice of the peace and constable, and later served as mayor of Fayetteville.

In 1818, Cornelius McGroarty, a native of Ireland, came from Cincinnati to join his other compatriots, and purchased the land where Fayetteville now stands. Soon, other Irish immigrants came to town, including John Ballard, who was engaged in the 1798 rebellion in Ireland and served in Napoleon's army at Waterloo. McGroarty's own son, Stephen, became a hero during the Civil War, attaining the rank of colonel and the reputation as a brave and gallant soldier. The McKittricks, McCloskeys, and Thompsons also came, establishing families that helped the Irish Catholic community grow to a population of 390 inhabitants by the time of the census of 1880. St. Aloysius Academy, a private Catholic school for boys, was established in 1850 to see to the education of boys between the ages of six and fourteen years.

The village of Fayetteville was incorporated in 1868, and the lilting Irish names of Fitzpatrick, McCafferty, McConn, McCaffrey, and McCarthy continued to grace the roster of village officials for decades to come.

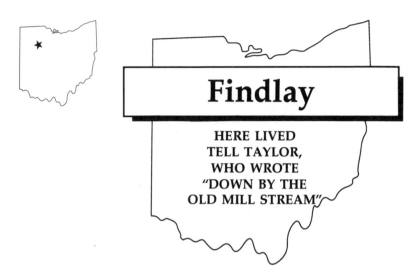

Findlay

HERE LIVED
TELL TAYLOR,
WHO WROTE
"DOWN BY THE
OLD MILL STREAM"

FINDLAY *(Hancock County)*

In 1835, Michael Misamore built a mill, the first frame structure in Amanda Township, Hancock County, Ohio, along the banks of the beautiful Blanchard River. The mill was run by water power, which was described in an early history book as "uncertain, through freezing in winter and low water in summer. Nevertheless, it was a great boon to the pioneers of the surrounding country, who often had to travel long distances through forest, with a small grist, ere the little ones could taste the luxury of a wheat cake."

While providing the little ones a taste of a wheat cake was the mill's main purpose, romance proved to be a more lasting product. In 1910, Tell Taylor was inspired to write of the mill on the Blanchard River one of the most famous songs of all time, *Down by the Old Mill Stream.* Taylor, born on a farm near Vanlue and reared and educated in Findlay, moved to New York in 1897 and, with two other men, opened one of the first publishing houses on Tin Pan Alley. It was on a return visit to Findlay in 1908 that he wrote the famous song. Taylor returned to Findlay for good in 1922, and is buried in Van Horn Cemetery near Vanlue, along the river that he loved and made famous. Today, there is no trace left at all of the old mill, but the stream that gave rise to the song is still meandering through the beautiful countryside of Hancock County, Ohio.

TELL TAYLOR
1876 — 1937

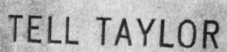

AUTHOR·COMPOSER·PUBLISHER
WHOSE INSPIRED SONG
DOWN BY THE OLD MILL STREAM
CONTINUES TO GIVE PLEASURE TO
MILLIONS AND TO ENDEAR HIS
MEMORY IN THE HEARTS OF HIS
FRIENDS AND NEIGHBORS OF HANCOCK
COUNTY

THEIR VIRTUES ON TABLETS OF LOVE+MEMORY
·ERECTED ·1939· BY
FINDLAY LODGE N⁰ 75 B.P.O.ELKS

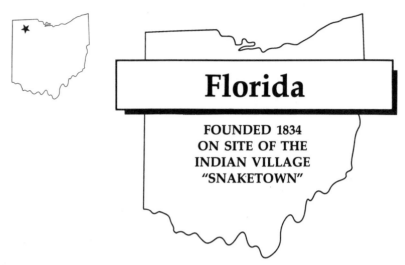

Florida

**FOUNDED 1834
ON SITE OF THE
INDIAN VILLAGE
"SNAKETOWN"**

FLORIDA (Henry County)

Florida's historical marker is probably one of the most photographed in the state, particularly when the wind-blown snow has drifted up to its edge. How Florida got its name, however, remains a mystery, as does the Indian village of Snaketown, on which the village purports to be founded.

There is no question that Florida has a past steeped in history. William Bowen built the first double log cabin in a clearing here on the north bank of the Maumee River in 1831, and it became known as "Hunter's Inn." Just three years later the town of Florida was founded. Florida's glory years were from 1842-1854, when it was a booming canal town, supporting 16 saloons, a grist mill, slaughter house, two hotels, an ashery, a wagon factory, blacksmith shop, shoe store, and more. Much less is known about its predecessor, Snaketown, but it is not for lack of trying.

As part of the village's sesquicentennial celebration in 1984, an archeological dig was sponsored by the Ohio Humanities Council. The goal of the dig was to find the site of Snaketown, named for the Shawnee Chief Captain Snake. The Indian village was occupied by Snake and his followers from about 1786 until its abandonment in 1794 in the face of the army of Gen. Anthony Wayne. Various writings had placed the village somewhere along the Maumee between Independence and Waterville, and the dig commenced at the edge of Florida. Six weeks later, after finding projectile points, Shaker remnants, animal bones, and a forty-foot canal boat, the workers had yet to find conclusive evidence that Snaketown existed at the site of present day Florida.

Today, while we know little of Snaketown, we know that Florida declined after the railroad bypassed her in 1854, and that her canal heritage still lives in the watered section of the canal between Florida and Independence.

Fort Jefferson

SITE OF
FRONTIER POST
BUILT BY
ARTHUR ST. CLAIR
1791

FORT JEFFERSON *(Darke County)*

At the junction of two streams in Darke County, Mud Creek and Prairie Outlet, stands an obelisk made of field stones that marks the site of Fort Jefferson, built by Gen. Arthur St. Clair in 1791. It was from this fort that St. Clair's forces marched into the worst disaster any American troops had encountered up to that time, and to this fort that the few stunned survivors managed to straggle back.

St. Clair had been charged by President Washington to crush the Indian uprisings and violence in the Ohio Country. He planned to march to the Miami villages and destroy them, erecting a series of forts along the way for security. Fort Jefferson was one such fort, and the last one built before the disaster at the site of what is now Fort Recovery.

Fort Jefferson was described as "35 yards square with a 'good' bastion at each corner. Barracks and storerooms formed the outer walls, while a powder magazine, bullock pen, and fenced garden were located outside the fort." By October 24th, construction had reached the point that the garrison could finish the task. St. Clair named the fortification "Fort Jefferson" after the secretary of state, Thomas Jefferson. Leaving a small defensive force behind, St. Clair and more than nine-hundred men marched off to disaster on the banks of the upper Wabash (see Fort Recovery).

Today, the site of Fort Jefferson, located at the town of the same name, is a state historical site.

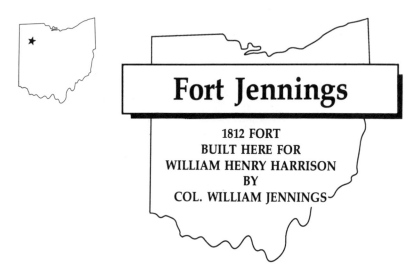

Fort Jennings

**1812 FORT
BUILT HERE FOR
WILLIAM HENRY HARRISON
BY
COL. WILLIAM JENNINGS**

FORT JENNINGS *(Putnam County)*

On September 21, 1812, Lt. Col. William Jennings received orders from Gen. William Henry Harrison to march his Kentucky troops down the Auglaize River from Fort St. Mary's toward Fort Defiance. His assignment included the erection of an intermediate post and the protection of supplies headed for Defiance, but after marching thirty miles, signs of Indians were observed. The troops began building blockhouses along the banks of the Auglaize, and camped in tents. When word came that they were not needed at Defiance, the men completed the fort at their encampment and named it Fort Jennings.

It is not certain just how substantial Fort Jennings was. Crudely constructed, the walls and blockhouses offered little protection from the weather, and with the chinking between logs constantly falling out, the main duty of the men was to keep the fires going for warmth. The monotony of life at a supply fort was voiced by one militiaman who wrote, ''We had the same unpleasant, uninteresting round of escorting convoys and provisions in advance of us.'' The fort was to house 40,000 rations for Gen. Harrison, with one ration consisting of 1 1/4 lb. beef, 18 oz. bread, and 1 gill of rum, whiskey, or brandy. In addition to escorting the convoys, other tasks at the fort included building boats, smoking meats, and making cartridges.

Fort Jennings was never attacked by Indians or British, yet ten men died of swamp illnesses and were buried in a small cemetery near the stockade. When the end of the War of 1812 came, the fort was abandoned and left to deteriorate.

Fort Loramie

SITE OF LORAMIE'S
TRADING POST AND
GENERAL WAYNE'S
FORT LORAMIE
1795

FORT LORAMIE (Shelby County)

The area around Fort Loramie in Shelby County was long contested by the French and the English. In 1749 Celeron de Bienville was sent by France to bury engraved leaden plates at the mouth of every stream he passed, thereby claiming all the land north and west of the Ohio River for France. The English responded that same year by building their first settlement in Ohio, a trading post at the Miami Indian village of Pickawillany along the banks of the Great Miami River. The French retaliated by destroying Pickawillany in 1752. Peter Loramie, a French-Canadian, set up a trading post nearby at present day Fort Loramie, and did a handsome business with the Wyandottes and Shawnees.

Loramie had such a strong influence with the Indians that his post was seen as a threat by the Americans in 1782. The Shawnees had been conducting raids across the Ohio River against white settlements in Kentucky, and George Rogers Clark led over a thousand mounted Kentuckians into Ohio against the Shawnees. Along with attacking the Indian towns, Clark's forces destroyed Loramie's Store, the principal supplier of the Shawnees. After the post was burned, Gen. Clark reported that "the property destroyed surpassed all idea we had of Indian stores."

Peter Loramie himself was not at the store when the attack came, but had managed to escape. Under agreement with the Indian commissioner, he led several hundred Shawnees out of Ohio to a reservation west of the Mississippi. In 1794, Anthony Wayne built a fort at the site of Loramie's trading post, and named it Fort Loramie. The spot where Loramie's Store stood continued to be a landmark for years to come, and was even included as a reference point in delineating the Greenville Treaty Line in 1795 (see Greenville). In later years, Fort Loramie would enjoy the commerce that came with the Miami and Erie Canal, and today Lake Loramie, built to supply water for the canal, is a popular recreation area.

Fort Recovery

SITE OF
GENERAL ST. CLAIR'S
DEFEAT, 1791;
GENERAL WAYNE'S
FORT, 1793

FORT RECOVERY (Mercer County)

It was just before sunrise on the snowy morning of November 4, 1791. Sent by President Washington to still the Indian attacks along the frontier, the army of Gen. Arthur St. Clair had encamped on the banks of the Wabash River. Suddenly, out of the stillness of early morning came the war whoops of the Indian forces led by Blue Jacket, Little Turtle, and Simon Girty. The unprepared soldiers were completely overwhelmed, and 631 men gave their lives that day.

Two years later, Gen. Anthony Wayne, called by the Indians the "general who never sleeps," returned to the site of the defeat. His advance men were greeted by the horrible sight of bones scattered throughout the area, including over 600 human skulls. Before construction of the new fort could begin, these remains had to be buried. Wayne called his new fort "Fort Recovery," and aptly named it was. On June 30, 1794, one of the largest forces ever to engage the American Army attacked the fort. On the site of previous disaster, the forces of Gen. Wayne prevailed. Two months later, the war was over with Wayne's victory at Fallen Timbers, opening the way for settlement of the Ohio Country.

Today, on the square in the town of Fort Recovery, stands a 93 foot high granite shaft, authorized by Congress, that entombs the fallen heroes "who, as advance guards, entered the wilderness of the west to blaze the way for freedom and civilization." Nearby is a reconstruction of the old fort, including two blockhouses, one of which contains a museum. The site is operated by the Ohio Historical Society.

Reconstructed Fort Recovery

Fostoria

**HOME OF
CHARLES FOSTER
Congressman,
35th Ohio Governor
and Secretary of the
Treasury**

FOSTORIA (Hancock/Seneca/Wood Counties)

Charles Foster literally grew up in the country store that his father built in 1832 in the middle of northwest Ohio's Black Swamp. The store was in a double log cabin, with the residence in one end and the store in the other. Two feuding hamlets, Rome and Risdon, were nearby, and by 1854, when tempers had cooled sufficiently that the citizens could meet without drawing blood, they united into one community. They named their new town Fostoria in honor of the storekeeper C.W. Foster, who by now was running the biggest country store in the state.

The younger Foster briefly attended the Norwalk Academy, but an illness in the family caused him to leave the institution and formal education forever. When the Civil War broke out, Foster accepted a commission with an Ohio Regiment, but his parents prevailed upon him not to go, as he was their sole surviving son. Back at the store, he extended credit to every family in the neighborhood with a son in the Union Army, a practice he maintained during the entire war.

Foster enjoyed a marked popularity, and was elected to Congress for the first time in 1870. After serving several terms, he was nominated for governor by the Republicans in 1879. It was a most unusual campaign, with the Democrats calling Foster "Calico Charlie," a derisive comment referring to his staying at the dry goods store during the war. As is often the case, this tactic boomeranged. Foster's supporters had entire towns festooned in calico, and marching bands dressed in it, neckties were made from it, and even newspapers were printed on it. The popular Foster won the governorship by 17,000 votes, and two years later he was reelected by 25,000 votes. President Benjamin Harrison later tapped Foster to be secretary of the treasury in 1891, a position he served with distinction.

Frankfort

SHAWNEE INDIAN VILLAGE, 1774.
Old Town Founded By John McNeill 1816.
Frankfort, 1827.

FRANKFORT *(Ross County)*

The present community of Frankfort is located on the former site of the Indian village of Old Chillicothe. There has been a considerable amount of confusion surrounding the Indian villages of Chillicothe, for five different Shawnee towns in Ohio went by that name. The Shawnees were divided into clans, or septs, one of which was the Chalahgawtha sept from which the name Chillicothe is derived. The principal town of each sept was named for the clan, and whenever a sept moved to a new location, the name of their town followed. Piqua, Westfall, Hopetown, Oldtown, and Frankfort are present-day Ohio towns that stand on the site of former Shawnee Chillicothes.

The Shawnee village at present Frankfort dates back to at least 1774, when Indian forces massed here to fight the Battle of Point Pleasant. Thirteen years later, Simon Kenton led a retaliatory raid against the Indians here for their attacks on white settlers near his Kentucky settlement at Kenton's Station. The Indians fled into the forest, leaving their cornfields to be burned by the white attackers. In 1793, Nathaniel Massie and Duncan McArthur reached Old Chillicothe as part of a survey crew, but withdrew in the face of Indian menacing. Two years later, they returned and nearly perished in a terrific storm that dropped three feet of snow. Their journey became known as "the starving tour," as thirty men had to survive extreme cold for four days on just two turkeys.

When the white settlement of Chillicothe was established, the Shawnee town nearby was largely abandoned. Eventually, John McNeil moved into the area and laid out Oldtown on his farm in 1816. The town was incorporated in 1827, the same year that its post office was established, necessitating a name change to Frankfort because another Ohio post office had the name of Oldtown.

84

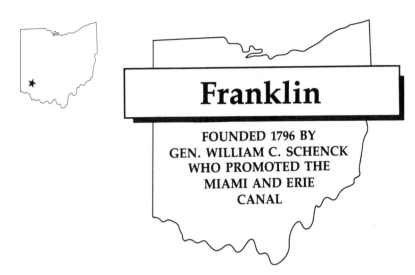

Franklin

**FOUNDED 1796 BY
GEN. WILLIAM C. SCHENCK
WHO PROMOTED THE
MIAMI AND ERIE
CANAL**

FRANKLIN (Warren County)

William Cortenus Schenck was a young man of twenty, just out of Princeton and grappling with his choice of careers. One moment he thought law, the next medicine. But when his uncle presented him with the opportunity to travel from his home in the east to the wild west of Ohio, he readily accepted. Uncle John Cumming was a friend of Judge Symmes, who had purchased all the land between the Miami Rivers. The land needed surveyed, and William set out in that year of 1793 with a party of explorers bound for Ohio. He was commissioned a lieutenant in the Hamilton County Militia, but took ill and returned home a few months later. Uncle John soon urged his nephew to go back to Ohio, where the best land would go to the ones who knew where it was. William was instructed to keep his uncle informed, and with a gift of surveying tools from Uncle John, he became one of the best surveyors in the West.

William was especially fond of the land where Franklin now stands, and in 1796 he and Daniel Cooper bought the land and laid out the town. Soon, half a dozen cabins stood in the forest at Franklin. Settlers came by flatboat on the Ohio, plagued by low water that grounded them and by spring floods that nearly wrecked them. Schenck himself lived in Cincinnati, and in 1803 became a member of the first Ohio Senate, but shortly thereafter he moved to Franklin, where he became a land agent, surveyor, and legal advisor for his townsmen. He also received a commission as a general.

Ohio was becoming interested in the possibility of constructing a canal, and in 1816 Schenck was appointed by the governor to survey a route from Lake Erie to the Ohio River. In 1821, after making an impassioned speech to the legislature in support of the project, he was stricken ill and died, a young man of only forty-eight. Gen. William Schenck was buried in Franklin's Woodhill Cemetery.

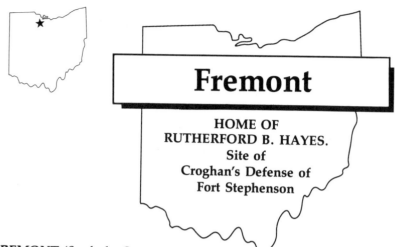

Fremont

**HOME OF
RUTHERFORD B. HAYES.
Site of
Croghan's Defense of
Fort Stephenson**

FREMONT (Sandusky County)

"It will not be among the least of General Proctor's mortifications that he has been baffled by a youth, who had just passed his twenty-first year. He is, however, a hero worthy of his gallant uncle, General George Rogers Clarke." So read the report written by Gen. William Henry Harrison about the extraordinary performance of Maj. George Croghan at the Battle of Fort Stephenson in 1813. Ironically, only days before the battle, Harrison had written a letter relieving the young major of command for disobeying his orders to retreat in the face of the enemy, an order he soon rescinded.

Croghan had received the orders to abandon the fort too late to carry out the order, as the Indians that were massing made such a move impossible. Instead, Croghan determined to protect the fort, and refused British General Proctor's demand to surrender. Croghan had a force of only 160 men to face the combined British and Indian strength of more than three thousand. To make matters worse, Fort Stephenson had only one piece of ordnance, a puny six-pounder cannon named "Old Betsy." Croghan ordered his men to fire and then move the red-hot cannon from port to port as fast as possible, giving the impression that the fort was better armed. He also correctly anticipated the angle of attack against the fort, and concentrated his defense at that section. A barrage of rifle fire forced the rushing attackers into a ditch, and "Old Betsy," which had been moved to a position that had command of the ditch, opened fire. The British retreated, and Maj. Croghan had won an important victory, suffering the loss of one man. George Croghan became a national hero, was promoted to lieutenant colonel, and received a gold medal from Congress.

George Croghan is buried beneath an impressive monument in Fremont's Birchard Library Park, the site of Fort Stephenson, and "Old Betsy" stands guard in the northwest corner of the park. Nearby is Spiegel Grove, home of Rutherford B. Hayes, which is now a state historical site (please see Delaware for Hayes information).

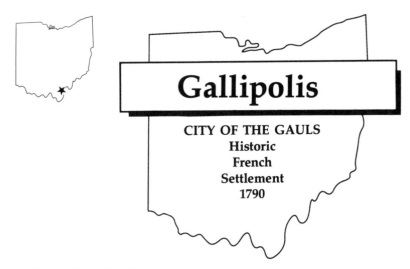

Gallipolis

CITY OF THE GAULS
Historic
French
Settlement
1790

GALLIPOLIS *(Gallia County)*

"A climate wholesome and delightful, frost even in winter almost entirely unknown, and a river called, by way of eminence, the beautiful, and abounding in excellent fish of vast size. Venison in plenty, the pursuit of which is uninterrupted by wolves, foxes, lions or tigers. A couple of swine will multiply themselves a hundred-fold in two years, without taking any care of them." So read the beautiful brochure describing the Ohio Country presented by Joel Barlow and William Playfair to the French in Europe. With the Bastille, and the guillotine, falling, several hundred Frenchmen chose to seek their fortune in this garden of Eden called Ohio. Unfortunately, Playfair absconded with the funds that were to be used by the Scioto Company to pay for this land, and no one told the French that their Eden was unbroken wilderness, infested with rattlesnakes, not suitable for farming, and home to Indians who at the time were engaged in hostilities toward the whites.

When the French emigres landed in America in 1790 and learned that their deeds were of no value, some stayed in the East, but others continued on to "paradise," where 80 crude cabins awaited them, protected against Indians by breastworks anchored at each corner by a blockhouse. The new settlement was named Gallipolis, City of the Gauls, but even this was not yet theirs. To add insult to injury, the land had to be purchased again from the Ohio Company, as it fell outside the Scioto Company lands.

Congress, in an effort to help rectify this debacle and demonstrate that America had a heart, allocated 24,000 acres of land in present-day Scioto County for the French, but most of the French, no match for the wilderness, headed for eastern cities, St. Louis, or New Orleans. Today the six-acre Gallipolis City Park marks the site of the original settlement of Gallipolis.

87

THE FRENCH SETTLERS AT GALLIPOLIS, DIRECT FROM PARIS, CUTTING DOWN TREES.

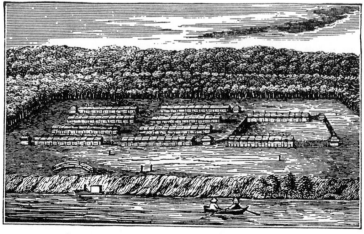

GALLIPOLIS, *i. e.*, CITY OF THE FRENCH, IN 1790.

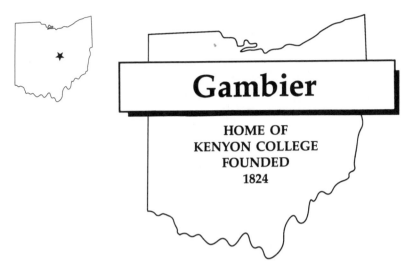

Gambier

**HOME OF
KENYON COLLEGE
FOUNDED
1824**

GAMBIER (Knox County)

Philander Chase was born in New Hampshire in 1775, graduated from Dartmouth in 1795, and in 1817 moved to the frontier state of Ohio. Chase, who had become the first Protestant minister in Louisiana and would become the first Episcopal bishop of Ohio, was intent on establishing a college in Buckeyeland, and went to England to raise funds for his new school. With great effort, Chase succeeded in raising $30,000. Among his benefactors were Lord Kenyon, Baron of Gredington, for whom the college is named, and Lord Gambier, for whom the town is named.

Upon his return to Ohio, Chase bought 8,000 acres of land in Knox County and, in 1824, founded Kenyon College, the first private institution of higher learning in Ohio. In the middle of the college's land was located the village of Gambier, laid out in 1826. The expenses of living in Gambier in the early days were considered small, with annual charges for instruction, $30; board at the college table, $40; rent in a room with a stove, $4; and rent in a room with a fireplace, $6.

Kenyon's reputation grew throughout the century, and the college numbered among its graduates Edwin M. Stanton, Lincoln's secretary of war, and President Rutherford B. Hayes. Lorin Andrews, Kenyon's president when the Civil War broke out, was the first volunteer to the Union army.

Today, Kenyon is noted for its world famous literary magazine, *The Kenyon Review,* and for the Kenyon Festival Theater, one of the country's top professional summer theaters. Actor Paul Newman and the late Swedish Prime Minister Olaf Palme are more recent graduates of Kenyon. Approximately 1,600 full time undergraduate students now study on the beautiful campus at Gambier.

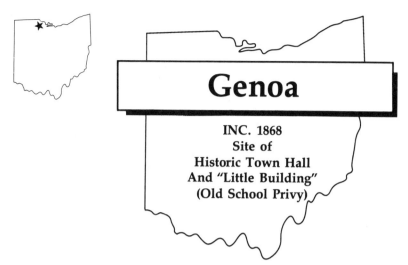

Genoa

INC. 1868
Site of
Historic Town Hall
And "Little Building"
(Old School Privy)

GENOA (*Ottawa County*)

Genoa is home to two sites on the National Register of Historic Places, the Town Hall/Opera House and the Old School Privy.

The Town Hall was built in 1885, and the Opera House, located on the second floor, was built the following year. The Hall was used not only for a theater, but for the yearly caucuses, medicine shows, and even a coroner's inquest of the town's first murder. Placed on the National Register of Historic Places in 1976, the Hall earned a place in Chesley's Collection of Historic Theatres in 1983.

Also on the National Register is Genoa's famous outhouse, known commonly as "The Old School Privy." Located on the grounds of Camper Elementary School, this simple but elegant building is one of the last privies of its kind. Built in 1870, this Romanesque Revival brick outhouse, if located away from the school, could itself be mistaken for an old one-room schoolhouse.

The quality of design in these two buildings reflects the pride that Genoa had in its civic buildings in the last quarter of the nineteenth century.

Georgetown

**GENERAL
ULYSSES S. GRANT
Lived Here From
1823 Until 1839**

GEORGETOWN (Brown County)

Hiram Ulysses Grant was born on April 27, 1822, in Point Pleasant, Ohio, a Clermont County village along the Ohio River (see Point Pleasant). His father, Jesse, a tanner by trade, moved the family from their little frame home a year later, settling in Georgetown where the elder Grant built a tannery. Hiram attended a two-room schoolhouse in Georgetown, but seemed to favor play over study. He was a frequent visitor at the home of Dr. and Mrs. Bailey, and when he informed his father that the Bailey's son was leaving West Point, Jesse Grant had his congressman arrange for Hiram to take young Bailey's place. The application mistakenly read "Ulysses Simpson" instead of "Hiram Ulysses," and thereafter he became known as "United States," "Uncle Sam," and "Unconditional Surrender" Grant.

Following his graduation from West Point, Grant floundered, but the Civil War brought him an unexpected resurrection. In spite of rumored drinking bouts, Lincoln stayed with him, saying, "I can't spare this man. He fights." And fight he did, forcing the Confederate surrender at Vicksburg and ultimately accepting the surrender of Lee at Appomattox. He was as gracious in victory as he was skillful in battle, allowing the Confederate officers to keep their swords and the soldiers their horses for spring plowing. Grant became the first four-star general since George Washington, and went on to the White House in 1868, where he served two terms. His political record was less inspiring than his military one, and, although he never personally profited, his administration was wracked by scandal.

It was said that part of Grant's effectiveness in war was his ability to write orders in clear prose. In his last years, Mark Twain encouraged Grant to write his *Personal Memoirs,* and although wracked by the pain of throat cancer, he managed to complete them just a few days before his death on July 23, 1885. Considered to be a masterful work, sales of the book provided a comfortable life for his widow.

Gnadenhutten

**EARLY MORAVIAN
MISSION SETTLEMENT
Site of 1782 Massacre
Of 90 Christian
Indians**

GNADENHUTTEN *(Tuscarawas County)*

Abraham, the chief of the Christian Moravian Indians, knew this March night in 1782 would be the last that he and his followers would spend alive. Just one day earlier Col. David Williamson had approached the Indians while they were gathering corn in their fields and promised them protection at Fort Pitt. After accepting their weapons, the colonel had them tied up, then told them that they were to be put to death by the troops as a lesson to their Delaware brothers. The colonel had "mercifully" granted Abraham's plea that the Moravians be allowed to spend this night in prayer before the "sentence" was to be carried out. Undoubtedly, Abraham spent his last hours regretting his faith in the Americans, whom he had defended when the Delawares warned him of their treachery.

Ninety-two prisoners were held in two buildings, the men and boys in one, the women and girls in the other. All were bound with their hands behind their backs, spending the long night in terror and prayer. When daylight came, twenty soldiers entered the room, and Capt. Charles Builderback, who had won the right in a drawing to begin the slaughter, walked up behind Abraham and crushed his skull with a mallet. Around the room the troops went, delivering fatal blows to the Indians who stood facing the walls. Similar sickening sounds came from the building next door. Soon, all the Moravians lay dead and scalped, with the exception of two boys who had escaped to warn the others at Schoenbrunn of the devastation that was headed their way. The atrocity inflamed the frontier, angering Indians and whites alike. The Delawares would later avenge the murders, but it was not Col. Williamson who would pay the price (see Bucyrus).

Today, a memorial to the Indian Massacre stands in the village of Gnadenhutten, and the single grave of the Indian martyrs is marked by a simple stone.

Granville

SETTLED 1805
Home of
Denison University,
Founded 1831.

GRANVILLE *(Licking County)*

"Granville is a spot where learning welcomes you as you enter, looks down upon you from the hills as you pass through, and bids you farewell as you leave," wrote a passerby through the village a century ago, and still today it is an appropriate description for the New England-like village huddled beneath the college on the hill.

In the autumn of 1805, 234 persons from Granville, Massachusetts, arrived on the 28,000 acres of land they had purchased in Ohio. Naming their new town Granville in honor of their former home, they set about building a community that would grow into one of Ohio's most beautiful villages. In 1831, the Baptist church in the center of town welcomed the thirty-seven new arrivals to the Granville Literary and Theological Institution, the forerunner of Denison University. The church housed the school in that first year while the school buildings were being built, but tragedy struck before the school was ever occupied. A fire in 1832 destroyed the uninsured college, and the struggle for funds began anew. The directors offered to name the college after anyone who would donate $10,000, and in 1853 it was named for William S. Denison of Adamsville.

Like other Ohio colleges in the 1850's, Denison struggled and almost left Granville. The forces of the Baptist denomination rallied, however, and soon the college was relocated to its present spot on the hill overlooking the village. The struggling theological department was dropped in the 1870's, with the school devoting its curriculum to science and liberal arts. In 1900, the female Shepardson College that had emerged from the Young Ladies Institute in Granville became part of Denison University.

Today, Denison is a four-year private coeducational liberal arts school with a full time enrollment of about 2,100 students.

Greenfield

NAMED IN 1799
BY ITS FOUNDER,
GEN. DUNCAN McARTHUR,
FOR ITS
GREEN PLAINS

GREENFIELD *(Highland County)*

(For information on General McArthur, please see McArthur, Ohio.)

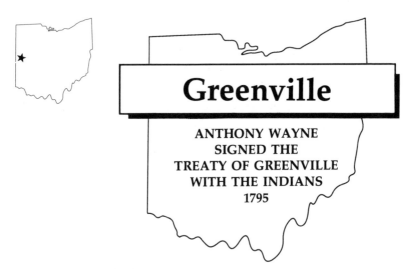

Greenville

**ANTHONY WAYNE
SIGNED THE
TREATY OF GREENVILLE
WITH THE INDIANS
1795**

GREENVILLE (Darke County)

Following the Battle of Fallen Timbers at present Maumee, Gen. Anthony Wayne had returned to Fort Greenville to await the Indian tribes arrival in the summer of 1795. As June passed into July, the wisely patient Wayne greeted the arrival of twelve tribes totaling more than 1,300 men. The great chiefs of the Indian nations, among them Tarhe the Crane, Blue Jacket, Black Snake, and Black Hoof, gathered around the council fires to discuss the terms of the peace that was to govern the Ohio Country. White wampum belts of peace were exchanged to show the sincerity and good faith of the speakers.

The terms of Wayne's peace were bitter ones for the Indians, yet the great chiefs knew they had little alternative but to accept them. The Indians were to cede to the United States about two-thirds of present day Ohio, retaining the northern third as Indian territory. They also were to retain the right to hunt and fish throughout the Ohio Country to the Ohio River. In exchange, the Indians received $1,666 for each tribe, plus an annual payment to each tribe of $825. On August 3, 1795, the chiefs and Gen. Anthony Wayne signed the Treaty of Greenville, opening much of Ohio to settlement.

"I fervently pray to the Great Spirit that the peace may be permanent and holds us together in bonds of friendship until time is no more," said Wayne. But a decade and a half later, a young chief who had refused to attend the treaty meeting would lead a confederation of Indian tribes against the settlers and soldiers once again. His name was Tecumseh.

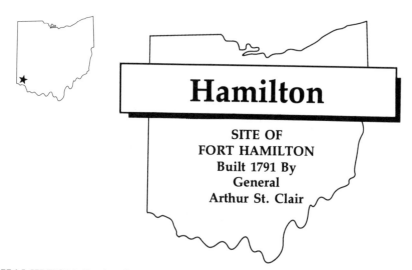

Hamilton

SITE OF
FORT HAMILTON
Built 1791 By
General
Arthur St. Clair

HAMILTON (Butler County)

Fort Hamilton, constructed by Gen. Arthur St. Clair in 1791, was one of a number of forts constructed in the first years of the 1790's in an effort to defeat the Indians and open the Ohio Country for settlement. Following by a year the crushing defeat of Gen. Josiah Harmar, hopes were high that this new army under St. Clair would erase the painful memory of Harmar's expedition and quiet the anxiety felt along the frontier. After much delay, St. Clair finally marched his troops out of Fort Washington (now Cincinnati), but it was an ill-prepared force, undisciplined, and followed by a group of women, children, and lovers who were quickly consuming the army's few rations. When the force reached the crossing of the Great Miami River twenty-three miles north of Fort Washington, St. Clair stopped to build the first fort in the series, and called it Fort Hamilton.

Fort Hamilton was a rectangular fort, with twenty-foot high double palisades and a ditch surrounding it. It served as a stopping place not only for St. Clair, who went on to a major defeat at the site of Fort Recovery, but also for Anthony Wayne's forces who stayed here for a short time two years later on their way to victory at the Battle of Fallen Timbers.

The fort was abandoned by 1797, and on the site of Fort Hamilton grew the city that took the name of the fort, Hamilton, Ohio.

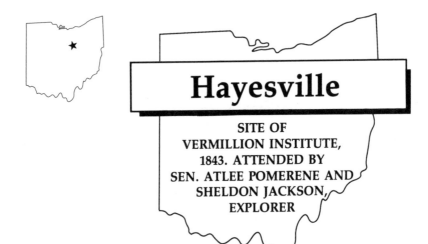

Hayesville

SITE OF
VERMILLION INSTITUTE,
1843. ATTENDED BY
SEN. ATLEE POMERENE AND
SHELDON JACKSON,
EXPLORER

HAYESVILLE (Ashland County)

The Vermillion Institute had its origin in Hayesville as a Baptist institution, but, not proving successful for that denomination, passed into the control of the Wooster Presbytery. Under the able guidance of Dr. Diefendorf, a pastor from Nashville, Ohio, the school flourished and became one of the leading Presbyterian schools in the country. At its peak, the school had an enrollment of 600 students. When Dr. Diefendorf resigned, the school floundered, but rebounded upon his return. He would soon resign again to take a post in Nebraska. In his absence, the difficulties again arose, and he again agreed to return. Unfortunately, he died before reassuming the presidency of the school. The experience of the Vermillion Institute provides graphic evidence as to why Dr. Diefendorf was considered one of Ohio's ablest educators.

Among the students at Vermillion were Atlee Pomerene (see Berlin) and Sheldon Jackson. After attending Vermillion, Jackson went on to become a noted missionary and educator, serving throughout the upper Midwest and in Indian Territory. In 1885, he was appointed superintendent of schools in Alaska, where he observed the starving condition of many of the Alaskan natives. He proposed introducing reindeer to the area, and the training of the natives as herders. He eventually established eight stations with 1,700 reindeer, and was involved in a life-saving operation as a result. In 1897, eight whaling vessels were trapped in the ice of the Arctic Ocean. On orders of the secretary of the treasury, the deer at two of the stations were taken to the vessels, thereby saving the whalers from starvation.

Higginsport

**WHITE BURLEY
TOBACCO
FIRST GROWN IN OHIO
NEAR HERE
DURING CIVIL WAR**

HIGGINSPORT (Brown County)

Higginsport, an Ohio River town, is located in the tobacco-growing region of southern Ohio, and Brown County has long prided itself on the quality of its tobacco. The "White Burley" chewing tobacco of Brown County has a special fame, having first been grown here during the Civil War. It was noted as "of fine quality and highly valued as a superior chewing tobacco." White Burley was discovered in 1864 by Joseph Fore on the farm of Capt. Fred Kautz, a Civil War soldier. Fore had obtained some burley seeds from George Barkley, which surprisingly produced some plants that were almost milk white. They were at first thought to be damaged, but grew as vigorously as the other plants, so were therefore transplanted with the others.

When the white plants were mature, they were cut and hung separately. After curing, they were "very bright and fine in texture, with a superior quality." The seeds were saved, and became the basis of the famous White Burley tobacco of Brown County.

In 1964, the White Burley Tobacco Monument Marker was erected in Pleasant Township in celebration of the centennial of White Burley's discovery.

Hillsboro

**HOME OF
ELIZA JANE THOMPSON
Early Temperance
Crusader**

HILLSBORO *(Highland County)*

It was three days before Christmas in 1873, and Dr. Dio Lewis had finished a lecture to a group of Hillsboro women on the evils of alcohol, drawing on his experience with an intemperate father. His address touched a sympathetic nerve with the women in attendance, and shortly thereafter more than fifty women signed a solemn compact which read: "With God's help, we will stand by each other in this work, and persevere therein until it is accomplished; and see to it, as far as our influence goes, that the traffic shall never be revived." On Christmas morning, a double line procession of more than seventy-five women made their way from church to the drug stores and saloons where liquor was sold. Trembling at her immodesty, Mrs. Eliza Jane Thompson, daughter of a former governor and wife of a judge, was the first to kneel in prayer on the floor of the barroom. After praying and singing hymns, the women apprised the shocked saloon keeper that they would be back the next day.

The women continued in their rounds until all the saloons and drug stores had been visited. Ultimately, all the saloon keepers either chose other occupations or left town, with the exception of a Mr. Dunn, who sued the women for obstructing his business. He won the case, but was awarded only $5.00.

The movement begun in Hillsboro became the Women's Temperance Crusade, a forerunner of the powerful Women's Christian Temperance Union (WCTU). And as for Mr. Dunn, he remained an oasis in the dry desert of Hillsboro. When repeal came in 1934, the State of Ohio opened a liquor store in the former quarters of the unrepentant Mr. Dunn.

SINGING BEFORE A SALOON.

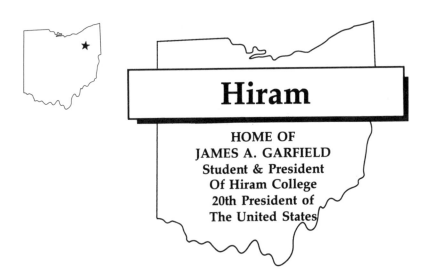

Hiram

**HOME OF
JAMES A. GARFIELD
Student & President
Of Hiram College
20th President of
The United States**

HIRAM *(Portage County)*

In 1849, a group of men interested in establishing a school affiliated with the Disciples of Christ met in the home of A. L. Soule. After two other meetings, it was agreed to establish a school, albeit an academy instead of a college, leaving only its location unresolved. It is said that while visiting Hiram, the delegation observed the town physician, lean and lank, ride by on a horse than was even leaner and lanker. Someone quipped that "a township that can't afford sickness enough to keep a doctor better than that is just the place for the school." The school opened in 1851 as the Western Reserve Eclectic Institute, received its charter in 1867 as Hiram College, and was rebuilt and enlarged in 1886. This four year private liberal arts college now has a full time undergraduate enrollment of about 1,200 students, and boasts among its illustrious graduates and former college presidents James A. Garfield, the 20th president of the United States.

"Tell me, Burke, do you not feel a spirit stirring within you that longs to know - to do and to dare - to hold converse with the great world of thought and hold before you some high and noble object to which the vigor of your mind and the strength of your arm may be given?" So wrote James A. Garfield, then Hiram College president, in a letter to his student, Burke A. Hinsdale, dated January 15, 1857. Perhaps Garfield was holding before himself the high and noble object of the presidency at that time, and perhaps he helped inspire Hinsdale to reach new heights, for when James A. Garfield became the 20th president of the United States, B.A. Hinsdale was the president of Hiram College.

(For more information on James A. Garfield, please see Mentor, Ohio.)

Hudson

**FOUNDED 1799.
Site of Western Reserve
College, 1826.
Now Home of
Western Reserve Academy**

HUDSON (Summit County)

Hudson was founded in 1799 by Connecticut pioneer David Hudson, who had come to northeast Ohio, the "Western Reserve of Connecticut," from New England. Laid out with a village green and distinguished by its white frame buildings, Hudson long had the reputation as the quintessential New England village in Ohio.

In 1826, Western Reserve College, the first college in northern Ohio, was founded in Hudson by a group of men who had been instrumental in developing the territory. Hudson was chosen over Cleveland for the college site, as Cleveland was a lake port city considered "full of temptation for the innocent student." Although the school primarily emphasized an education in the classics and preparation for the ministry, it was strong in the sciences as well. In 1836, Western Reserve College constructed the third observatory to be built in the country, and the observatory's founder, Professor Elias Loomis, played a key role in the refining of the weather charts used around the world today.

In the meantime, Cleveland was a growing city with an improving reputation and bent on having its own university. When Leonard Case, Jr. bequeathed a large sum of money for the purpose of establishing a scientific school in Cleveland, representatives of the new Case School Of Applied Science met with officials of Western Reserve College to discuss sharing a tract of land. Amasa Stone, Cleveland banker and railroad builder, offered to pay for the removal of Western Reserve College to Cleveland, and in 1882 the school left Hudson for good.

Following the departure of Western Reserve College, the beautiful campus in Hudson became home to Western Reserve Academy, a highly rated secondary school. In 1967 Western Reserve University and the Case Institute of Technology officially became Case Western Reserve University in Cleveland.

Huron

**LEADING
OHIO BUILDER
OF STEAMSHIPS
IN THE 1830's.**

HURON (Erie County)

The 1830's were a time of intense activity along the Lake Erie shore. With lake trade booming, the villages that were located at the mouths of rivers on Lake Erie were scrambling to meet the demand for ships to sail the lake waters. Sloops, schooners and barques all plied Erie, but the steamships were the queens of the waterway. The steamer *Walk-in-the-Water* inaugurated the steamship era on the lake in 1818, but this ship from Black Rock on the Niagara River met a tragic end three years later when she was destroyed in a storm off Buffalo. Fortunately, all passengers were saved.

Huron, located where the Huron River empties into Lake Erie, has a natural harbor that gave rise to its shipbuilding industry. Among the many steamships built at Huron is one that gained quite a degree of celebrity, but for a tragic reason. The *Sheldon Thompson*, built at Huron for $16,000, was pressed into service in the Black Hawk War, and in 1832 was chartered to ferry troops under the command of General Winfield Scott. While sailing across the lake from Buffalo, she was hit by an outbreak of cholera. Panic swept the ship, and the dead were cast overboard while anchored in the harbor at Chicago. With the bodies still visible in the clear water the next day, the ship had to keep moving. Other ships fled in terror from the *Sheldon Thompson*, which suffered the loss of nearly one hundred men.

In 1834, the disease that raged around the lake struck Huron itself, killing many residents and causing many others to flee. Finally, when the Milan Canal drew away much of Huron's business, the community entered a period of quietude. Today, tourism is one of Huron's leading industries.

Ironton

ONCE CENTER OF
SOUTHERN OHIO'S
WORLD LEADING
PIG IRON
INDUSTRY

IRONTON *(Lawrence County)*

Ironton is located in the center of the Hanging Rock Iron Region of southern Ohio. The area was wilderness up to 1826, when John Means built a charcoal furnace, dubbed the "Union," near his home and began making pig-iron. Within twenty years, the area was home to twenty-one charcoal furnaces, and that number would double again within the next few decades. Surrounding each of the furnaces were "furnace estates," ranging from 5,000 to 10,000 acres, on which grew the trees that supplied the 15,000 cords of wood yearly that kept the charcoal fires burning. Grouped at each furnace was a community of about seventy-five families directly involved with the operation of the furnace. The Iron Railroad, a thirteen mile long track that connected these isolated furnaces, transported iron and supplies back and forth to the Ohio River. In 1849, Ironton was laid out as the terminus of this little railway, and two years later it became the county seat.

The pig-iron produced by these furnaces was considered to be the best in the world, and the best of the best was that from the Hecla Furnace, three miles east of Ironton. During the Civil War, Hecla's iron was used solely for casting ordnance, but its chief use during peace time was for the manufacture of railroad car wheels. The average life of an ordinary car wheel was about 80,000 miles, compared to the 200,000 miles expected of a Hecla wheel.

The last charcoal furnace operating in the area was the Pine Grove Furnace. Perhaps its longevity was due in part to its being the first furnace to demonstrate that a blast furnace could successfully shut down on the Sabbath. Cynics suggested that the furnace owners were not themselves so religious, but the Sundays-off practice attracted "a class of furnace attendants more respectable and conscientious, and more devoted to the interests of their employers."

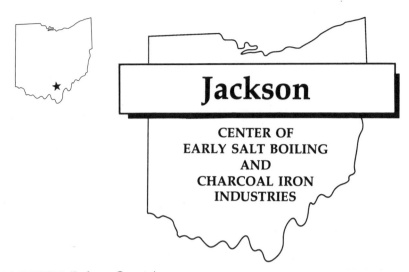

Jackson

**CENTER OF
EARLY SALT BOILING
AND
CHARCOAL IRON
INDUSTRIES**

JACKSON (Jackson County)

Before the arrival of white settlers to this part of the country, Indians would come here to make salt, often accompanied by white captives, including, at different times, Daniel Boone and Jonathon Alder. The first whites to make salt here for themselves did so in 1798. The "Old Scioto Salt-works" that gained fame at the turn of the nineteenth century was located in Jackson County along the banks of Salt Creek, a stream that fed the Scioto River. Wells were sunk about thirty feet to draw the water, which was then boiled away in huge iron kettles, leaving behind the fine white crystals so important for seasoning and meat preservation. The salinity of the water was not considered great, requiring up to fifteen gallons of water to make one pound of salt. From the kettles the salt was loaded onto packhorses and carried to other settlements where it would fetch up to four dollars a bushel. Sometimes the buyers would come to the salt works, but they risked falling prey to the rowdy boilers. One traveler, intent on revenge after having his saddlebags thrown into the furnace on an earlier visit, loaded another pack with gunpowder on a return trip. The expression "shooting one with a pack saddle" became common in the region.

Salt was such an important commodity that Congress set aside a six-mile square area for the use of the state, and in 1804 the Ohio legislature passed an act regulating the management of these salt works. Later, other salt springs that were more accessible and of a higher salinity were found, and in 1824 Congress authorized Ohio to sell these lands "and apply the proceeds to such literary purposes as the Ohio legislature may think proper; but to no other purpose whatever."

Charcoal iron, another principal industry of Jackson County, is described elsewhere (please see Wellston).

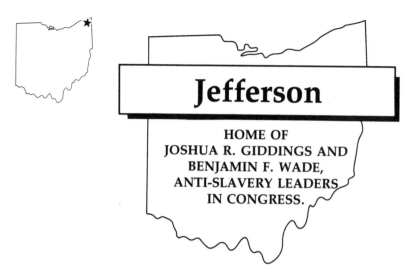

Jefferson

HOME OF
JOSHUA R. GIDDINGS AND
BENJAMIN F. WADE,
ANTI-SLAVERY LEADERS
IN CONGRESS.

JEFFERSON (Ashtabula County)

"The little village of Jefferson, which then counted hardly more than seven hundred inhabitants, was the home of Giddings and Wade, and was the center of a most extraordinary amount of reading and thinking. Outside of Massachusetts, I do not believe that an equal average of intelligence could have been found among all sorts and conditions of men, who were there of an almost perfect social equality." This is the way the town of Jefferson was described by William Dean Howells, famed Ohio author.

Joshua Giddings was born in 1795, and grew up on the Ohio frontier in the Western Reserve. Mostly self-educated, he tramped forty miles through the wilderness to study law with Elisha Whittlesey (see Canfield), and established a successful legal practice in Jefferson. In 1838, two years after the House of Representatives invoked the infamous "gag rule" to stifle debate on the slavery issue, Giddings was elected to Congress. Ardently antislavery and pro-free speech, Giddings joined the attack against the gag rule, and for introducing antislavery petitions he earned the censure of the House. Undaunted, the fiery Giddings resigned his seat, and was overwhelmingly reelected by his home district. In 1844, the gag rule was revoked by the House.

While Giddings served in the House, his protege and law partner, Ben Wade, was leading the Radical Republicans in the Senate, having been first elected to that body in 1850. "Bluff Ben" advocated the immediate emancipation of the slaves during the Civil War, and felt Lincoln was too lenient toward the South. The three term U.S. senator was elected president pro tem of the Senate in 1867, and narrowly missed becoming president when the impeachment of President Johnson failed by one vote, there being no sitting vice-president.

Allies and partners in life, Giddings and Wade remain close in death, buried near each other in the town cemetery.

Johnstown

FOUNDED 1813
Famous Mastodon
Remains
Discovered Here,
1926

JOHNSTOWN (Licking County)

Ten thousand years ago, much of Ohio was covered by an ice sheet up to 5,000 feet thick. Ice Age animals, including giant beavers, saber-tooth tigers, wild horses, mammoths and mastodons, roamed near the southern edge of the ice. Nomadic Paleo-Indians, working together in groups, may have stalked the giant creatures along the glacier's edge. When the climate began to warm, the ice started melting, and the glacier retreated northward. Many animals moved north with the glacier, but for others, including the mastodon, the warmer climate sounded the death knell. Mastodons became extinct in Ohio.

On August 12, 1926, eight thousand years after the last of its kind walked the earth, two farmers in Johnstown, Ohio uncovered the complete skeletal remains of a mastodon in a farm field, transforming the normally sleepy village into the center of national attention. Before the summer was over, Model T's would be lined up for miles along the old dirt road that ran by the farm, and photo and parking concessions would be flourishing. Unfortunately for Johnstown, the skeleton that had been buried for millenia in Licking County would vanish from Johnstown in a matter of weeks - a businessman from Newark, who had purchased the bones for $3,000 a few days after their discovery, sold them to the Cleveland Museum of Natural History for $5,300. All attempts to have the bones returned to Johnstown have failed, and today visitors to the museum in Cleveland can see the reassembled skeleton of the famous Johnstown Mastodon on display.

While complete mastodon skeletons are rare (only about a dozen have been found in the state), all may not be lost for Licking Countians wishing to display a native mastodon. On December 12, 1989, near Heath, another mastodon was discovered while workers were digging a pond for a golf course. Perhaps this will be the mastodon that didn't get away!

Kalida

**FIRST PUTNAM COUNTY
SEAT, 1834-1866.
Home of Putnam County's
Pioneer Days
Celebration**

KALIDA (Putnam County)

On September 6, 1873, a group of the old pioneers of Putnam County met at Kalida to form the Putnam County Pioneer Association to "perpetuate the early history of our county." The organization was to meet annually on the first Saturday in September at Kalida, with membership limited to those persons resident in the county prior to 1840. From these meetings came a collection of stories worthy of passing on to future generations, and to achieve this, the group published two pamphlets of Reminiscences, the first in 1878 and the latter in 1886. Reading some of these early reminiscences, one can imagine the laughter and frivolity that accompanied these day-long Pioneer Day Celebrations.

"H.S. Knapp became at an early day editor of the Kalida *Venture*," goes one reminiscence. "He went one Sunday to a camp meeting at Columbus Grove, in a wagon, with his wife. They were newly married. Started to return together on horseback and got dumped into a mud-hole. Knapp tried to pull his wife out but failed. Backed his horse; wife caught horse's tail and was pulled out. The *Venture* appeared next morning with editorials short and crabbed."

The Society has changed over the years. The meeting date was changed to the first Saturday after Labor Day in 1962, and the membership was opened to anyone interested in the Society. The tone of the celebrations also changed, with "pageants" being introduced in the 1940's. Reenactments of schools in the 1890's, 1840's wedding ceremonies, and the constructing of the first plank road in the county were among the pageants introduced on Pioneer Day. The organization continued to grow, and in 1970 the Society acquired the former Methodist Church to use as a museum.

Today, the former Putnam County Pioneer Association is the Putnam County Historical Society.

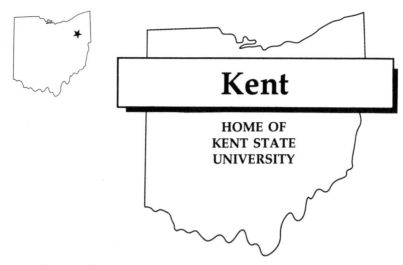

Kent

HOME OF
KENT STATE
UNIVERSITY

KENT *(Portage County)*

"Shortly after noon on May 4, 1970, on a grassy knoll behind Taylor Hall and the Prentice Hall parking lot, a contingent of Ohio National Guardsmen opened fire for a period of thirteen seconds, striking thirteen Kent State University students, some of whom were nearby, others of whom were distant. Four students were killed, one was permanently paralyzed, and the others were wounded in varying degrees of severity. The students were shot as the guard was responding to a demonstration on the campus. Four days of protest (against the U.S. invasion of Cambodia) ended in tragedy. The loss of the students killed and wounded was a pivotal moment in the history of Kent State University." These words are introductory to the college bulletin of Kent State, a school whose very name evokes intense emotion across the country. Allison Krause, Jeffrey Miller, Sandra Scheuer, and William Schroeder were the names of the students killed. After the shootings, campuses across the nation erupted, many closing for the remainder of the spring term.

Twenty years later, plans go forward for an on-campus memorial to the fallen students. The university's library has dedicated a Memorial Room that holds materials relating to May 4, and the University's Center for Peaceful Change has instituted an academic program with its own major to help today's students learn from the tragic events of May, 1970.

Kenton

HOME OF
LT. JACOB PARROT
First Congressional
Medal of Honor
Winner

KENTON (Hardin County)

Kenton is one of three Ohio communities claiming an Andrews Raider of Civil War fame on its historical marker. Kenton was hometown to the youngest raider of the group, Jacob Parrot, a nineteen year old private. The famed Andrews Raiders were awarded the first Congressional Medals of Honor for a daring raid into the South during the Civil War (please see McComb for details of the raid), with Parrot being awarded the first medal because of his age. Lt. Jacob Parrot of Kenton survived the war, and died in 1908. He is buried in Kenton's Grove Cemetery beneath a marker that reads "Lieut. Parrot was honored by Congress with the first medal issued for distinguished bravery."

On July 12, 1990, the 127th anniversary of President Lincoln's signing the bill establishing the Medal of Honor, the descendants of Jacob Parrot presented the medal to Congress in formal ceremonies attended by Speaker of the House Thomas Foley, Senate Majority Leader George Mitchell, and 33 Medal of Honor recipients. The ceremony brought to a conclusion the family's search for an appropriate place to display the medal, and helps fulfill their desire to keep alive the role of the Andrews Raiders during the Civil War. The first Congressional Medal of Honor has a new home in a climate-controlled display case in the House Crypt in the Capitol Building in Washington, D.C. Since Jacob Parrot received that first medal, 3,392 members of the armed forces have been awarded the nation's highest military award for valor.

Kettering

HOME OF JAMES M. COX
Governor of Ohio, 1913-15,
1917-21 and of
CHARLES F. KETTERING,
Inventor

KETTERING (Montgomery County)

James M. Cox, Ohio's first three term Democratic governor, is considered by many to be in the top rank of Ohio's modern-day governors, bringing to his first administration some of the greatest reforms the state had ever seen. Penal reform, child labor laws, improved rural education, agricultural experimentation, workmen's compensation, and the Conservancy Law (a response to the disastrous flood of 1913) were but a few of the initiatives addressed during his governorship, which rode into office on the crest of the Progressive Movement in Ohio in 1912.

James Cox was born on his father's farm on March 31, 1870, and he went on to be a school teacher, printer, reporter, congressman, governor and publisher of the *Dayton Daily News* and *Springfield News.* At the end of his first term, he was nominated by his party for reelection in 1914, running on his record of "promises fulfilled" and a pledge of "legislative rest." An apparently weary electorate defeated his bid for a second term that year, but two years later he was returned to office for two more terms.

Cox's performance as Ohio governor earned him the Democratic nomination for president in 1920, with a young Franklin D. Roosevelt as his running mate. His Republican opponent was another Ohio newspaper publisher, Warren G. Harding (see Marion), who won the election. Cox retired from politics until he was appointed by Roosevelt to the World Economic and Monetary Conference in London in 1933. He added to his extensive newspaper holdings and wrote his autobiography before his death in 1957.

(Please see Loudonville for Charles F. Kettering.)

Kingston

TRADITIONALLY INGSTOWN.
Founded in 1816 by
Thomas Ing, A Tailor
and Tavern Keeper.
Incorporated 1834

KINGSTON *(Ross County)*

Zane's Trace had created an overland route from Wheeling to Maysville, and almost immediately businesses and communities started blossoming along the trail. Among the services most in demand along the early road were taverns. With travel through the forest painfully slow, frequent overnight accommodations were needed, and the log roadside taverns filled the need for room and board. The smaller taverns of the day had only a lower room and a loft into which the traveler ascended by a ladder or stairs. In the loft would be found four or five beds, and in the event that both sexes needed to share the loft, a curtain would be drawn between them.

Sometime after 1805, Thomas Ing bought a forty acre plot of land along the main route between Lancaster and Chillicothe and located the village of "Ingstown" upon it. In 1816, the town was regularly laid out and renamed Kingston. Mr. Ing obtained a license to establish the first tavern here in 1817, and also served as the town's first tailor. Soon, new arrivals were setting up businesses at Kingston to serve the traffic along the stage route, including a second tavern "for the special accommodation of the traveling public." It was a distinguished clientele that they served. With the route through Kingston being part of the main road from the southwest to the nation's capital, many notables came through town. Henry Clay, President Monroe, Felix Grundy, and ex-President Santa Anna of Mexico were but a few of the illustrious guests who stopped in Kingston for a meal or lodging.

Kirtland Hills

FOUNDED AS KIRTLAND 1817
Home of First
Mormon Temple
In The
United States

KIRTLAND HILLS *(Lake County)*

Rising high above the surrounding countryside on a bluff overlooking the east branch of the Chagrin River stands one of the most interesting and storied buildings of the Western Reserve, the first Mormon Temple in the United States, erected by the Prophet of Mormon and his followers in the year 1833. The three story temple, inspired by a detailed vision of Prophet Joseph Smith, dominates the skyline from all directions, the crushed china and glass in the stucco glistening in the sunlight. Inside, twelve pulpits arranged into three tiers dominate opposite walls, in accordance with Smith's vision. No simple frontier church, this temple has stood for more than a century and a half. Smith, however, barely lasted here until the church was completed, fleeing in advance of a mob in 1838.

Smith hailed from New York, where he had been led by the spirit in 1823 to uncover a lost scriptural record of Mormon recorded on golden plates. He translated them into the Book of Mormon, and soon attracted a following. Sidney Rigdon, an influential preacher from the Western Reserve, was converted to Mormonism and convinced Smith to return to Ohio with him. In the open frontier society of Ohio, the Mormon Church, known as the Church of Jesus Christ of Latter-Day Saints, grew at a rapid pace. The curious from far and wide made their way to Kirtland, some to mock and most to believe. When the temple was completed after three years of work, a frenzy of religious fervor ensued at the dedication.

While the pace of conversions was quite satisfactory, financial problems arose, and when the church bank failed it engendered resentment and rumor around Kirtland. Smith would later write, "We were obliged to secrete ourselves to elude our pursuers, who continued their race more than two hundred miles from Kirtland, armed with pistols and seeking our lives." Smith met his death at the hands of a mob in Illinois, but Brigham Young, who helped build the Kirtland temple, led the brethren to Utah and founded Salt Lake City.

111

Lancaster

**BIRTHPLACE OF
WILLIAM T. SHERMAN
Civil War
General**

LANCASTER (Fairfield County)

William T. Sherman, who along with Generals Grant and Sheridan formed the "Ohio Triumverate" that led the Union Army to victory, was born on February 8, 1820 in Lancaster. His father admired the courage and humanity of the great Indian chief, Tecumseh, and so named his boy William Tecumseh Sherman. The name was prophetic, for William was destined to follow Tecumseh as a military genius, although a Presbyterian preacher at first balked at baptizing the child with a "heathen" name.

William's father, Charles Sherman, an Ohio Supreme Court justice, was stricken suddenly by cholera in 1829 and died, leaving a widow with eleven children. Thomas Ewing took in "Cump," and sent him to West Point when he was sixteen. After a fling with banking and law after graduation, he took a position at a military academy in Louisiana. Sherman, however, sensed that a long and bitter war was in the wind, and returned north to fight for the Union.

Sherman's brilliant military career is most noted for his "March to the Sea." Casting aside excess baggage and equipment and planning to live off the land as they marched, the troops cut a swath through the South from Atlanta to the sea. Upon gaining Savannah, Sherman sent his famous message to Lincoln: "I beg to present to you as a Christmas gift the city of Savannah with 150 guns and plenty of ammunition and about 25,000 bales of cotton."

The birthplace of William Tecumseh Sherman stands yet today on E. Main St. in Lancaster.

Lebanon

**HERE LIVED
THOMAS CORWIN
Governor and
United States
Senator**

LEBANON *(Warren County)*

Thomas Corwin was born in Kentucky in 1794, and the family moved to Ohio when Tom was four years old. With funds enough to keep only Tom's brother in school, Tom, an able student, was consigned to work on the family farm. Among his tasks was transporting produce to market in Cincinnati by wagon, and during the War of 1812, he drove his wagon filled with supplies for the army of Gen. William Henry Harrison to a camp on the St. Mary's of the Maumee. He thus earned the appellation "Wagon Boy," which served him well in the homespun campaign of 1840 when Harrison won the presidency and Corwin the governorship of Ohio.

In 1844, Corwin was elected to the U.S. Senate, where his sympathy for the slave, his foresight, and his courage culminated in 1847 in one of the most courageous speeches ever delivered on the floor of Congress. Perceiving the popular War with Mexico as an attempt to extend slave territory, Corwin alone dared speak against it. "If I were a Mexican, I would tell you, 'Have you not room enough in your own country to bury your dead men? If you come into mine, we will greet you with bloody hands, and welcome you to hospitable graves'." He then added prophetically, "Should we prosecute this war another moment...the North and South are brought into collision on a point where neither will yield... and we will plunge the sister States of this Union into the bottomless gulf of civil strife!"

"Our country, right or wrong," was the angry retort to Corwin's speech. While Corwin was denounced as a traitor and burned in effigy, the spark was struck that grew into the conflagration of civil war, for the Mexican War did not truly end until the surrender at Appomatox. Corwin left the Senate in 1850 to serve in the Treasury Department, and retired in 1852. In 1858 and 1860, he was again elected to Congress, and served as minister to Mexico during Lincoln's first term. Thomas Corwin, wagon boy and profile in courage, died in 1865 and was buried in Lebanon Cemetery.

LENA *(Miami County)*

Albert B. Graham was born on a farm near Lena on March 13, 1868, and became one of the three students in the first graduating class of Lena-Conover High School in 1885. He decided to devote his life to education, and went on to attend normal school (teacher-training school) after high school. As a teacher in a one-room schoolhouse, and later as township superintendent, he was dedicated to providing his students with a healthy learning environment. He believed in free self-expression, but rejected free and unlicensed actions "with the Devil as the only tutor."

On January 15, 1902, while Graham was the superintendent of the rural schools of Springfield township of Clark County, Ohio, he formed the first agricultural club for boys and girls in the United States. The "Boys and Girls Experiment Club" later was to become 4-H Club, meaning "Head, Heart, Health, and Hands." Saying that he never intended to be "a teacher of parrots," Mr. Graham envisioned the club as a means to teach the future generations to think responsibly and critically, and to lead rather than merely repeat. The major role that 4-H plays yet today in shaping young people's lives is testament to Mr. Graham's foresight.

Mr. Graham's contributions extended beyond the founding of 4-H. He served as the first Director of Agricultural Extension in Ohio, and, as a member of the National Education Association, was one of a committee of five meeting in Los Angeles that developed the plans for junior high schools. One of the first such schools in the country opened in Columbus in 1907.

Mr. Graham, father of 4-H, died on January 14, 1960, and was buried in Fletcher Cemetery, Fletcher, Ohio.

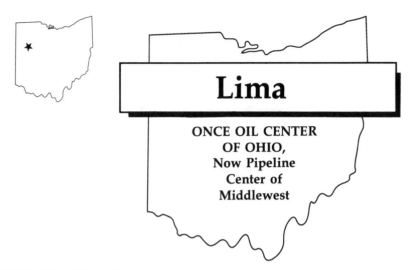

Lima

**ONCE OIL CENTER
OF OHIO,
Now Pipeline
Center of
Middlewest**

LIMA *(Allen County)*

In the spring of 1885, Mr. B. C. Faurot was drilling for gas at his paper mill in Lima. If his well did not strike gas, he would settle for water - after all, he could always buy fuel, but a lack of water for his paper mill would be a serious difficulty. When the drill reached a depth of 1,251 feet, however, it was not water but oil that soaked the ecstatic mill superinten- dent. The news spread like wildfire that oil had been found in Lima!

Material arrived from Toledo to "shoot the well," which was accom- plished by lowering two tin cans of explosives into the hole, followed by nitroglycerine. While people lined the railroad tracks for a good view, the charge was set off and oil shot 75 feet into the air. Unfortunately for Mr. Faurot, the well would produce only thirty barrels a day, but it brought the oil industry to Lima, the site of the largest oil-fields in the world up to that time.

Within two years, there were seventy wells in the city of Lima, and several hundred in the entire Lima field. Prosperity followed the oil, and in 1887 President Baxter of the Lima Board of Trade gushed: "Last night a bank in the city paid 1,800 checks to skilled labor. We have a daily production of 20,000 barrels of oil. We have a system of public schools as near perfection as can be made. We go to the handsomest little opera house in the West. For a nickel we can ride two miles on a splendidly equipped electrical street-railroad. As to natural gas, we already have enough to set the ordinary village crazy."

In 1888 Standard Oil undertook to lay 210 miles of pipe from Lima to Chicago at a cost of $2,000,000. An oil producer would usually lease an entire farm and had the right to lay pipe through the fields, paying the owner about 1/6 of each barrel. When Lima's heyday as a producer passed, it remained as a pipeline center.

Lisbon

**BIRTHPLACE OF
MARCUS A. HANNA
Industrialist
and
Political Leader**

LISBON (Columbiana County)

Marcus A. Hanna was born in Lisbon in 1837, and rose to prosperity through his business interests in coal, iron, and shipping. His wealth put him in a position to have political influence, and the Cleveland industrialist wielded this influence in a most effective manner, being called "the closest thing to a national 'boss' in American history."

Hanna first noticed a young man named William McKinley in 1876 when McKinley was defending workers accused of violence at one of Hanna's mines. Genuinely fond of McKinley, he became his political "manager" when McKinley found himself gerrymandered out of his congressional seat, and under Hanna's able guidance, McKinley was elected Ohio governor twice, in 1891 and 1893.

After McKinley's governorship, the Hanna-McKinley team set their sights on the White House. Hanna masterminded McKinley's nomination at the 1896 Republican convention, and organized McKinley's successful front porch campaign for the presidency. Theodore Roosevelt thought Hanna a backstage promoter who sold McKinley "like a patent medicine," yet in spite of Hanna's reservations, Roosevelt was on the ticket with McKinley in the 1900 election, and ascended to the presidency upon McKinley's assassination.

Hanna moved onto the political stage himself when he entered the U.S. Senate in 1897, and it was widely thought that he would challenge Roosevelt for the nomination in 1904. This was not to be, for Mark Hanna died in February of that year, just a few months before the Republican convention.

Lithopolis

HOME OF
THE WAGNALLS
MEMORIAL
FOUNDED 1924

LITHOPOLIS *(Fairfield County)*

"Dreams long dwelt on amount to prayers and prayers wrought in faith come true." These words, found inscribed in stone at the Wagnalls Memorial in Lithopolis, are taken from Mabel Wagnalls book *Rosebush of a Thousand Years.* Mabel was the only child of Adam Wagnalls, co-founder of the Funk and Wagnalls Publishing Company, and his wife Anna, both natives of the village of Lithopolis. Mabel, although born in Kansas in 1869 and educated in part in Europe, considered Lithopolis her home, and it was while she was living here that she corresponded with O. Henry, whose own literary career was launched at the nearby Ohio Penitentiary in Columbus. Among her other friends were Oley Speaks (see Canal Winchester), Houdini, and Edwin Markham. Mabel, a concert pianist, wrote piano compositions and books based on music, among her works *Stars of the Opera* (1898), *The Light in the Valley* (1925), and *The Mad Song* (1926). Miss Wagnalls married Richard Jones in 1920, and resided on Long Island.

In 1924, Mabel Wagnalls Jones established the Wagnalls Memorial Library in Lithopolis in memory of her parents. The memorial, a beautiful Tudor-Gothic building of native freestone, houses an auditorium, three libraries, meeting rooms and two tower rooms. Handwrought light fixtures, handmade tables, chairs and desks, and beautiful stained glass windows adorn the facility, and original paintings of John Ward Dunsmore and poems of Edwin Markham are on display at the memorial. The original letters from O. Henry to Miss Wagnalls can also be seen at the library.

Mabel Wagnalls died in New York City in 1946, leaving her estate of $2,500,000 to be used by the people of Lithopolis to operate the library and endow a scholarship fund. Still available to students of Bloom Township, the fund has assisted more than 1,650 students to attend colleges across the country. Mabel Wagnalls, her parents, and husband are buried in the Lithopolis Cemetery.

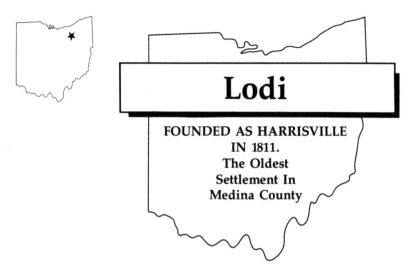

Lodi

**FOUNDED AS HARRISVILLE
IN 1811.
The Oldest
Settlement In
Medina County**

LODI (Medina County)

After the Connecticut Land Company divided the lands it had surveyed in the Western Reserve (see Warren), it allotted two tracts to a group calling itself the Torringford Land Company. In turn, the Torringford Land Company subdivided its land for sale to others, and selected Joseph Harris as its agent. Young Harris left his home in Randolph, Portage County, Ohio in the fall of 1810, following the southern line of the Western Reserve until he reached the area that is now known as Lodi. Here, he went about the task of clearing a spot in the woods, and after a few weeks labor he had managed to erect a crude log cabin in the forest. Having thus begun the first settlement in Medina County, Harris returned to Randolph to gather his wife and baby and bring them to their new home.

The Harris party, consisting of Harris, his wife and baby, an eleven year-old boy, four sleds and four teams of oxen, reached their new home on a snowy February 14, 1811. For the Harris's, like the other early pioneers in the Reserve, it was a lonely life, their land having been selected by lottery and often quite distant from any others. The nearest neighbors to the Harris's were seventeen miles away in Wooster. Growth was slow, and by the end of that first year, Harrisville was a settlement of just five men, two women, two boys, three log huts, seven yoke of oxen, a horse and two dogs. Isolated and exposed, the news that the War of 1812 was breaking out and the Indians were attacking settlers was bad news indeed, and it was decided to abandon Harrisville and return to Portage County for the duration of the war. When the war ended only Harris and one other family came back to Harrisville, and the struggle began anew. Harris's persistence paid off, and by 1818 thirty-five families were in the settlement.

Joseph Harris, the pioneer of Medina County, spent the rest of his life in Harrisville, dying in 1863 at the age of eighty-one.

118

Logan

**FOUNDED 1816 BY
GOVERNOR THOMAS
WORTHINGTON
WHO ESTABLISHED
LOGAN'S FIRST
MILLS**

LOGAN *(Hocking County)*

Logan was founded in 1816 by Thomas Worthington, the sitting governor of the state and the "father of Ohio statehood" (see Worthington, Ohio). At the time of Logan's founding, the area was part of Ross County, in which Worthington resided. He purchased eighty acres for the rather large sum of $1,000, this being the first in his ultimate acquisition of nearly 2,000 acres in what was to become Falls Township. The township takes its name from the great falls of the Hocking River located just above Logan, a natural feature that was to rescue Worthington's investment.

After platting his new town in 1816, Worthington needed to attract settlers who had been traveling toward the mills of other towns in the region. Harnessing the power of the falls on the Hocking, Worthington built two mills in 1818, one a sawmill for the cutting of lumber, the other a grist mill for grinding grain into flour and meal. Worthington's position as governor may also have been helpful in creating Hocking County from parts of Ross, Athens, and Fairfield. As with any county, a county seat is needed, and Worthington's offer of the proceeds from nineteen lots in Logan to build a courthouse was accepted, making Logan the seat of Hocking County. Worthington also built a jail at his own expense, and set aside one lot to be used as a public market.

Logan's growth was rather slow until the completion of the Hocking Canal. On an October day in 1840, the canal boat *A. McCaw* arrived in Logan carrying visitors to hear a campaign speech by Thomas Corwin (see Lebanon, Ohio). This first arrival opened the doors to Logan's prosperity along the banks of the Hocking Canal. Today, canal locks are still visible southeast of Logan near the county line, and farmers still come to town on Tuesdays and Fridays to offer their wares at the public market on the original lot set aside by the town's founder in 1816.

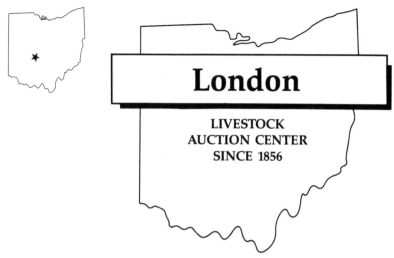

London

LIVESTOCK
AUCTION CENTER
SINCE 1856

LONDON (Madison County)

The London Live-Stock Sales
by Hon. John F. Locke (1889)

The live-stock sales at London have justly obtained a wide distinction throughout the Central and Western States among cattle and horse dealers. Early in 1856 a few of the leading cattle dealers met in London for the purpose of arranging for monthly sales in London (rather than shipping herds east). It was agreed to hold the first sale on the first Tuesday in March, 1856, and thereafter on the first Tuesday of every month. The first sale was held in March, 1856, and have continued regularly for over thirty years. But four sales have been missed - the July sale, 1863, when the "fall of Vicksburg" was celebrated; the October sale, 1863, being election day, and a very exciting one, being in the celebrated Vallandigham campaign; the July sale, 1865, being the Fourth of July, in celebration of the "downfall of the rebellion," and the September sale, 1868, on account of the "cattle plague."

The day before the sale, various droves of cattle may be seen coming on the roads to London. About 10 o'clock of the day of sale from two to three thousand people have assembled on the streets to witness the sales and do trading that has been put off until "Salesday." The public square near the courthouse is the market place. Often three or four droves are being sold at the same time, and the hue and cry of the noisy auctioneers is strange and amusing to one unfamiliar with it.

There is no indication that the sales will cease, nor is there any good reason why they should. They have accomplished well the purpose intended, and have reflected great credit upon Madison County, and all feel a just pride in them.

Lorain

BIRTHPLACE OF
ADMIRAL ERNEST J. KING
Commander In Chief
U.S. Fleet
World War II

LORAIN *(Lorain County)*

Admiral Ernest J. King, born in Lorain in 1878, graduated from Annapolis in 1901 and went on to become an admiral in 1941. When the Japanese bombed Pearl Harbor in 1941, King was made the commander in chief of the U.S. Fleet, and soon after was given the post of Chief of Naval Operations - the first time one man had simultaneously held both positions.

Admiral King was considered to be a crusty, extremely professional military man, described by President Roosevelt as "so tough he shaves with a blowtorch." King's leadership was crucial to the Allied victory at sea during World War II: he favored aircraft carriers over battleships, and his use of small escort vessels blunted the German threat to Allied convoys.

Admiral Ernest J. King died in New Hampshire in 1956.

121

Loudonville

HOME OF
CHARLES F. KETTERING
Inventor,
Scientist,
Humanitarian

LOUDONVILLE (Ashland County)

Charles Kettering was born on a farm north of Loudonville in Ashland County in 1876, and, after graduating from college in 1906, moved to Dayton. After working at the National Cash Register plant for three years, he left to independently develop his ideas. It has been said that this man, more than any other, "put ladies in the driver's seat." In the early years of the automobile industry, driving was seen as a dirty and dangerous business, not so much for the hazards of other vehicles on the road, but for the hazard of just getting one's own vehicle underway. The old engines had to be turned over by hand, and the hand crank was responsible for broken arms, broken wrists, and the occasional tossing of a would-be driver into mudholes or worse. It is easy to imagine the happy reception Charles Kettering's invention, the automobile self-starter, received when Cadillac introduced it to the motoring public in 1910.

After selling his first order of self-starters to Cadillac, Kettering and E.A. Deeds started a new concern called the Dayton Engineering Laboratories Company, which would become known worldwide as Delco. Among Delco's products was Kettering's independent electrical generator that brought power and light to many farms prior to rural electrification in the 1930's. For the relief Charles Kettering brought to motorists, farmers, and others, he is seen as one of the nation's greatest inventors.

Louisville

"CONSTITUTION TOWN"
Originator of
Ohio's Annual
Constitution Day
September 17

LOUISVILLE (Stark County)

"WE THE PEOPLE of the United States, in Order to form a more perfect Union, establish Justice, insure domestic Tranquility, provide for the common defence, promote the general Welfare, and secure the Blessings of Liberty to ourselves and our Posterity, do ordain and establish this Constitution for the United States of America." On September 17, 1787, after a long, hot summer of laborious work in Philadelphia, the Constitutional Convention completed its work, signed the Constitution, and submitted it to Congress.

September 17th, the day the Constitution was signed, never attained the status of July 4th, and the date now generally passes unnoticed across the country - with the exception of Louisville, Ohio. In 1951, Mrs. Olga T. Weber, concerned that the freedoms guaranteed Americans under the Constitution were being taken for granted, began passing out patriotic literature in her hometown. Copies of the Bill of Rights, the Constitution, and other materials were distributed throughout Louisville by Mrs. Weber, and on September 17, 1952, Mrs. Weber organized the first "Constitution Day" program at the high school. A speech by Representative Frank T. Bow highlighted the day's events. The idea of a "Constitution Day" continued to gain steam, and in 1953 Governor Frank Lausche proclaimed September 17 as "Constitution Day" in Ohio. Three years later, the Congress of the United States, at Louisville's request, asked President Eisenhower to designate the week of September 17-23 as "Constitution Week," and in 1955 it was so designated. In 1957, the village council proclaimed Louisville "Constitution Town."

The observance began by Mrs. Weber grew into a week-long festival that is observed each September in Louisville. Mrs. Weber herself lived to see the silver anniversary of her day in 1977 before her death the following year.

Loveland

**FIRST SETTLED BY
COL. THOMAS PAXTON
IN 1796.
Incorporated
July 21, 1876**

LOVELAND (Hamilton/Clermont/Warren Counties)

Many towns along the route of Gen. Anthony Wayne's march against the Indians in 1794 trace their origins to soldiers who were involved in the campaign. The beautiful countryside through which the troops marched beckoned them to return when the hostilities ceased, and with the Indian wars over, many of Wayne's soldiers did return to establish settlements. Among these soldiers was Col. Thomas Paxton, who commanded an advance guard of soldiers on Wayne's expedition. Col. Paxton, who also served as an officer in the Revolutionary War, had the valuable skill of a surveyor, and located hundreds of Virginia military land warrants between the Scioto and Little Miami Rivers.

Col. Paxton arranged to purchase 1,200 acres of land on the east bank of the Little Miami in 1794, and two years later he and his family came to establish the first settlement in Clermont County. The Paxton house, surrounded by a stockade, became the center of social life for the earliest pioneers. Col. Paxton died in 1811 at the age of seventy-seven.

While Col. Paxton established the first settlement, the town that bore his name was laid out on this spot by Col. William Ramsey in 1849, and a year later he laid out the town of Loveland. The two towns later became one when the town of Loveland was incorporated in February, 1876. Loveland prospered at the junction of the Cincinnati and Marietta and Little Miami Railroads, and soon extended itself into two neighboring counties, Warren and Hamilton. The well-to-do were attracted to Loveland over a century ago, as recorded in an 1880 history: "A large portion of its inhabitants are business and professional men of Cincinnati, noted for their enterprise, intelligence, and love of the beautiful in nature, who have reared elegant villas and palatial mansions along the beautiful river-side."

Madison

BIRTHPLACE OF
FREDERICK B. OPPER
Cartoonist Creator
of
"Happy Hooligan"

MADISON (Lake County)

Frederick Opper, born in Madison on January 2, 1857, was considered in his day to be the dean of American cartoonists and caricaturists. He attended public school in Madison, and began his working career as a boy of fourteen at the *Madison Gazette*. In 1873, he moved to New York City and took a job in a mercantile establishment. He sketched in his free time, and managed to sell some humorous sketches to *The Comic Monthly* and other publications. In 1881, he joined the staff of *Puck*, where he worked for eighteen years drawing tramps, actors and political cartoons. In 1899, he took a position with William Randolph Hearst's *New York Journal*, where he created his most famous character, Happy Hooligan, the happy, gentle tramp with a tin can on his head who attracted a large following. Happy Hooligan and other Opper characters reached millions of readers through Hearst's chain of newspapers.

Opper was also a noted political cartoonist, and during the William McKinley campaign of 1900, he created a series called "Willie and his Papa," which depicted Mark Hanna (see Lisbon) as "Nursie" to "Pa Trusts." Opper drew for Mark Twain, and illustrated *"Aesop's Fables."* Considered an influential force in shaping public opinion, Opper continued working for the Hearst papers until 1933, when failing eyesight brought his career to an end.

Frederick B. Opper died in New Rochelle, N.Y. on August 27, 1937.

Malta

**HOME OF
JAMES BALL NAYLOR
Author of
Historical Novels
Of Early Ohio**

MALTA (Morgan County)

James Ball Naylor has been credited with bringing more attention to the Muskingum Valley through his books than any other man up to his time. However, Naylor, as proficient a writer as he was, was not primarily an author, but a physician.

Naylor was born in Penn Township, Morgan County, on October 4, 1860. When he was yet a young child, his father was killed in the Civil War. He attended school in the district before going off to the Marietta Academy for a few months, but with his heart set on the medical profession, he returned to Malta to teach in the country schools in order to raise funds. Then it was off to Columbus to attend Starling Medical College, from which he graduated in 1886. After many years as a physician in Malta, he concluded the last fourteen years of his practice by serving as the district health commissioner in Morgan County until 1934.

While Naylor had a great love of medicine, he had an equal love for his homeland and its history. For eight years he wrote a column for the *Marion Star,* and in 1893 he wrote his first book of verses entitled *Current Coins Picked up at a Country Railway Station* under the pen name S. Q. Lapius. The semi-autobiographical *Ralph Marlowe* brought his literary talents to the attention of the public for the first time.

Dr. Naylor continued publishing his works until 1935. A reading of some of his titles reveals the affection he had for his Ohio home. *Under Mad Anthony's Banner, In the Days of St. Clair, Songs from the Heart of Things, Old Morgan County, The Sign of the Prophet,* and *A Book of Buckeye Verse* are but a few of the books that he published in his lifetime.

James Ball Naylor died on April 1, 1945.

Malvern

**BIRTHPLACE OF
THEODORE N. VAIL
Father of Railway Mail
And Long Distance
Telephone Services**

MALVERN (Carroll County)

Theodore Newton Vail was born at Malvern on July 16, 1845, and began his career in communications in Morristown, New Jersey, where, as a boy, he was employed as a clerk in a drug store. In the drug store was a telegraph office, and Vail learned telegraphy in his spare time. He eventually became a telegraph operator for the railroad, and it was in this industry that he made the first of his two major achievements.

Vail, while a postal clerk with the railroad, developed a system of sorting, tying, and labeling bundles so they could be thrown off the trains at connecting stage lines, rather than going through the slower process of being sorted by postmasters at connecting points. After numerous promotions, Vail inaugurated the fast mail service, a benchmark in American mail delivery. Swift moving express trains, carrying only mail and making few stops, provided the service. The cars were painted white, and bore the words "The Fast Mail." Each car was named for a state governor, which was lettered in gold on the car's side.

In 1875, a new invention, called by some "Graham's talking toy," drew Vail away from the mails and into the telephone industry. Vail is credited with being the genius that organized the telephone system in the United States. General manager of the Bell Telephone Company in 1878, he established local companies across the country, then hooked them together with a long distance network. Hundreds of competing companies entered the industry upon the expiration of Bell's patents. As president of American Telephone and Telegraph (AT&T), he brought as many competitors as he could into the fold, and cooperated with independents by making the long-distance lines available to them. The relationship of AT&T and its constituent companies, however, continued to be a thorny problem for a century.

Theodore Vail died in Baltimore on April 16, 1920.

Manchester

FOUNDED 1791
First Settlement
Within Virginia
Military
District

MANCHESTER (Adams County)

"The first settlement within the Virginia military tract, and the only one between the Scioto and Little Miami until after the treaty of Greenville, in 1795, was made in this county, at Manchester, by the then Col., later, Gen. Nathaniel Massie. Massie, in the winter of the year 1790, determined to make a settlement in it, that he might be in the midst of his surveying operations and secure his party from danger and exposure. In order to effect this he gave general notice in Kentucky of his intention, and offered each of the first twenty-five families, as a donation, one in-lot, one out-lot, and one hundred acres of land, provided they would settle in a town he intended to lay off at his settlement. His proferred terms were soon closed in with, and upwards of thirty families joined him. After various consultations with his friends, the bottom on the Ohio River, opposite the lower of the Three Islands, was selected as the most eligble spot. Here he fixed his station, and laid off into lots a town, now called Manchester, at this time a small place, about twelve miles above Maysville (formerly Limestone) Kentucky. This little confederacy, with Massie at the helm (who was the soul of it), went to work with spirit. Cabins were raised and by the middle of March, 1791, the whole town was enclosed with strong pickets firmly fixed in the ground with block houses at each angle for defence.

Thus was the first settlement in the Virginia military district and the fourth settlement in the bounds of the State of Ohio effected."

— Henry Howe, *Historical Collections of Ohio,* 1889.
(See also Washington C.H.)

Mansfield

HOME OF JOHN SHERMAN
Author of Sherman
Anti-Trust Act.
Secretary of the Treasury.
Secretary of State.
U.S. Senator.

MANSFIELD (Richland County)

John Sherman, brother of Gen. William Tecumseh Sherman, was born in Lancaster, Ohio, the son of Charles R. Sherman, Ohio Supreme Court Justice. After the sudden death of his father, eight year-old John was sent to Mt. Vernon to be raised by a cousin. John would later move to Mansfield to study law with another brother, Charles, and in 1844 he opened a law office in the community. During William's spectacular career in the military during the Civil War, John was providing crucial civilian leadership in Washington.

John Sherman was first elected to Congress in 1855, and served several terms in the U.S. Senate. During the war, he considered resigning his seat to join the army, but Lincoln convinced him to stay in Congress. Under President Rutherford B. Hayes, Sherman served as Secretary of the Treasury, where he was credited with bringing stability to the nation's currency by making greenbacks redeemable for gold. President McKinley appointed Sherman Secretary of State, but it was during his term as U.S. Senator that he made his most famous contribution to the nation, the Sherman Anti-trust Act of 1890.

The idea that what was good for "Big Business" was good for America had long prevailed, since it was believed that the prosperity at the top would provide benefits throughout the society. By the last decade of the nineteenth century, however, it appeared that monopolies were strangling competition and controlling state and national politics to an unhealthy degree. In 1890, U.S. Senator John Sherman gave his name to the national anti-trust bill that made restraint of trade in interstate and foreign commerce illegal, one of the many accomplishments of his storied career.

Mantua

**NAMED BY
JOHN LEAVITT
AFTER A FAMOUS
ITALIAN CITY**

MANTUA (Portage County)

Mantua township, located in the Western Reserve county of Portage, had its origin as the property of the "Suffield, Cuyahoga & Big Beaver Land Company," a group of sixteen Connecticut men who had purchased land here and elsewhere in "New Connecticut" (see Conneaut). The company sent David Abbott to survey the township into 420 acre tracts, and Abbott, like other surveyors of the time, became a prominent citizen in early Ohio, serving in the state's constitutional convention in 1803. The township of Mantua was officially organized on March 5, 1810, and given its name by John Leavitt in honor of Napoleon, who had captured the Italian city of Mantua in 1796.

Mantua township claims the distinction of being home to the first settler in Portage County, Abraham Honey, who made a clearing and put up a cabin in 1798. Honey was joined the following winter by Elias Harmon, who had been traveling in the company of Benjamin Tappan and David Hudson from New York. The three men parted company, with Tappan going on to establish Ravenna, Hudson to found the town that would bear his name, and Harmon to the clearing where Honey's cabin stood. Elias Harmon became the United States Marshal here in 1810, and his census of that year found a total population in Mantua of 152 people, up from the twenty-seven in 1806, but down from the 254 people listed upon the founding of the township earlier that year. A reading of the deaths in Mantua from 1799 to 1825 reveals some of the hardships encountered in establishing communities in pioneer Ohio: Mrs. Anna Judson, a newly married woman, became the township's first death after being given arsenic by mistake on July 2, 1804, and Jacob Blair was killed in the raising of a house in 1807.

Marblehead

**OLDEST LIGHTHOUSE
IN CONTINUOUS SERVICE
ON GREAT LAKES
LOCATED HERE.
Built 1821-22**

MARBLEHEAD (Ottawa County)

Up until 1820, the nighttime shore of Lake Erie was hidden by darkness, with the occasional campfire the only sign marking the shore. Navigators would have to be extremely careful, trying to stay within sight of moonlit land lest they run aground on one of the many sand bars at the rivers' mouths, or crash on a rocky outcropping. Then, lighthouses appeared in 1820 at Conneaut, Ashtabula, and Fairport Harbor, and in the next year the rocky point at the Marblehead Peninsula was likewise marked by a light.

The Marblehead Lighthouse was constructed at the "roughest point on Lake Erie," with an uninterrupted sweep of 200 miles. It was the first permanent building at Marblehead, constructed by Sanduskian William Kelly. The lighthouse welcomed its first keeper in 1821 in the person of Benajah Wolcott, a Revolutionary War veteran who had come from Connecticut with the first survey team. It would take a rugged individual to maintain the light at Marblehead. Fierce winds blowing across the shallow water of Lake Erie would toss storm-driven spray into the lighthouse window sixty-seven feet above the ground.

As time went by, the floor of the lake was thoroughly charted, harbors marked, and shipping channels dredged. Modern navigational equipment did much to tame the lake. But while much has changed, the Marblehead Lighthouse, gleaming brilliant white in the sunshine by the blue Lake Erie waters, still delights the passersby on the ferries and pleasure boats as it guards the rocky shore.

Courtesy Natalie Bredbeck

Marietta

**FIRST ORGANIZED
SETTLEMENT IN
THE NORTHWEST
TERRITORY
1788**

MARIETTA (Washington County)

It can be said that Ohio was born in Boston at the Bunch of Grapes Tavern, for it was there on March 1, 1786 that Gen. Rufus Putnam, Manasseh Cutler, and nine others met to form the Ohio Company. Putnam had been leading a group of Revolutionary War veterans seeking to be paid for their military service with western lands, and Congress was sympathetic to a plan that would have the frontier settled by men who could defend their settlements from Indian attacks while at the same time settling a debt to the men. Congress agreed to sell the Ohio Company a million and a half acres north and west of the Ohio River for $500,000 down and an equal amount when the survey was complete.

On April 2, 1788, forty-eight New Englanders, destined to become known in Ohio as the "Forty-eight Immortals," began their voyage by flatboat down the Ohio River, landing on April 7 at the mouth of the Muskingum River across from Fort Harmar. Jarvis Cutler, the sixteen year old son of Manasseh Cutler, leaped ashore from the "Union Galley" (later renamed the "Mayflower") and became the first of the party to reach the site of the pioneer settlement in the Northwest Territory. The men initially proposed that the new village be named Adelphia, which means "brotherhood," but these veterans of the Revolution finally decided on Marietta in honor of Marie Antoinette, a gesture of gratitude for France's support during the Revolutionary War.

Arthur St. Clair, governor of the territory, arrived to preside at Marietta while the Campus Martius fort was being erected to shelter the officials and protect the settlers. "No colony in America was ever settled under such favorable auspices," said George Washington, referring to the able leadership of his Revolutionary fellows and founders of Marietta. Today, Campus Martius serves as a museum of pioneer life, with Gen. Putnam's house, the first in Ohio, preserved within its confines.

132

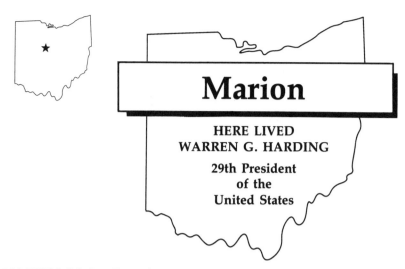

Marion

HERE LIVED
WARREN G. HARDING

29th President
of the
United States

MARION *(Marion County)*

Warren G. Harding was a kind, amiable man, one who got along well with others. Among his friends were Thomas Edison, Harvey Firestone, and Henry Ford, and the four would often go camping together. Yet, after his death, it was only with great difficulty that a high ranking Republican could be persuaded to attend the dedication of this former president's tomb.

Warren Harding was born in Blooming Grove in Morrow County in 1865, and as a child moved to Caledonia in Marion County. After attending Ohio Central College, he became the publisher of the *Marion Star* newspaper. He was elected to the Ohio Senate in 1898, held the post of lieutenant governor, and then went on to the U.S. Senate. At the deadlocked Republican National Convention in 1920, Harding was selected as a compromise candidate on the tenth ballot in the proverbial "smoke-filled room." In the presidential election, he waged a popular "front porch campaign" and won over fellow Ohioan James Cox in a landslide.

While Harding was never accused of profiting from the corruption in his administration, his blind trust in several of his appointees would cost him his reputation. As he became aware of the misdeeds within his administration, his health suffered, and while on a trip across the country in 1923, he became ill and died of a stroke.

In recent years, Harding has been seen as more of a hapless victim of his own trusting nature than as a corrupt man. After his death, his body was returned to his hometown, and he now lies buried in the impressive Harding Memorial in Marion, Ohio, near the home where he conducted his famous front porch campaign.

Martins Ferry

**BURIAL PLACE
OF
EBENEZER ZANE
Builder of
Zane's Trace**

MARTIN'S FERRY (Belmont County)

Walnut Grove Cemetery in Martin's Ferry is the final resting place of Ohio pioneer Ebenezer Zane and his also famous sister, Elizabeth. A Virginian by birth, the adventurous Ebenezer moved westward when twenty-one years old, and eventually arrived at the mouth of Wheeling Creek in Virginia (now West Virginia). He made a small settlement which grew into the frontier village of Wheeling. During the Revolution, Zane defended the town against the British and Indians, an engagement in which his sister Betty helped save Wheeling's Fort Henry. In 1796, Ebenezer laid out the first continuous road in Ohio, known as "Zane's Trace" (see Aberdeen).

Ebenezer and Betty Zane are buried in a cemetery overlooking the Ohio River across from Wheeling. On Ebenezer's tombstone is found the inscription "The first permanent inhabitant of this part of the Western World, having first begun to reside here in the year 1769. He died as he had lived, an honest man." Betty Zane's grave marker reads "Elizabeth Zane, Heroine of Fort Henry," memorializing her courage in carrying a supply of gunpowder to Fort Henry from a nearby house while the fort was under attack by the British and Indians in 1782.

Marysville

LOG CABIN, SYMBOL OF
PRESIDENT HARRISON'S
CAMPAIGN,
WAS ORIGINATED HERE,
1840

MARYSVILLE (Union County)

The campaign of 1840 has been called "the most extraordinary political contest ever waged in the United States," and it was this exceptional campaign that brought Ohio and the term "Buckeye" to the forefront of the nation. Gen. William Henry Harrison of Ohio was his party's candidate for the presidency, but an opposition newspaper felt Harrison was eminently unqualified, noting that "he was better fitted to sit in a log-cabin and drink hard cider, than rule in the White House." Many Ohioans took this as a resounding, though unwitting, endorsement, and posters appeared picturing Harrison sitting by the door of a log cabin drinking cider, its walls festooned with coonskins and strings of buckeyes. A large procession on the way to the State convention in Columbus included a number of unusual devices designed to represent their party, and from Union County appeared an actual log cabin in the parade. Built of buckeye logs, it was situated on a wagon pulled by horses, and from the roof of the cabin rang out a song written by native son Otway Curry, accompanied by his flute:

"Oh where, tell me where, was your buckeye cabin made?
'Twas built among the merry boys who wield the plough and spade.
Where the log cabins stand in the bonnie buckeye shade."

"Oh what, tell me what, is to be your cabin's fate?
We'll wheel it to the capital and place it there elate,
For a token and a sign of the bonnie Buckeye State."

The Buckeye log cabin from Marysville helped propel William Henry Harrison into the White House, and forevermore established the people of Ohio as Buckeyes in the eyes of their countrymen.

Massillon

NAMED FOR THE
COURT CHAPLAIN
OF LOUIS XIV,
JEAN-BAPTISTE
MASSILLON

MASSILLON (Stark County)

Massillon, born of the Ohio & Erie Canal, traces its heritage back to the village of Kendal, which is now part of Massillon. Kendal was laid out in 1811 by New England Quaker Thomas Rotch as a refuge for his sickly wife, Charity, and a place to raise his 400 sheep, which he had driven in front of his carriage from Connecticut to Stark County. The plat of Kendal included 99 lots, and the surrounding area of about 2,500 acres was dedicated to the raising of Spanish merino sheep.

Among the early citizens of Kendal was James Duncan, a retired New England ship captain who owned land on the east side of the Tuscarawas River. When the Ohio legislature passed the canal building act in 1824, a bitter struggle ensued between landholders on either side of the river to have the canal routed through their property. Duncan won out, and contracts were signed at his Kendal residence on January 18, 1826 to dig 44 sections of the canal along the east side of the river. Duncan shortly thereafter added to his land holdings and laid out a town of 165 lots, dwarfing the town of Kendal, and recorded his survey at Canton on December 7, 1826. Mr. Duncan, being the husband of the former Eliza T. Vilette, a cultured French speaking woman, agreed to his wife's request to name his town Massillon in honor of Jean-Baptiste Massillon, a noted French Catholic Bishop in the days of Louis XIV.

James Duncan and George Wallace commenced building the canal on the east side of the river, with a half mile section built by Aaron Chapman. Chapman's advertisement for laborers cautioned that "Those who cannot work without whisky need not apply." It is said that Chapman's section was better built and more quickly done than the other sections. On August 25, 1828, the canal opened from Akron to Massillon with the arrival of the canal boats *Allen Trimble* and the *State of Ohio*, touching off celebrations punctuated by cannon firings that lit up the nighttime sky.

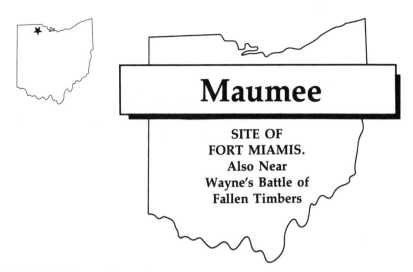

Maumee

SITE OF
FORT MIAMIS.
Also Near
Wayne's Battle of
Fallen Timbers

MAUMEE (Lucas County)

For the third time, an American general was leading his forces toward the Miami Indian villages from Fort Washington at present day Cincinnati. The first expedition, in 1790, was led by Gen. Harmar, who was summarily defeated. The following year, Gen. Arthur St. Clair marched from Fort Washington, building Fort Hamilton and Fort Jefferson before meeting disaster on the Wabash River at the site of the future Fort Recovery (see Fort Recovery). And now in 1794, Gen. Anthony Wayne was nearing the goal in this third campaign, having beaten the Indians at Fort Recovery and establishing Fort Defiance (see Defiance).

Wayne's troops marched to within four miles of British Fort Miamis, a post that had been rebuilt by the English in 1785 from an abandoned French trading post, and served as an outpost for their position at Detroit. The post was a thorn in American territory, and had been offering aid and encouragement to the Indians in their attacks upon Americans. The area near the fort was littered with fallen trees, and it was here that the Battle of Fallen Timbers commenced. After considerable maneuvering, the final skirmishes took place within sight of the British soldiers within the fort, yet the British kept their gates closed and offered no assistance to the defeated Indians who approached for aid. After the battle, Wayne burned the grain and vegetables growing outside the fort, then considered attacking the fort itself, for he had orders from the President giving him such discretion. Wisely, he turned his back on Fort Miamis and its frustrated soldiers and marched back to Fort Defiance and then on to Fort Greenville (see Greenville). The following summer, a permanent peace treaty was signed at Fort Greenville that opened the Ohio Country for settlement.

An impressive statue commemorating Wayne's victory at Fallen Timbers overlooks the Maumee River at a site administered by the Ohio Historical Society.

McArthur

FOUNDED 1815.
Named For
General Duncan McArthur
Congressman,
Governor

McARTHUR (Vinton County)

The site where McArthur now stands was forest prior to 1815, with only two log cabins nestled among the trees. The first settlers in the area worked quarries in the northern part of the county for millstones, and two roads intersecting here made it a natural stopping place. In 1815, a town was laid out on this site by Moses Dawson, Levi Johnson, Isaac Pearson, George Will, J. Beach, and Samuel Lutz, and named McArthurstown in honor of Duncan McArthur, war hero, legislator, and future Congressman and governor. The name was changed to its present form in 1851 by an act of the state legislature.

Duncan McArthur was an early pioneer of Ohio, having entered the Scioto Valley with General Nathaniel Massie as a chain-bearer on Massie's surveying crew in 1793. He soon became an assistant surveyor and assisted Massie in the laying out of Chillicothe. As was the case with many early surveyors, he attained great land holdings and wealth.

McArthur was second in command in Hull's campaign of 1812 that ended in a shameful surrender at Detroit, yet his personal courage in the expedition led to his being elected to Congress upon his return from captivity. He soon quit Congress to rejoin the fray, and was commissioned a brigadier-general. McArthur received the command of the Northwest Army upon Harrison's resignation in 1814. When the war ended, Detroit was in the Americans' hands, and McArthur was its defender.

McArthur served two terms in Congress, and in 1830 was elected governor of Ohio. He is buried alongside governors Worthington, Tiffin, and Allen in a historic cemetery in Chillicothe.

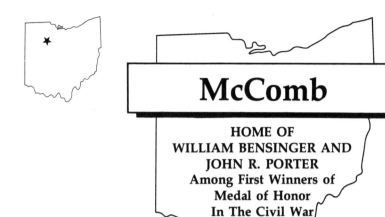

McComb

**HOME OF
WILLIAM BENSINGER AND
JOHN R. PORTER
Among First Winners of
Medal of Honor
In The Civil War**

McCOMB (Hancock County)

On April 12, 1862, at Big Shanty, Georgia, a daring raid began that was to capture the imagination of a nation. Twenty-two soldiers from the North, mostly Ohioans, had penetrated into northern Georgia, intent on stealing a locomotive and using it to burn bridges behind them as they made a run for the North. When the crew from the confederate locomotive *The General* detrained to eat breakfast, the raiders seized the train and headed north, attempting to destroy confederate supply lines. Pursuit began immediately, and the great chase did not end until ninety miles later, when the locomotive ran out of fuel and the soldiers were forced to abandon the train. All were captured, and eight of the men were executed for the deed at Atlanta in June, 1862. Eight others escaped confinement, and the remaining raiders were later paroled. All the participants were awarded the Congressional Medal of Honor, the first recipients of this distinguished honor.

William Bensinger and John R. Porter, two of the Andrews Raiders, are buried in McComb's Union Cemetery. Porter was one of the men who escaped confinement, and Bensinger was exchanged to the North almost a year later. Captain Bensinger's Medal of Honor can be seen at the McComb Library.

139

McConnelsville

**A LEADING
SALT PRODUCING
CENTER
1820-1840**

McCONNELLSVILLE (Morgan County)

McConnellsville, the county seat of Morgan County nestled in the Muskingum River Valley, dates back to the early years of the nineteenth century as an important salt-making center. Salt was an essential commodity of pioneer life, and its scarcity was a great inconvenience to the earliest settlers. In 1795, a few miles above McConnellsville in Muskingum County, a source of salt was located at Salt Creek, and shortly a party of men arrived from Marietta to establish a salt-producing company in the Muskingum Valley.

"Twenty-four kettles were bought in Pittsburgh and transported by water to Duncan's Falls, and thence by packhorses about seven miles to the salt licks," reads an early county history. "A well was dug near the edge of the creek, fifteen feet deep, down to the rock that formed the bed of the stream, through the crevices in which the salt came to the surface. The trunk of a hollow sycamore tree three feet in diameter was settled into the well and bedded in the rock below, so as to exclude the fresh water. A furnace was built of two ranges, containing twelve kettles in each, a shed erected over the furnace, and a small cabin for the workmen. The water from the well was raised by a sweep and pole.

"By the aid of one man to chop and haul wood, with a yoke of oxen, they could make about one-hundred pounds of salt in twenty-four hours, requiring 3,600 gallons of water... Thus was made the first salt in the Muskingum Valley."

Salt was first made down river near McConnellsville around 1820, and for the next twenty years the smoke of the salt-furnaces hung in the valley from the county line above to three miles south of McConnellsville, and, according to the 1840 census, Morgan County was Ohio's premier salt producer.

Medina

HOME OF
A. I. ROOT
Founder of
The Bee Industries
1865

MEDINA (Medina County)

Amos Ives Root was busy working one day in 1865 when a swarm of bees happened to fly over his head. A fellow worker asked A. I. what he would give for them, and A. I., never dreaming that the man would be able to capture them, answered "a dollar." To Mr. Root's astonishment, the man returned with the bees. Within a few years, Mr. Root had a thousand hives, and had invented a new beehive that permitted honey to be extracted without damaging the hive. He authored and published books and magazines devoted to beekeeping, including *The ABC's of Bee Culture,* which he printed by windmill power in his backyard. At his many talks about bees, he would announce that he had found a cure for his baldness, open a drawer, and a swarm of bees would issue forth, covering his head.

Not surprisingly, A. I. Root was considered an eccentric by his fellow townsmen. He began his career as a jeweler, then developed a traveling "electricity show," demonstrating the wonders of electricity. Unsuspecting members of the audience would be taught to "dance" by wearing his "galvanic slippers," metal shoes worn on sheet metal while receiving a charge. He introduced the forerunner of the bicycle, the velocipede, on the town square, where he fell several times before making it look enjoyable.

Bicycling got into his blood almost as much as beekeeping. He would ride as many as 70 miles through northeast Ohio, and eventually met two bicycle mechanics from Dayton named Orville and Wilbur Wright. He was on hand September 20, 1904 when they flew their craft, and he wrote an article about it. It was rejected by publishers as too far-fetched, but now the article can be found at the Smithsonian Institution, undoubtedly the scoop of the century.

A.I. Root died in 1923 at the age of 82. He was, in the words of the local paper, "a strange man, a likeable man."

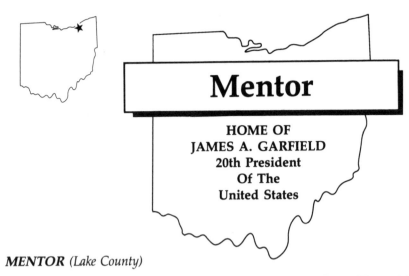

Mentor

HOME OF
JAMES A. GARFIELD
20th President
Of The
United States

MENTOR (Lake County)

James A. Garfield was born in a log cabin in Orange Township, Cuyahoga County, Ohio on November 19, 1831. He was to become the last American president that could rightfully claim such a humble birthplace. As a boy, he worked as a muleskinner on the Ohio & Erie Canal, driving the mules that pulled the boats along the canal. After graduating from Williams College in Massachusetts in 1856, he returned to Ohio to take a job as a teacher at the Western Reserve Eclectic Institute, later to be Hiram College (see Hiram, Ohio). He rose to the presidency of the school just one year later. The school was affiliated with the Disciples of Christ, and Garfield served as a lay minister for the denomination.

Garfield joined the new Republican Party in 1859, and was admitted to the Ohio Bar and elected to the Ohio Senate that same year. When the Civil War broke out, Garfield distinguished himself as a capable soldier, rising to the rank of major general by war's end. He was elected to Congress during the war, and left "Lawnfield," his Mentor home, to hold his Congressional seat for eighteen years. In 1880, the Ohio legislature appointed him to the U.S. Senate, but he was to occupy the White House instead.

The 1880 Republican Convention was a battle between James G. Blaine and U. S. Grant for the nomination. On the 36th ballot of the deadlocked convention, the personable Garfield emerged as the Republican candidate, and he went on to become the 20th President of the United States. Of Ohio's eventual eight presidents, he would be one of four to die in office. On July 2, 1881, just four months into his term, Garfield was shot in a Washington railroad station by Charles Guiteau, a demented office seeker who shouted, "I am a Stalwart and now Arthur is President!" Garfield lingered in agony for 80 days before dying on September 19, 1881.

The body of the slain president was brought back to Ohio by special train, and he was buried in Cleveland's Lakeview Cemetery.

J. A. Garfield

Barnard, Photo., 1887.

LAWNFIELD.

Miamisburg

SITE OF
LARGEST CONICAL
INDIAN BURIAL MOUND
IN EASTERN
UNITED STATES

MIAMISBURG (Montgomery County)

Beginning about the year 1000 B.C., a relatively sophisticated culture of prehistoric Indians inhabited the upper Ohio Valley, including the present site of Miamisburg. We do not know by what name this group called themselves, but today we refer to them as the Adena people, named after Thomas Worthington's estate near Chillicothe where remnants of this culture were first unearthed. The Adena, like their successors the Hopewells, were generally referred to as the "Moundbuilders" by the early settlers of Ohio, who came across literally thousands of burial mounds scattered throughout the region.

While many of the mounds were relatively small and contained a single burial, the mound at Miamisburg is huge. With a height of over 68 feet and a base that covers three acres, it is the largest conical Indian mound in the eastern United States. One of the first excavations into the mound occurred in July, 1869, when a number of residents sunk a shaft six feet in diameter from the top of the mound down to its base. Inside the mound they found a human skeleton in a sitting position, facing east, and later excavations found burials on several levels. We have learned from these excavations that the Adena were a hunting and gathering people who lived in semipermanent villages. They maintained a vast trading network, exchanging Ohio flint for copper and mica, which they used to fashion beautiful ornaments. Among the most prized archeological finds are the famed Adena pipes, fashioned into human shapes.

The Adena vanished from Ohio sometime between 100 and 300 A.D., leaving behind their burial mounds as monuments to their time in Ohio. Today, the Miamisburg Mound is a state historical site administered by the Ohio Historical Society.

143

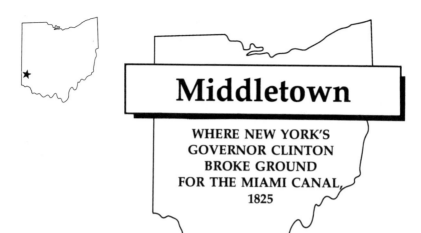

Middletown

**WHERE NEW YORK'S
GOVERNOR CLINTON
BROKE GROUND
FOR THE MIAMI CANAL,
1825**

MIDDLETOWN (Butler County)

Ground-breaking ceremonies in Ohio's early years were times of great joy and merriment, and the two main ingredients of these festivities were alcohol and gunpowder: the former for innumerable toasts, the latter for resounding salutes. The Fourth of July was the favored date for such ceremonies, but Governor DeWitt Clinton of New York, the father of the famous Erie Canal, was not available to be in Middletown that day. He was elsewhere in Ohio, breaking ground for the Ohio & Erie Canal. The folks of Middletown would have to wait two weeks for Governor Clinton to lift the first spadeful of earth here, but on July 21, 1825, it was Middletown's turn to fire her guns, and the Miami Canal, the first section of the Miami & Erie Canal, was underway. Ohio was about to be transformed from a backwoods frontier state to an industrial center with ties to the rest of the world.

The Miami Canal was to run from Cincinnati to Middletown, with later sections extending the canal to the Maumee River and on to Toledo. The canal was built in sections as money became available, with the first section connecting directly to market outlets - if the funds dried up, the completed section would still be useful. On July 1, 1827, water was let into the canal at Middletown, and by July 4 it was deep enough to float the canal boat *Samuel Forrer*, named in honor of the canal's chief engineer. In early December, the canal was navigable from Cincinnati to Middletown, and in 1845, the Miami & Erie Canal stretched from the Ohio River to Lake Erie.

Today, Middletown proudly boasts a number of markers and memorials to her glory days along the old canal.

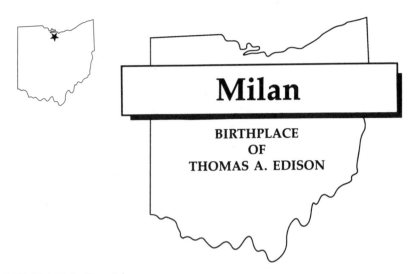

Milan

**BIRTHPLACE
OF
THOMAS A. EDISON**

MILAN (Erie County)

Thomas Alva Edison was born in a small brick house that clings to a hill overlooking Milan's old canal basin. The year was 1847, and Milan was bustling with the business that went with the canal. "Land schooners" filled with wheat lined up for miles to unload at Milan's wharves, and warehouses bulged with goods. The streets were filled with canal characters and colorful language, yet the beautiful Greek Revival houses lent a dignified air to this New England-like community. Milan's days as a world-class port for grain exports was limited, however, and when the railroad by-passed the town, its population went elsewhere. This included the Edisons, who moved to Port Huron, Michigan.

In an oft-repeated theme, Edison, like many other geniuses, did not perform well scholastically. Called slow and unadaptable by his teachers, he was taken out of school and taught by his mother, and he soon built a chemistry lab in his home. He was fascinated by telegraphy, and when he rescued the son of a stationmaster, he was rewarded with an apprenticeship as a telegraph operator. He went on to invent a stock ticker and mimeograph machine before moving to Menlo Park, N.J., where he invented the phonograph.

Edison's most famous invention is the incandescent light, which he invented in 1879 after 6,000 experiments, proving his motto that "genius is one percent inspiration and 99 percent perspiration." He also proved the saying that "no man is a prophet in his own land" when he visited his birthplace in Milan decades after inventing the light bulb and found it still lit by candlelight. Edison eventually bought the house in 1906, and brought his good friends Harvey Firestone and Henry Ford to travel these country roads with him, remembering childhood events. Thomas Edison died in 1931, after amassing 1,300 patents. His birthplace in Milan is a national historic landmark and museum.

Milford

**HOME OF FIRST
METHODIST CLASS
IN NORTHWEST
TERRITORY,
1797**

MILFORD (Clermont County)

Francis McCormick, a veteran of the Revolution and soldier under Lafayette at Yorktown, left Kentucky in the year 1795, his aversion to human slavery compelling him to seek a new home north of the Ohio River. He settled just north of the site of Milford, an early milling center along the Little Miami River. It was here that Rev. McCormick, a giant of a man with a kindly expression, decided to organize his pioneer neighbors into the first Methodist society in the Old Northwest Territory. McCormick held church services in his log cabin, perhaps the first such church in Ohio, and one of his congregation, Ezekiel Dimmit, became the first Methodist class leader, holding classes in his own cabin in the fall of 1797. Soon this first group of twenty pioneers was joined by Rev. Philip Gatch, who, a quarter of a century earlier, had become the first native-born preacher to ride a Methodist Circuit in America.

The message of Methodism was spread along the frontier by preachers on horseback called circuit riders, and in 1800, Rev. Henry Smith became the first preacher assigned to Milford, which was part of the just-established Miami Circuit of the new Western Conference. The Miami Circuit included all the country along the Miamis as far north as the settlements extended. For twenty years, church meetings were held in the humble cabins of the pioneers or outdoors in beautiful groves of trees, referred to as "God's first temples." These first temples served until 1818, when the society built a sturdy frame meeting house of staunch timber in Milford, to be followed by another larger one in 1836. These permanent houses of worship served the congregations well, but spelled the beginning of the end of the circuit riding preacher.

Milford Center

**UNION COUNTY'S
FIRST SEAT
OF GOVERNMENT
Founded 1816**

MILFORD CENTER *(Union County)*

The settlers who moved into these Darby Plains in the early years of the nineteenth century were moving into a desolate area known as "The Barrens." It was considered an almost worthless wet paririe, where the dense prairie grass grew to a height of over eight feet. The land was poorly drained and was covered with water most of the year, but, as is characteristic of prairies, the land became dry in the fall and subject to raging prairie fires. The fires were essential for the survival of the prairie, with its sea of waving grasses and beautiful wildflowers, but they slowed settlement and endangered people.

One of the earliest settlements in the area was along the banks of Big Darby Creek, and the name of the present town, Milford Center, provides an excellent thumbnail sketch of the town's evolution. Sturdy frontiersmen had settled along the banks of the Big Darby in the earliest years of the 1800's, and in order to socialize and do business with each other, they cleared brush from along the banks. The crossing became known as "Darby Ford." In 1810, George Reed built a mill along the stream, and the settlement became known as "Mill-Ford." Later still, when the community was vying to become the county seat, it added "Center" to its name to attract additional residents, giving the town its present name of "Milford Center."

Today, Milford Center is a sleepy little village along the banks of the scenic Big Darby Creek, and the county seat is in Marysville.

Millersburg

**PLATTED 1824.
Now In The Heart
Of
Amish Country**

MILLERSBURG (Holmes County)

Millersburg, the county seat of Holmes County, was laid out in 1824 by Charles Miller and Adam Johnson, and today it is the center of one the largest Amish populations in the United States. The Amish, an offshoot of the Mennonites, broke from that denomination in the seventeenth century to follow Swiss Mennonite Bishop Jacob Amman, and in 1727 moved to Pennsylvania. In 1807, a group of the Pennsylvania Amish traveled down the Ohio River seeking new lands, and after searching through Iowa, Illinois, Indiana, and Ohio, they settled upon the Killbuck and Tuscarawas Valleys of east-central Ohio.

The Amish have kept themselves separate from modern society, eschewing modern mores and conveniences. Called the "plain people," they dress as their ancestors did centuries ago, the women wearing simple long dresses of flax, the men somber homespun clothes, bearded beneath broad brimmed hats. Using neither electricity nor automobiles, they have nevertheless prospered, using horse drawn buggies and farm implements. The Amish take care of their own, do not participate in any governmental programs, and band together to rebuild when fire or other disaster strikes a community member.

Amish children rarely attend school beyond the eighth grade, feeling that further education interferes with the simple life, and a 1972 Supreme Court decision backed their right to only a rudimentary education. One-room schoolhouses are in evidence along the dirt roads, but churches are not, for the Amish take turns hosting the services in their homes or barns. The existence of such a pre-industrial agricultural community in the midst of twentieth century America has drawn the interest of outsiders, and while providing a market for some Amish goods, the resulting tourism is seen by some as a threat to their way of life.

148

Millville

**1866 BIRTHPLACE OF
KENESAW MOUNTAIN
LANDIS
First Baseball
Czar**

MILLVILLE *(Butler County)*

Kenesaw Mountain Landis was born in Millville on November 20, 1866, and named for the Civil War battle where his father was wounded. Landis was a federal judge in Chicago prior to being tapped as the first commissioner of baseball, and had earned some recognition when he fined Standard Oil of Indiana a record $30 million dollars in a rebate case, a decision that was later overturned.

In 1920, the club owners of major league baseball decided to replace the three member commission that had overseen the game with a one man "czar," hoping to restore a measure of integrity and trust in the national pastime. Only a year before Judge Landis took the reins, the nation had been shocked at the revelation that eight Chicago White Sox players had apparently conspired to throw the 1919 World Series at the behest of gamblers, an incident that was to go down in history as the infamous "Black Sox Scandal."

The stern, craggy-faced judge turned out to be the perfect man for the job, and he ruled baseball with an iron fist until his death in 1944. During his tenure he was recognized for restoring confidence in the game, and on several occasions he banned players from the game for life for rules violations. He even ordered that the proceeds of a World Series game be donated to charity when the game was called for no apparently good reason.

Kenesaw Mountain Landis, baseball's first czar, is enshrined in the Baseball Hall of Fame.

Mingo Junction

**MINGO INDIAN
VILLAGE SITE
WHERE
GEORGE WASHINGTON
CAMPED, 1770**

MINGO JUNCTION (*Jefferson County*)

In the fall of 1770, George Washington felt compelled to make an arduous journey through the Ohio Valley by way of canoe. The reason for the journey was two-fold: first, to locate the bounty lands for the officers and soldiers of the Virginia Regiment before an English land company preempted the claims, and second, to satisfy his own interests in the lands of the Ohio Valley.

Washington kept meticulous diaries of his travels, describing the scene with a surveyor's eye. His entry of October 22, 1770 reads: "The water from little Beaver Creek to the Mingo Town, in general, is swifter than we found it the preceding day. The Hills which come close to the river opposite to each bottom are steep; in many places, rocky and craggy. The River along down abounds in Wild Geese and several kinds of ducks. We killed five wild Turkeys today." At the Mingo Town, Washington found "60 odd Warriors of the Six Nations going to the Cherokee country to proceed to war against the Cuttawba's."

Washington also faithfully recorded the details of the weather during his travels, and noted that the day he reached the Mingo Town was "very raw & cold. Cloudy, and sometimes snowing and sometimes raining." The weather was only a minor concern to the party, however, as the journal entry goes on to say that "upon our arrival at the Mingo Town we received the disagreeable news of two traders being killed at a town called the Grape Vine Town, 38 miles below this; which caused us to hesitate whether we should proceed or not." The Indians confirmed that one man was killed, but did not believe their people had done it. At two o'clock the next afternoon, uncertain as to their safety, Washington and his party set out again in their canoe, leaving behind the Mingo Town that would one day be known as Mingo Junction, Ohio, and paddling into possible danger downstream (see Powhatan Point).

150

Minster

**FOUNDED 1832
AS STALLOSTOWN
ON LAKE LORAMIE,
Former Miami-Erie
Canal Reservoir**

MINSTER (Auglaize County)

In 1832, a group of German immigrants had made their way to Cincinnati, hoping to acquire land in Ohio where they might make a settlement. Their leader, F.J. Stallo, had investigated land just three miles north of another German community that was being established at the same time, and so on September 8, 1832, he went to the Piqua land office to purchase the land. A drawing was held for each of the 144 lots that had been platted in "Stallo's Town," after which Stallo was to execute a deed for each purchaser. Unfortunately, he died before executing the deeds, throwing the orderly process into chaos that took years to straighten out.

After Stallo's death, the German settlement continued to grow. In 1848, the name of the town was changed to Minster in honor of Muenster, Germany, the homeland of many of the early residents. The streets were given such names as Frankfort, Hanover, Zweibruken, Vienna, and Berlin, but a later council, making a move toward Americanizing the community, changed the names to Clay, Washington, Jackson, Jefferson, Monroe, and Adams.

The coming of the canal through Minster brought increased prosperity. Nearby was Lake Loramie, a reservoir built to feed the Miami & Erie Canal. A grist mill was built along the feeder canal, and in town the shipping and pork-packing industries were flourishing. But riding the canal boats was another cargo that brought death to Minster in the 1840's. Cholera was following the transportation routes of America, and Minster was hit especially hard. "People died so rapidly that immediate burial could not be given them," chronicled one source. Strangely, all the cholera cases were limited to the east side of the canal.

Today, Lake Loramie is a state park where many canal features remain, and Minster is an orderly community that proudly reflects its early heritage as a German settlement.

Montpelier

**BIRTHPLACE OF
DR. PAUL A. SIPLE
Polar
Explorer**

MONTPELIER (Williams County)

Sixty-thousand Boy Scouts wanted to go to the South Pole with Admiral Richard E. Byrd on his first expedition to the Antarctic, but only one could be selected in the national competition. After a first review, the field was narrowed to 100, then down to six. Now it was up to the admiral himself to interview each of the remaining half-dozen scouts, and pick one to accompany him on a journey of a lifetime. He chose Paul Siple, a nineteen year-old Eagle Scout from Erie who had been born and raised in the small farming community of Montpelier, Ohio. It was a good choice, for Paul Siple would go on to earn the nickname "Mr. Antarctica" and grace the cover of Time Magazine.

The year of that first expedition was 1928, but it would not be the last expedition for Siple. He would return to the pole time and again, eventually spending 64 months there over four winters and ten summers. During one of these expeditions, Siple and his party camped directly on the South Pole for eight months and became the first men to spend the entire dark, six-month winter in Antarctica. The average temperature of minus 76 degrees, and the winter low of minus 120, gave him ample opportunity to study the effects of wind and cold. There he developed what he considered his most important achievement, the wind chill index.

Paul Siple died of a heart attack at the age of 58 in 1968. In his hometown of Montpelier, a plaque adorns the house where he grew up on Empire Street, and a marker at the town hall reads "Dr. Paul Allman Siple, Born 1908 in Montpelier, Ohio; Died 1968 in Arlington, Va. Scientist, polar explorer, inventor, and author. Honored by educators, governments, industry, international scientists."

MORROW COUNTY
BIRTHPLACE OF
WARREN G. HARDING
29th President
Of The
United States

MT. GILEAD *(Morrow County)*

(Please see Marion, Ohio.)

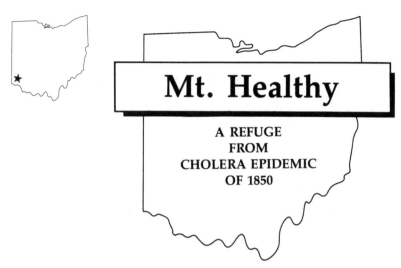

Mt. Healthy

A REFUGE FROM CHOLERA EPIDEMIC OF 1850

MT. HEALTHY (Hamilton County)

Mt. Healthy was founded in 1817 by John La Boiteaux and Samuel Hill, who named it Mt. Pleasant. The town went by this name for many years, but when a conflict arose with the post office as a result of another town already having that name, the residents chose Mt. Healthy, perhaps in gratitude that their community was spared from the terror that struck Cincinnati in the late 1840's.

Cholera was the most feared and awe-inspiring pestilential disease of the nineteenth century, and four times in that century the deadly disease swept much of the globe. America was first visited by the second global epidemic, which rose from near the Ganges in India in 1826, ravaging all of that country before following a caravan route into Europe and Russia. It crossed the Atlantic in 1832 aboard a ship crowded with immigrants that landed in New York. The United States was reached again by the disease in 1849, infecting all of the country east of the Rockies. Ohio's new canal system, national road, and the Ohio River offered an improved transportation route for the disease as it spread into and beyond the state.

In Cincinnati, 8,500 people died from cholera in 1849, about one of every fourteen residents. The disease ran such a rapid course that "a healthy man at day break may be dead and buried at night fall." Poor sanitation and infected water supplies were an open invitation to the spread of cholera, which left its sufferers dehydrated, with a subnormal temperature, vomiting and in circulatory collapse. The fatality rate of the disease ranged from 30 to 80%, with death sometimes occurring within hours.

Although the disease exacted a terrible toll in human life, it led to improved sanitary conditions that have made cholera virtually unheard of in America today.

154

Mt. Pleasant

QUAKER YEARLY
MEETING HOUSE
ERECTED 1814

MT. PLEASANT *(Jefferson County)*

The Quakers trace their origins back to England where, in 1647, a lay preacher named George Fox began preaching the doctrine of a "Christ within," proclaiming that revelation is experienced directly by the individual without mediation by the church. This "inner light" experience frequently was accompanied by trembling, giving rise to their being called "Quakers", although they referred to themselves as the Religious Society of Friends. Persecuted for their beliefs in England, the Quakers came to America and set up congregations -called "Meetings" - in Rhode Island by 1661. Soon, there was a sufficient number of Meetings to organize a Yearly Meeting, or a confederation of Meetings within an area. Opposed to slavery and insisting that the Indians be treated as equals, the Quakers refused to bear arms against others. William Penn's "Holy Experiment" attracted the Quakers westward to Pennsylvania, and in 1800 several hundred Friends had made their way to Ohio.

In 1814, the Quakers built their first Yearly Meeting House west of the Alleghenies at Mt. Pleasant. The large brick structure was capable of seating up to 2,000 people, and served five "quarterly meetings" in Pennsylvania, Ohio, and the Indiana Territory. Mt. Pleasant became an important antislavery center, where Charles Osborn published *The Philanthropist* in 1817, the first antislavery newspaper in the country. For nearly a century, the Mt. Pleasant Meeting House served the industrious Quakers of the region, and in 1909 the last regular yearly meeting was held there.

The state of Ohio acquired the Mt. Pleasant Meeting House in 1950, and today it is a state memorial operated by the Ohio Historical Society.

Mt. Sterling

HOME OF
JOHN W. BRICKER
Governor and
United States
Senator

MT. STERLING (*Madison County*)

John W. Bricker was one of modern-day Ohio's most popular governors and the first Republican governor to serve three consecutive terms. The feat is even more impressive in that it was accomplished during the Franklin D. Roosevelt years when Democrats were dominating the political scene.

John Bricker was born on September 6, 1893 on a small farm in Madison County, and attended one-room rural schools until entering Mt. Sterling High School. It was said of him by one Republican leader, "I have never known anyone except Bricker whose friends have thought from the time he was 18 years old that he would some day be governor."

Bricker's political career began in Grandview in 1920, where he served as village solicitor. He was elected to his first statewide position in 1932 as attorney-general in a race that saw the Democratic gubernatorial and presidential candidates win by large margins. In 1938, pressing the theme that "Ohio Needs a Change," he won the governorship by more than 118,000 votes.

The success of Bricker during a time of Democratic domination drew the interest of Republicans across the nation, and in 1944 he was the vice-presidential candidate on his party's unsuccessful ticket. The popular Bricker went on to the U.S. Senate in 1946, and was reelected in 1952.

"The individual citizen must again be conscious of his responsibility to his government and alert to the preservation of his rights under it," said Bricker at his first inauguration as governor. "No superman or dictator can point the way to the better life we seek. It is a democratic task. The leadership must be of the many, of people of high character and good purpose. Such leadership is undramatic but safe. By it, democracies can serve and build."

John Bricker died on March 22, 1986, and was buried in Columbus' Greenlawn Cemetery.

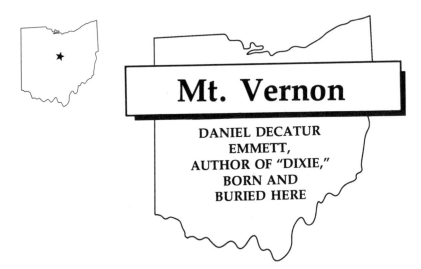

Mt. Vernon

**DANIEL DECATUR
EMMETT,
AUTHOR OF "DIXIE,"
BORN AND
BURIED HERE**

MT. VERNON (Knox County)

"In Dixieland, I'll make my stand, to live and die in Dixie" sang out the troops of the Confederacy during the Civil War. *Dixie* was the marching song of the south, and inspired hundreds of thousands of southerners during the war. Had it been widely known that a staunch Unionist from Ohio had written the song, its acceptance as the virtual anthem of the south would probably have been questionable; and the author himself, when the song became popular in the south, did not widely boast that he had written it.

Daniel Decatur Emmett of Mt. Vernon, Ohio was in New York City in September of 1859. A struggling minstrel, he had been asked to write a new song for opening night. The song he wrote was *Dixie.* When it was played in New Orleans in the spring of 1861, it brought down the house, and shortly thereafter was adopted by the Confederacy. It was said that even Lincoln loved the song, and it remains popular to this day.

Dan Emmett was the author of several other well-known songs, including *Turkey in the Straw* and *Old Dan Tucker,* songs which, like *Dixie,* are still familiar. In Emmett's later years, he returned to Mt. Vernon, where he sold copies of his songs to eke out a meager living. Daniel Decatur Emmett died in 1904, and is buried in Mt. Vernon.

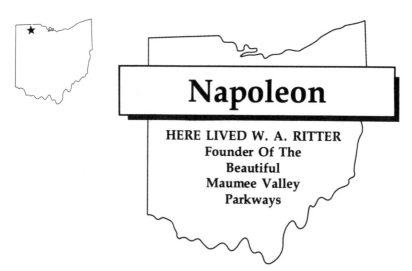

Napoleon

HERE LIVED W. A. RITTER
Founder Of The
Beautiful
Maumee Valley
Parkways

NAPOLEON (Henry County)

Napoleon, the seat of Henry County, is situated in the beautiful and historic Maumee Valley. Centuries ago, French voyageurs explored this region, and it was through this valley that Gen. Anthony Wayne led his forces to victory over the Indians in 1794. The valley again witnessed the marching of troops when Gen. William Henry Harrison beat back the British in the War of 1812. Within a few decades, the Maumee Valley would be transformed from a military route to a commercial one with the arrival of the Miami and Erie Canal that flowed along the river to Lake Erie. The town of Napoleon was settled in the valley by French and German pioneers, and it was the French who prevailed in naming the community Napoleon.

Warren A. Ritter was born in Henry County on April 25, 1878 and completed his education at the local high school. He served as a soldier in the Cuban and Philippine Wars, and his childhood along the banks of the old canal in the Maumee Valley perhaps helped influence him to serve as an engineer on the Panama Canal in 1904. A few years later he returned to Napoleon to become the postmaster, and he also organized the Napoleon Chamber of Commerce. But it was Mr. Ritter's love of landscaping, an interest he held since he was a boy, that earned him a place on Napoleon's historical marker.

W. A. Ritter, while serving as a commander in the Civilian Conservation Corps, formulated a vision of a series of parks along State Route 24 in the Maumee River Valley between Toledo and Defiance. With the construction of these parks, the Maumee Valley was again being transformed, this time from the site of an abandoned and deteriorating canal to the scenic jewel of northwest Ohio. Today, State Route 424, a state scenic highway, undulates through the valley and is part of the historic Anthony Wayne Parkway.

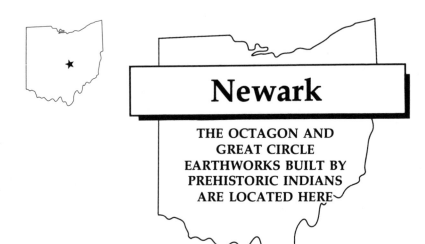

Newark

THE OCTAGON AND
GREAT CIRCLE
EARTHWORKS BUILT BY
PREHISTORIC INDIANS
ARE LOCATED HERE

NEWARK (Licking County)

For a period of about 700 years, from 200 B.C. to 500 A.D., this area of central and southern Ohio was the hub of a broad trading network of prehistoric Indians that stretched from Kansas to the east coast and from Michigan to Florida. Called Hopewell by us, these groups fished, hunted, gathered, and grew a few crops. Mystery surrounds much of their lives, and their demise, for the Hopewell culture largely vanished from the territory around 500 A.D.

When the earliest white men entered this region, they were baffled by the vast earthworks that they found. Some attributed them to a vanished race of superior men, others thought they were left behind by the lost tribes of Israel. Even the Indians who lived in the area were mystified by the mounds. Today, we have only a few remnants of the Hopewell surviving, including what is left of the Newark earthworks.

The original Newark earthwork complex was a vast enterprise, covering four square miles. If size was an indicator of importance, this was one of the most important sites for the Hopewells. The mounds, shaped in circles and octagons, were connected by causeways, and it is believed that the Hopewells came to these enclosures for ceremonial and trading purposes. Its location near Flint Ridge may indicate that this earthwork was used as a trading center for Ohio flint, which was exchanged for copper, mica, and silver. Recent studies suggest that the Octagon Earthworks may have been a lunar observatory that served as a calendar.

What brought the end of the Hopewell culture is not known. Epidemics, conquerors, and climatic changes have all been suggested as theories, but the mists of time still veil the Hopewell disappearance. Today, the 50 acre Octagon Mound and the 20 acre Circle Mound survive, sharing their grounds with a golf course.

New Athens

SITE OF
FRANKLIN COLLEGE
1825-1927.
Now Part Of
Muskingum College

NEW ATHENS (Harrison County)

The founding of a college on the Ohio frontier at New Athens dates back to 1817, when Scotch-Irish Presbyterians came from Pennsylvania to the hills of eastern Ohio and founded Alma Academy. The academy was upgraded to a college in 1825, going by the name of Alma College for two years when the name was again changed, this time to Franklin College. In the 1800's, Franklin College educated more Presbyterian ministers than any other college west of the Appalachian Mountains, and her alumni roll is a distinguished one. George McCook, one of the famed Fighting McCooks and later attorney-general (see Carrollton), John Bingham, prosecutor of Lincoln's assassins (see Cadiz), and Joseph Ray, famous mathematician, were among those who attended Franklin College.

Like other institutions in the state, Franklin became embroiled in the slavery debate of the nineteenth century, the internal dispute so intense that it literally divided the college. New Athens had for a while the distinction of having two colleges, Franklin College and the pro-slavery off-shoot, Providence College. Providence was very short-lived, and Franklin soon bought it out.

Franklin failed to evolve from its classical model of education, and when the railroad by-passed New Athens, the college languished. After conferring nearly 700 degrees between 1825 and 1908, the school was reduced to providing only "normal school" courses. In 1926 the Board of Trustees passed a resolution that read in part, "whereas Franklin College after nearly a century of service is without faculty and without students" a union with Muskingum College (see New Concord) is desired. And so a final merger took place in 1927, with Franklin's alumni welcomed into the Muskingum Alumni Association and her archives becoming an integral part of the archival collection of Muskingum College in New Concord.

New Concord

HOME OF MUSKINGUM COLLEGE AND JOHN GLENN, JR., FIRST AMERICAN TO ORBIT THE EARTH

NEW CONCORD (Muskingum County)

By 1827, Zane's Trace was becoming obsolete as the new National Road came at a snail's pace from Cumberland into Wheeling and then on into Ohio. The route in part followed Zane's Trace in eastern Ohio, but dropped away into the valley at Crooked Creek. Traffic by-passed the few cabins and the Old School Presbyterian Church on Pleasant Hill to follow the new road into the valley, and in 1828 Judge David Findley laid out the village of Concord here, settled chiefly by Scotch-Irish Presbyterians. "New" was added two years later to secure a post office, the former name already designating a town in Geauga County.

New Concord grew up with education on its mind. Judge Findley, the town proprietor, had been a trustee at Union Academy on Pleasant Hill, and the townspeople desired a school in their new village. In 1836, New Concord's first academy opened, drawing from nearby Franklin College (see New Athens) seven of its first twelve students. A year later Muskingum College was incorporated and opened its doors to seventeen pupils, presumably the same seventeen who had just completed the winter term at the academy. The college grew on little more than Scotch-Irish faith in its early years, plagued by the same financial hardships that dogged other early Ohio colleges. In 1838, the first building at the college went up, complete with construction short-cuts necessitated by economy. It stood only until 1851, when it was destroyed by fire. It was soon rebuilt, and part of it is incorporated in Paul Hall. The four year liberal arts school now has an enrollment of about 1,100 students.

In addition to Muskingum College, New Concord is proud to claim John Glenn, Jr., who became the first American to orbit the earth aboard Friendship 7 on February 20, 1962. Glenn, who along with the Wright Brothers and Neil Armstrong form the Ohio Triumvirate of Flight, went on to serve in the United States Senate.

New Holland

**SETTLED 1818
AS FLEMINGSBURGH
BY PENNSYLVANIA DUTCH,
HOLLANDERS AND
GERMANS**

NEW HOLLAND *(Pickaway County)*

Pickaway County is divided into two distinct regions that are clearly visible with a glance at a county map. The western part of the county is divided into irregularly shaped townships with roads that are more likely to follow natural features such as streams and valleys, while on the east side of the county one sees a neat rectangular pattern to the townships, with roads generally running on straight east-west and north-south courses. The dividing line between these areas is the Scioto River that served as the eastern boundary of the Virginia Military District. The Virginia Military District was surveyed using a "metes and bounds" system customary to Virginia (see Washington C.H.), while the east side of the county, lying outside the Military District, was surveyed in the regular fashion used by the rest of the state. The west side developed at a slower pace, due in part to the large surveys in that section that made settlement by persons of smaller means difficult. Attendant to this were the number of tenant farmers there working for absent Virginia landholders, a system that proved less satisfactory for growth than actual ownership of the land.

Into the western edge of the county came John Fleming in the early 1800's. Fleming hailed from Virginia, and he and his wife built the first log cabin in the area and raised eleven children. The plat of the village, then called Flemingsburgh, was filed on September 2, 1818. When the village was incorporated in 1835, the name was changed to New Holland. A great deal of excitement came to the village during the Civil War, when Gen. Sherman's army took two days to pass through town. The army's covered wagons, following the old Zanesville-Cincinnati Trace (now Route 22), were pulled by four-mule teams, and created quite a stir for the townspeople as they passed through the old double-barrelled covered bridge that spanned the North Fork of Paint Creek.

New Lexington

**NEAR BIRTHPLACE
OF
JANUARIUS MACGAHAN,
"LIBERATOR OF
BULGARIA"**

NEW LEXINGTON *(Perry County)*

While it may be safely presumed that relatively few Ohioans know of Januarius Aloysius MacGahan, who now rests in a cemetery in New Lexington, it has been written that "the Bulgarians heard the voice of God in the burning words of MacGahan's descriptive writings, and hailed him as the Messiah of their race." Virtually unknown in Ohio, his grave has been a shrine to pilgrims from Bulgaria who journey to the small Ohio town to pay homage to one of the greatest figures in their history.

Januarius MacGahan was born on Pigeon Roost Ridge near this Perry County farm community in 1844. He aspired to be a teacher, but due to his youthfulness and lack of experience, he was turned down by the school board. Deeply disappointed, he left his home and embarked on a series of great adventures that eventually helped change the map of Europe and make his birthday a day of celebraton in Bulgaria.

In 1876, MacGahan accepted an assignment as a war correspondent in the Balkans to verify reports of Turkish atrocities. His descriptive accounts of the horrors committed against the Bulgarians brought into question England's support of the Turks, and opened the door for the Russians to intervene on Bulgaria's behalf. MacGahan rode with the Russian force of 100,000 soldiers that crossed the Danube, and was hailed by the Bulgarians as their liberator.

Following the end of the Russo-Turkish War, MacGahan stayed in Constantinople to rest and care for a sick friend. He fell victim to typhus, and died on June 9, 1878 at the age of thirty-three. His body was returned to America in 1884, and reinterred in Maplewood Cemetery in New Lexington. In 1928, MacGahan was admitted to the Journalism Hall of Fame at the Ohio State University.

MACGAHAN, the War Correspondent.

New Paris

REV. BENJAMIN HANBY
WROTE THE
CHRISTMAS SONG
"UP ON THE HOUSETOP"
HERE IN 1864

NEW PARIS *(Preble County)*

(Please see Westerville.)

New Philadelphia

SITE OF
RESTORED SCHOENBRUNN
Ohio's First
Christian Town
Founded 1772

NEW PHILADELPHIA *(Tuscarawas County)*

David Zeisberger had learned several Indian languages at the school he attended in Pennsylvania, preparing for his Moravian missionary service to the Indians. In 1771, he entered the Tuscarawas River Valley in Ohio seeking to establish a peaceful home for his mission, and was invited by the Delaware Chief Netawatwes to build the mission on land near a spring of sparkling water. Called Schoenbrunn, which is German for "beautiful spring," the mission became the first town in Ohio.

Within a year, the new community numbered almost 200 residents, and sixty log houses, a church and a school were erected. Chief Netawatwes took the Christian name of Abraham and led his people in a pledge of nonviolence against Indian and whites alike, but in the midst of frontier fighting, the Moravians were viewed with distrust by both their Delaware brothers and the American soldiers. The missionaries decided to abandon Schoenbrunn in the face of these hostilities, and after a final tearful church service, the building was burned to prevent its desecration. The band of Moravians moved to the new village of Lichtenau. Eventually, Schoenbrunn would be burned to the ground by marauding soldiers under Col. David Williamson, and Abraham, professing peace to the end, would be slain in a terrible massacre (see Gnadenhutten). David Zeisberger, after serving sixty years as a missionary, died in 1808 and was buried three miles south of New Philadelphia in the Moravian town of Goshen, the last home of the Christian Moravian Indians in Ohio.

Today, the town of New Philadelphia stands on the site of old Schoenbrunn, which has been reconstructed under the auspices of the Ohio Historical Society and is open to the public.

New Richmond

JAMES G. BIRNEY STARTED HIS FAMOUS ANTI-SLAVERY NEWSPAPER HERE IN 1836

NEW RICHMOND (Clermont County)

James G. Birney, a native of Kentucky and former slaveholder, moved to New Richmond in 1834, and began the publication of his newspaper, *The Philanthropist*, shortly thereafter. The newspaper was an antislavery publication, originally based more on religious principles than political ones. While publication of such a paper was all but impossible in Kentucky, Birney had the assurance of leading antislavery men that he would be protected from mob violence in his new location.

Birney moved his newspaper to Cincinnati in 1836, and became the focal point of controversy. Cincinnati at that time wished to stimulate trade with the south, and to develop a Charleston to Cincinnati railroad. Birney's sentiments were not seen as good business by many, and on July 30, 1836, a mob attacked his printer's office, destroying the press and scattering the type.

Birney became involved in another controversy that same year when he was convicted under a nearly obsolete 1804 law of "secreting a Negro," a girl named Matilda Lawrence, who had escaped from a steamer on the Ohio River. Her defense lawyer, Salmon P. Chase, later got the conviction overturned on appeal to the state supreme court.

In 1840, the antislavery forces formed a third political party, the Liberty Party, and ran candidates in the national election. James G. Birney was selected as the party's first presidential candidate, with Thomas Morris, also of Clermont County, as his running mate (see Bethel). The Liberty Party garnered few votes, and it was another Ohioan who made the journey to the White House - William Henry Harrison.

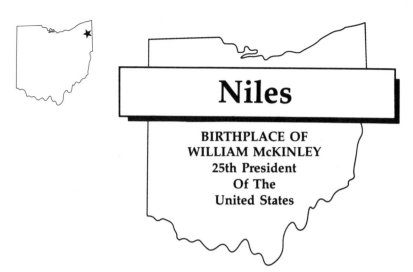

Niles

BIRTHPLACE OF
WILLIAM McKINLEY
25th President
Of The
United States

NILES (Trumbull County)

(Please see Canton, Ohio.)

North Bend

HOME OF WILLIAM HENRY
HARRISON, 9th President Of
The United States.
BIRTHPLACE OF
BENJAMIN HARRISON,
23rd President

NORTH BEND *(Hamilton County)*

William Henry Harrison holds the distinction of being named on more Ohio communities' historical markers than any other individual. Born in Virginia, Harrison entered the army in 1791 and became an aide to Gen. Anthony Wayne, distinguishing himself at the Battle of Fallen Timbers. After defeating the Indians of Tecumseh's federation at Tippecanoe, his reputation as a great Indian fighter was firmly established, and under his leadership the western frontier was secured during the War of 1812. It was Harrison who received the immortal communication from Oliver Hazard Perry, "We have met the enemy and they are ours," thereby ending the British threat on Lake Erie. Gen. Harrison went on to serve as an Ohio congressman and senator before embarking on the famous "hard cider and log cabin" campaign of 1840 that made him the ninth president of the United States. Unfortunately, his rugged reputation could not save him from contracting pneumonia at his inauguration, and on April 4, 1841, just one month after assuming office, President William Henry Harrison became the first president to die in office. He is buried beneath a towering hilltop monument in North Bend.

At the time of his death, President Harrison had a seven year old grandson named Benjamin back home in North Bend. After graduating from Miami University in 1852, Benjamin moved to Indianapolis, where he set up a law office prior to the outbreak of the Civil War. In 1881, Benjamin Harrison was elected to the United States Senate from Indiana, and in 1888, despite losing the popular vote, he defeated Grover Cleveland for the presidency, becoming the twenty-third president of the United States. He ran again in 1892, but this time lost the election to Cleveland. Harrison's wife passed away during the campaign, and after his defeat he returned to Indianapolis, where he died in 1901.

WILLIAM HENRY HARRISON,
Ninth President of the United States.

BENJAMIN HARRISON,
Twenty-third President of the United States.

North Olmsted

HOME OF
THE FIRST
MUNICIPALLY OWNED
BUS LINE

NORTH OLMSTED (Cuyahoga County)

When the financially strapped Cleveland Southwestern Railway, which operated an electric streetcar line from Elyria through North Olmsted to Cleveland, suddenly announced that it was suspending service effective midnight February 28, 1931, Mayor Charles Seltzer had only one week to react to the crisis. One-hundred fifty riders would be stranded if nothing was done, so he called a council meeting to suggest that North Olmsted begin municipal operation of the bus line on March 1. Council agreed, and with just three days left before service was to be suspended, the mayor put down several hundred dollars out of his own pocket on two used buses. The village clerk rushed to Columbus for two sets of license plates, which she obtained on the promise to send in the applications when the motor numbers were known. Meanwhile, workers were busily washing and painting the two buses, applying gallons of red and white paint to the coaches. At 5 a.m. on March 1, 1931, the pride of the North Olmsted Municipal Bus Line, the first such line in Ohio, rolled out of North Olmsted.

Robert Dunford would recall fifty years later what the day was like: "We had two small, 21-passenger buses from the General Motors Company, and the General Motors man was out there on Sunday morning, and he drove the first bus. I played conductor, and nobody had any change. I got a dollar bill from everybody that got on the bus. Then we got into Cleveland and sat there for a few minutes before we started back; and the company driver said to me, 'well, you're gonna be a driver, so get in there and drive'." And it was not only the drivers who drove in those early days - off duty police and firemen and part time park employees were also pressed into service. The five-cent local fare may have been one of the reasons for the popularity of the new line.

The North Olmsted Bus Line grew steadily over the years, and today operates forty coaches that carry a million-and-a-half passengers more than a million miles a year.

North Star

NEAR BIRTHPLACE
AND EARLY HOME OF
ANNIE OAKLEY,
"LITTLE SURE SHOT,"
BORN 1860

NORTH STAR (Darke County)

Phoebe Ann Moses was born in a log cabin near North Star, Ohio on August 13, 1860. Her father died when she was quite young, and soon the fields echoed with the crack of her rifle as she hunted game for her family. When Annie, as her sisters called her, was fifteen years old, she was put up to a shooting match with champion marksman and performer Frank Butler. The contest took place near Cincinnati at a place called Oakley, and when this teenaged girl won the match, the legend of Annie Oakley was born.

Annie and Frank Butler married a year later and began touring, putting on shooting exhibitions that eventually led to her starring in Buffalo Bill's Wild West Show. In 1883, she was introduced to Sitting Bull, who was convinced that, because of her great skill, she was possessed of, and protected by, the Great Spirit. He "adopted" her, and named her "Watanya Cicilia," or Little Sure-Shot.

Annie Oakley died on November 3, 1926. The *Greenville Daily Advocate* reported in its full front-page story, "Here, among the people of her native heath, she will ever be remembered for her winsomeness, her sincerity, and her love of the country in which she was born, and in whose broad expanse she chose to have her ashes laid. In the years to come, her grave will be a shrine for those who loved this woman, before whom the kings and rulers of the world bowed and paid tribute, and whom all honored."

Annie Oakley and Frank Butler, her husband of fifty years, are buried south of North Star in Brock Cemetery.

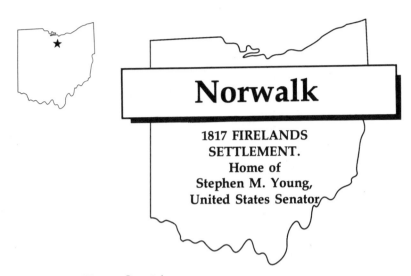

Norwalk

**1817 FIRELANDS
SETTLEMENT.
Home of
Stephen M. Young,
United States Senator**

NORWALK (Huron County)

On Independence Day, 1779, just off the coast of New Haven, Connecticut, there appeared the commanders of the British land and sea forces to issue a warning to the citizens of New Haven to repent "of the ungenerous and wanton insurrection against the soverignty of Great Britain." When the requested repentance was not forthcoming from the Americans, the British forces attacked the defenseless town, killing dozens of people, destroying houses, and taking prisoners, one of whom was the president of Yale. The fleet moved on to Fairfield, burning houses, churches and stores, then on to Norwalk, inflicting similar devastation. In 1781, the British troops returned to attack New London, led by Benedict Arnold, who was familiar with the town and its people. The suffering of New London, like the other towns, was terrible. People were left without homes and a means of making a living. After the war, the Connecticut legislature responded to the plight of the "Fire Sufferers" and granted them a half million acres in the western portion of the Connecticut Reserve in Ohio (see Conneaut). A generation passed before the Sufferers could take possession, and by then the original claimants were either dead or too old to travel. The Firelands, which now encompass Huron and Erie Counties, were largely settled by their heirs.

Norwalk, now the seat of Huron County, was wilderness when Elisha Whittlesey (see Canfield), Platt Benedict, and Frederic Fallig platted a town here in 1816, and Benedict's log cabin was the first structure built here in 1817. Like other towns in the Firelands named for the ravaged cities of Connecticut, the New England influence is everywhere. Considered one of the Reserve's most beautiful cities, Norwalk's West Main Street has a place on the National Register of Historic Places. In more recent history, Norwalk proudly claims Stephen M. Young, U.S. Senator 1959-71.

Oak Harbor

**OAK TIMBER
WAS SHIPPED
FROM THIS HARBOR
TO WORLD PORTS**

OAK HARBOR (Ottawa County)

Oak Harbor, contrary to what may be expected from its name, is located ten miles inland from Lake Erie in the middle of an agricultural area largely bereft of forest. However, like many other Ohio towns, its name provides evidence of the changes wrought in the state over the past century and a half. The community of Oak Harbor dates back to 1832 when it was platted along the north shore of the Portage River in Salem Township. The region was on the eastern edge of the Great Black Swamp, and featured swampy marshland adjoined by stands of oak, walnut, elm, poplar and other woods. Originally called Hartford, the town had to change its name to get a post office, the name of Hartford having been taken by another community. To emphasize the importance of the surrounding timber and the key role that the Portage River played in the town's commerce, Oak Harbor was selected as the village's new name.

The Portage River was Oak Harbor's link to the world, and the clearing of the timber around the village provided wood products that were shipped to various ports of the world. In town, the native timber gave life to a stave factory, a hoop factory, a planing mill, a wooden bowl factory, and a saw mill. Through her harbor aboard the *John Marshall* and *Mary Berkhead* went oak staves to Buffalo, lumber to Scotland for shipbuilding, and thousands of cords of wood to steamship ports for fuel. The town prospered, and many enjoyed their prosperity with excursions from Oak Harbor to the Lake Erie Islands aboard the pleasure craft that plied the Portage after the Civil War.

The 1870's saw the coming of the railroads to Oak Harbor, supplanting the harbor on the Portage River with iron rails and a station. The oak was also disappearing at the same time, with the community becoming an agricultural center. Today, Oak Harbor's name serves as a simple reminder of the town's historic past.

Oak Hill

**NEAR SITE OF
JEFFERSON FURNACE
WHERE IRON WAS MADE
FOR THE IRONCLAD
"MONITOR"**

OAK HILL *(Jackson County)*

The Hanging Rock region of southern Ohio, centered around Jackson County, was the leading producer of iron for implements and weapons in the United States in the mid-1800's. Iron produced in this region was noted for its exceptionally tough and durable quality, and nowhere was this more evident than in one of the ships made from the tough Hanging Rock iron, a ship that was destined to participate in one of the most famous battles in American naval history.

The *Merrimack*, a Union ship that had been sunk and then salvaged by the Confederates, was thought to be an invincible craft, and on March 9, 1862, a crowd had gathered to watch her finish off the ships of the Union blockade in the harbor at Newport News, Virginia. The day before, her ten heavy guns and iron-plated sides had proved too much for other Union vessels, as she sunk or crippled three of the wooden ships. But this day, she was to meet a ship like no other ever seen, a ship disparagingly called "a cheesebox on a raft." This low-riding ship with the revolving turret, named the *Monitor,* was also iron-plated, and when the *Merrimack* opened fire, the *Monitor's* iron repulsed the blow in a shower of sparks. The *Monitor's* return volley seriously weakened the *Merrimack's* plating, and after two hours of fighting, the *Merrimack* retreated.

A few weeks later, the Confederates destroyed the *Merrimack* when they evacuated Norfolk, and the *Monitor* would eventually sink in a storm off the North Carolina coast. This first battle of two ironclads brought to an end the days of wooden fighting ships forever, and again proved the superiority of Ohio's Hanging Rock iron.

Oberlin

HOME OF FIRST COEDUCATIONAL COLLEGE IN THE UNITED STATES

OBERLIN *(Lorain County)*

When Oberlin College was founded in 1833, it provided women "all the instructive privileges which hitherto have unreasonably distinguished the leading sex from theirs." However, the women did not actually fully share the curriculum with men, but had a "ladies'" curriculum that eliminated some subjects considered at the time too rigorous for "ladies' delicate minds." And while male graduates of the college received a baccalaureate degree, women received a certificate without a degree. But on September 6, 1837, four women applied for, and were granted, acceptance into the heretofore "gentlemen's curriculum" that would lead to a degree.

Mary Hosford, Mary Fletcher Kellogg, Elizabeth S. Prall, and Caroline Mary Rudd were the young student pioneers who began the course of study that made Oberlin the first co-educational college in the United States. While some minor concessions were made out of respect for the "delicacy of their gender" (such as being excused from a physiology class when a cadaver was introduced), and other courses considered inappropriate for women (such as rhetoric) required some compromise (the reading of their essays instead of unscripted oratory), the women endured the rigors of the same classical education provided the men.

On August 25, 1841, nine young men and three young women received their degrees from Oberlin College. The young women of Oberlin had made it possible for, in Mary Hosford's words, other young ladies to make their way "through the same path we have trod, peaceful and unmolested."

Today, Oberlin College is a thriving institution with an enrollment of about 3,000 students.

Ohio City

FIRST SUCCESSFUL
AUTOMOBILE
PRODUCED HERE
BY JOHN W. LAMBERT,
1891

OHIO CITY (Van Wert County)

It must have been a startling sight on that afternoon in 1891 when the doors were thrown open at Lambert's implement store and out rumbled a snorting, belching monstrosity that began chugging down the streets of Ohio City. Only a few in town had any idea what John Lambert was up to in his shed that adjoined the store, and one of those few, J. A. Swoveland, the town druggist, was privileged to witness the first test drive in the 80 foot showroom of the implement store. That done, the road test was next.

The streets of Ohio City were not prepared for such a vehicle. Tree stumps made the road an obstacle course, and while not presenting an inordinate problem to horses and buggies, they made for an exciting first drive in America's first gasoline-powered automobile. Described as more of a "slalom" event than a drive, Lambert maneuvered his vehicle around obstacles, certainly startling horses along the way. When on one of his sallies through town he lost control and struck a hitching rack (the world's first automobile accident), the future of such contraptions looked bleak in the eyes of many.

The future of Lambert's first car was, indeed, short lived. It was destroyed in a fire later in that same year, but Lambert was undaunted. He would go on to produce several marketable automobiles after moving from Ohio City. The friction-drive transmission would become one of his 600 patents in the automobile and gas-engine fields.

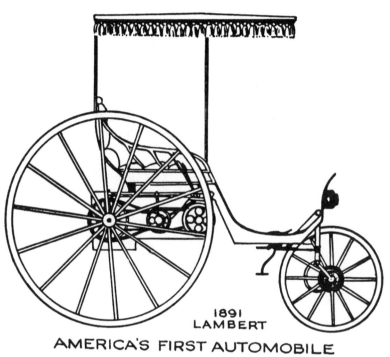

1891
LAMBERT
AMERICA'S FIRST AUTOMOBILE

Courtesy Brumback Library

Old Washington

SITE OF SKIRMISH
WITH GENERAL
JOHN H. MORGAN'S
CONFEDERATE
RAIDERS

OLD WASHINGTON *(Guernsey County)*

"This state is in imminent danger of an invasion," Ohio Gov. David Tod proclaimed as he mobilized the militia throughout southern Ohio. The "Thunderbolt" was bringing the Civil War to Ohio soil!

Gen. John Hunt Morgan, the "Thunderbolt of the Confederacy," had received orders in early summer of 1863 to conduct a raid from Tennessee into Kentucky, creating a diversion to distract Union troops and allow the Army of Tennessee to safely retreat from an untenable position. Following the raid, he was to return to Tennessee. Morgan had other ideas, however, and saw this as an opportunity to cross the Ohio River and bring the war north. With a force of 2,460 men, Morgan's Raiders moved into, and through, Kentucky, across the Ohio River into Indiana, and on July 13, 1863, were poised to invade Ohio.

Governor Tod's call for troops was answered by 55,000 Buckeyes, mostly untrained and undisciplined, but determined to protect their state and bring to an end Morgan's rampage. Once in Ohio, Morgan found "every man, woman, and child his enemy," "every hilltop a telegraph, every bush an ambush." Morgan's erratic path went through Harrison, Ripley, Piketon, Pomeroy, Old Washington and other towns, with his capture finally coming in Columbiana County, forty-six days after the raid began.

General John Hunt Morgan was sent to the Ohio Penitentiary in Columbus, but the prison was unable to hold the "Thunderbolt." He made a daring escape in November of 1863, but ten months later, while preparing to attack Union forces, he was surprised and killed by Federal troops near Greenville, Tennessee.

Oregon

HOME OF
PETER NAVARRE,
The Scout and AUTOKEE,
Chief of the
Ottawa Tribe

OREGON *(Lucas County)*

Peter Navarre made his way from Detroit to the mouth of the Maumee in 1807, where he erected a cabin and established a trading business with the Indians, buying furs on behalf of a Detroit trading house. After the War of 1812 broke out, Navarre was part of Gen. Hulls' surrender at Detroit, but went on to serve as a scout for Gen. William Henry Harrison toward the end of the war. His nighttime ride between Fort Meigs and Fort Stephenson (see Fremont) bearing messages for Harrison earned him a Congressional pension. Navarre died in 1874 at the cabin that he had built sixty-seven years earlier.

Among the Indians who lived in northwest Ohio was Autokee, the eloquent chief of the Ottawas. After the Indians were moved onto reservations, whites began preying on them in spite of governmental assurances of protection. The abused Indians bore these injustices with a dignity reflected in the poignant speech Autokee gave before a council attended by a government Indian agent. "The Great Father (the president) is good, but the white men fill his ears, and he cannot hear the red men call. The bad white men have killed our deer, trapped our otter and mink, have stolen our horses and abused our women, have camped on our land and called it their own, and when we tell them to go they hold up their rifles and say they will shoot. What must we do? We have waited many, many moons for our great father to drive these bad men from our land, but he has not done it, and if we drive them he will be angry with us. He has women, he has children; will he let bad men abuse them? No! He will not! Our Great Father is a great chief; he was at the great river when our British brothers from across the big water tried to take the country away from him, but he would not let them land. Our father is a great chief; he is brave; will he protect his red children? I have spoken."

In 1838, Autokee and his people received their answer when they were forced westward to a new reservation. The relatively young Autokee died just a few years later.

Ottawa

FOUNDED 1834
ON SITE OF
LAST OTTAWA INDIAN
RESERVATION
IN OHIO

OTTAWA *(Putnam County)*

The Ottawa tribe dates back in this part of Ohio to at least the middle of the eighteenth century, when their village of Tawas was visited by early French missionaries and traders. The Ottawas apparently maintained good relations with the French, and several Indian skeletons unearthed years afterward bore French-made silver crowns with etchings of bear and deer. It is thought that the crowns were made before the French and Indian War in 1756. The Jesuits, in attempting to Christianize the Indians, maintained a shrine in the wilderness nearby. Called "The Light House," the log chapel had a crude altar at one end before which stood a lamp that burned day and night for many years.

After the Americans took control of this land, they signed a treaty stipulating that "there shall be reserved for the use of the Ottawa Indians, but not granted to them, a tract of land on Blanchard's fork to contain five square miles," the center of which is now Ottawa. After bitter debate, the Ottawas reluctantly accepted the treaty. Life on the reservation was bittersweet: the area abounded in game, maple trees for making maple sugar were plentiful, and the river held a bounty of fish. But disease also visited the reservation, and small-pox killed a number of Indians. In 1833, the lands of the Reserve were put up for sale by the government to settlers, and the Indians were forced to move westward, where they were to again be ravaged by disease on the way to their new reservation.

The town of Ottawa was laid out on the site of the old reservation in 1834, and in July of that year Michael Row built the town's first hewed log house. Within a few short years, virtually all the Ottawa Indians were gone, with the exception of a few who stayed behind with white families. Today, Ottawa lies amid a vast agricultural area, and is the seat of Putnam County.

Ottoville

FOUNDED 1845
Named For
Rev. John Otto Bredeick
Originally Known As
Lock Sixteen

OTTOVILLE (Putnam County)

Settlement in this part of northwest Ohio was spurred more by the Miami & Erie Canal than by any other factor. All along the course of the "Big Ditch," settlers were arriving and small towns were springing up. At about the same time that Rev. John Otto Bredeick and a group of German Catholic pioneers were settling at Canal Construction Section 10 (see Delphos), a few other German Catholic families were locating themselves seven miles north along the banks of the Miami & Erie Canal at Canal Section 16. Intensely religious, these pioneers had to travel to Section 10 to fulfill their religious obligations. Seeing the hardships this created, especially for the children who had to travel for their religious instruction, Rev. Bredeick decided to establish a parish at their settlement. He bought forty acres of land from the government, and after reserving a portion for the building of a church, sold the rest. In his honor, the town was named Ottoville. In 1848, these few families at Ottoville were gathered into a parish.

With one parish at Section 10, and another seven miles away at Ottoville, Rev. Bredeick took on the hardships of travel himself. Riding horseback between the parishes, he came once a month to Ottoville, holding services in a two story frame building. The upper story was for the church services, and the lower floor was for the use of newly arrived settlers who needed temporary quarters. Rev. Bredeick guided the community of Ottoville for ten years until his death on August 19, 1858.

Confusion has surrounded Ottoville's original name of Section 16 for many years. For some unknown reason, "Lock 16" replaced "Section 16" somewhere during Ottoville's history. Lock 16 on the canal was actually at Acadia near Spencerville, and the lock at Ottoville is number 28.

Owensville

FOUNDED IN 1838
Birthplace of
Governor John Pattison
43rd Governor
of Ohio

OWENSVILLE *(Clermont County)*

Owensville, a Clermont County community of less than a thousand people, gave to the Buckeye State its forty-third governor, John M. Pattison. Governor Pattison was born on June 13, 1847, the son of a country merchant. His work in his father's store and on neighboring farms helped instill in him the values of hard work, honesty and moderation that would serve him so well, and his courage was demonstrated when he joined the 153rd Ohio Volunteer Infantry when but a boy of sixteen. Following the Civil War, he enrolled at Ohio Wesleyan University in Delaware, Ohio, where he managed to pay his way by working as a schoolteacher and on farms when not in class. In only twenty months he completed his course of study and graduated in 1869.

After embarking on a career in insurance and law, he was elected to the state legislature, but declined renomination to devote himself to his legal profession. Ten years later, he was again "drafted" by the Democrats into the race for the state senate, his reluctant candidacy garnering a record number of votes in Clermont County. Apparently resigned to his popularity, he went on to serve in Congress in 1891, helping secure for his constituents one of the first appropriations for rural free delivery of mail.

Back in Ohio, the Republicans had controlled the governor's office for fourteen years, but the winds of reform were blowing in 1905. Bossism was an issue on both the national and state scene, and John Pattison, an ardent temperance man and strict observer of the Sabbath, presented a clear alternative to the entrenched politics of the time. Although the Republicans won every other statewide office, Democrat Pattison was swept into the governor's office by a comfortable majority on the strength of his personal character. The campaign had taken a terrible toll on his health, however, and just six months after taking office on January 6, 1906, Governor Pattison died at his Milford home.

Oxford

HOME OF
MIAMI UNIVERSITY
Established
1809

OXFORD *(Butler County)*

Not unlike other early Ohio college towns, the idea of the college preceded the existence of the town in which it was located. Miami University, one of Ohio's first colleges, was conceived in 1803 by an act of Congress, permitting the Ohio legislature to select a township within the district of Cincinnati to be devoted to the support of a college. The township of Oxford was selected, and in 1816 the cornerstone was laid for the university. The main building was completed and opened in 1824, with room rent in the dormitory at $5 a year, including servant's hire. Miami, like other early colleges, suffered fianacial hardships, and placed this notice in an early catalog: "Tuition must be paid in advance; and if not paid by the student it is charged to the faculty." Robert Bishop, the college's first president, thought bells an extravagance, so the hours of the day were marked by the blowing of a bugle. Under Dr. Bishop, the school achieved such a high standard of excellence that it came to be known as "the Yale of the West."

Miami earned its sterling reputation with a faculty that included a number of noted educators, chief among them William Holmes McGuffey (see Youngstown). While McGuffey was at Miami, he wrote the first of his *McGuffey Readers*, books that would make him the "schoolmaster of the nation." His house at the campus is now the McGuffey Museum. Miami University is also the birthplace of the "Miami Triad" of national fraternities: Beta Theta Pi (1839), Phi Delta Theta (1848), and Sigma Chi (1852). Miami alumni include President Benjamin Harrison (see North Bend), and journalist Whitelaw Reid (see Xenia). When Harrison tapped Reid as his running mate in 1892, it represented the only time in American history that running mates on a presidential ticket were graduated from the same college.

Today, the beautiful campus at Oxford is home to about 16,000 students.

Painesville

**HOME OF
LAKE ERIE
COLLEGE
Founded 1857**

PAINESVILLE (Lake County)

Lake Erie College has its roots not in its beautiful campus at Painesville, but in Willoughby where it was given life as the Willoughby Female Seminary in 1847. The Willoughby Seminary itself evolved from Mt. Holyoke in Hadley, Massachusetts, which had been founded ten years earlier on a plan that would allow young women to perform domestic services at the school to keep the cost of tuition low. The Mt. Holyoke model soon spread west to Ohio, carried by a group of Mt. Holyoke graduates who opened the Willoughby Female Seminary. The school, in the midst of its prosperity, burned to the ground in 1856. The directors moved the school to Painesville after the fire, and from the ashes of the Willoughby Female Seminary rose the Lake Erie Seminary in 1857.

Lake Erie (Female) Seminary was opened in a new four story building that stands yet today as College Hall. It operated on the Mt. Holyoke plan with "style of living neat, but plain and simple, domestic work of the family to be performed by members of the school, and all surplus income to be cast into the treasury for the still further reduction of expenses the ensuing year." Bible study was a prominent part of the curriculum from the outset, but in 1898 the plan of study was enlarged and the school became the Lake Erie College and Seminary, granting the usual collegiate degrees.

Lake Erie College boasts the beautiful architecture for which the Western Reserve is famous. Foremost among the architect-builders of the Reserve was Painesville's Jonathon Goldsmith. In 1829, he built one of his finest Greek Revival houses for the town physician, Dr. John Mathews. Encroachment threatened this fine old house in the city, and it was later moved to the campus of Lake Erie College, where it can be seen today.

Lake Erie College is now a four year coeducational liberal arts college with more than 800 students.

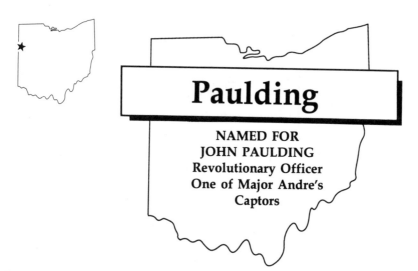

Paulding

**NAMED FOR
JOHN PAULDING
Revolutionary Officer
One of Major Andre's
Captors**

PAULDING (Paulding County)

Paulding County, with the town of Paulding as the county seat, is named for John Paulding, a native of Peekskill, N.Y. and a captor of Benedict Arnold's contact in treason, Major Andre. Paulding served through the Revolutionary War, and was reportedly taken prisoner three times; he died in 1818.

Three northwest Ohio counties are named in honor of Andre's captors, Paulding, Isaac Van Wart, and David Williams.

(For a description of Andre's capture, please see Van Wert.)

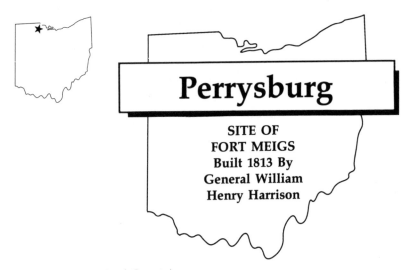

Perrysburg

**SITE OF
FORT MEIGS
Built 1813 By
General William
Henry Harrison**

PERRYSBURG (Wood County)

Fort Meigs, built during the winter of 1812-13 and named in honor of the Ohio governor, was strategically located along the banks of the Maumee River opposite the rapids. It was a large, strongly built fortification, but it was only with the cunning of Gen. William Henry Harrison that it was able to withstand two sieges of the British and Indians in the spring and summer of 1813.

Gen. Proctor had erected British artillery across the river from the fort on a bank sixty feet above the river. Included in the English weaponry were two awesome twenty-four-pounder cannons, and with his power and height advantages, Proctor assured Tecumseh and his Indians that Fort Meigs would soon be blown open and the Indians could storm into the fort. Harrison had other ideas, however, and he erected all of his large tents in a line inside the fort to hide his men from view as they dug trenches, creating two walls with the dirt. The first wall was twelve feet high and nine-hundred feet long, the second was a similar height and seven-hundred feet long. When dawn came on May 1, the British opened fire, and continued their barrage for several days. Inside the fort, the soldiers were burying their dead each night, and collecting the enemy cannonballs for reuse. When an emissary from Proctor came under white flag to demand the surrender of the fort, he saw little damage and no dead. Finally, after nine days of shelling and a growing disquietude among the Indians, the British withdrew to their Fort Malden.

Following a second brief siege on Fort Meigs in July, Proctor's troops moved on to Fort Stephenson (see Fremont), where they again met defeat. These victories coupled with Perry's triumph on Lake Erie led to the American victory in the west in the War of 1812. Today, Fort Meigs is one of the largest reconstructed walled forts in America, and contains exhibits of the War of 1812.

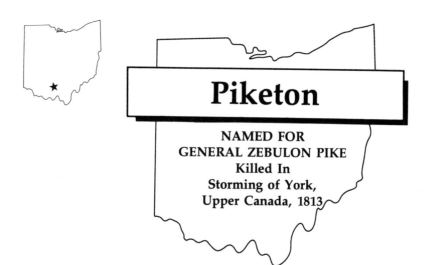

Piketon

NAMED FOR
GENERAL ZEBULON PIKE
Killed In
Storming of York,
Upper Canada, 1813

PIKETON (Pike County)

In a few instances, Ohio towns have taken their names from great Americans who otherwise had little connection to the Buckeye State. When these communities boast of the origin of their name on their historical marker, we have an opportunity to wander beyond our state's borders. Piketon, named after Gen. Zebulon Pike, allows us to range from the Rockies to Santa Fe, from the Rio Grande to Canada.

Zebulon Pike was born in New Jersey on January 5, 1779, the son of a Revolutionary War captain and soldier in St. Clair's defeat in 1791. An army "brat," Zebulon was an ensign in his father's regiment, and learned French, Latin, and mathematics. Following the Louisiana Purchase, Pike, now a lieutenant, was placed in command of an expedition seeking the source of the Mississippi River, a mission he accomplished in 1805 after much hardship.

In 1806-07, Pike literally reached the pinnacle of his explorations with the discovery of Pike's Peak in the Rocky Mountains. Shortly thereafter, his party trespassed onto Spanish lands and were taken as prisoners of the Spanish to Santa Fe, but were soon released. Pike's explorations, and his published accounts of them, excited many adventurous Buckeyes, who set out for this newly explored western land.

In 1813, Gen. Zebulon Pike led a force against York (now Toronto), Canada during the War of 1812. After taking control of a British fort, Gen. Pike was killed when the magazine of the fort exploded.

Piqua

**HOME OF
DON GENTILE
World War II
Army Air Force Ace
1920-1951**

PIQUA (Miami County)

A seven-foot statue stands on the public square in Piqua, and the plaque on its base reads "A One Man Air Force." "Ace of Aces" he was called by some, "Captain Courageous" by President Roosevelt. To the people of Piqua, he is Don Gentile, World War II Army Air Force Ace, and a product of their town.

Don Gentile was born in Piqua on December 6, 1920, and as a teenager was fascinated with flying. When the war came, Don itched to get into battle, and went to England to join other Americans in the Eagle Squadron flying Spitfires. He was the hottest fighter in the hottest fighter group, one of "Blakeslee's Bachelors," a group of unmarried men at the controls of P-51 Mustangs. They were the first group to fight over Paris and Berlin, and by the time Gentile transferred back to the U.S. Army Air Corps, he was on his way to establishing a reputation as one of America's greatest fighter pilots.

The final tally of Gentile's "kills" is uncertain, but he is credited with shooting down up to 30 enemy aircraft, many under extremely adverse conditions. He was the first U.S. flyer to break Eddie Rickenbacker's World War I record of 26 enemy planes destroyed, and among his numerous medals are the Distinguished Service Cross with cluster, Royal Air Force Pilot Badge, British Star, and many other honors bestowed by both the U.S. and foreign governments.

After the war, Gentile enrolled at the University of Maryland as an officer-student. On January 28, 1951, the 30-year-old pilot who had escaped death a hundred times over Europe was killed in a crash while on a routine training flight north of Andrews Air Force Base. He was given a posthumous promotion to the rank of major. In 1986, thirty-seven years after his death, the people of Piqua dedicated the statue of Don Gentile, called by Gen. Dwight Eisenhower his "One Man Air Force."

Plain City

FOUNDED 1818
BY ISAAC BIGELOW
ON EARLY
POST ROAD

PLAIN CITY *(Madison/Union Counties)*

The first attempt at settlement at what would become Plain City dates back to 1797, when Lucas Sullivant platted North Liberty, a town with several hundred lots situated along wide, spacious streets. Sullivant later became preoccupied with laying out another of his settlements at Franklinton, and North Liberty, while impressive on paper, languished, its population peaking at three cabins.

In 1811, the Post Road, a gravel road that would become part of the Worthington-Urbana Road, opened the area for settlers. Three years later, a seventeen year old boy named Isaac Bigelow trekked to Ohio from Pennsylvania on foot. He was on a business errand for his father, delivering payment to an uncle for land where Plain City now stands. He returned to Darby Township for good in 1818, and submitted a plat for a village that he would call Westminster. In 1823, his town was renamed Pleasant Valley.

Travelers making their way along the Post Road would often stop at "The Traveller's Inn," a log inn serving the hunters and trappers in the area. Slowly, other new businesses were established, and Bigelow himself opened a dry goods store. By the time the village was incorporated in 1842, a flour mill, blacksmith shop, post office, grocery store and hotel were among the businesses serving the residents of Pleasant Valley. The arrival of a trunk line railroad through the village in 1851 brought new growth to the farming community, and in that same year the town was again renamed, this time Plain City.

Isaac Bigelow died of pneumonia in 1857, and was buried in a now vanished cemetery between the Post Road and Big Darby Creek. A few miles west of town is a cemetery preserve bearing his name where the early pioneers rest beneath the rippling grasses and beautiful wildflowers that greeted them upon their arrival in the Darby Plains.

187

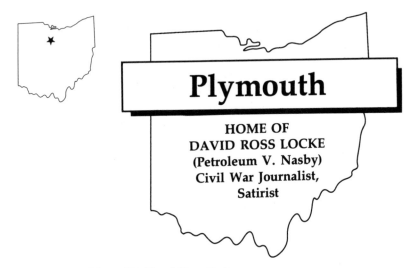

Plymouth

**HOME OF
DAVID ROSS LOCKE
(Petroleum V. Nasby)
Civil War Journalist,
Satirist**

PLYMOUTH (Huron/Richland Counties)

When Abraham Lincoln needed a moment of relief from the tensions of the Civil War, he did what thousands of other Americans did. He picked up the newspaper and read the ramblings of "Petroleum Vesuvius Nasby, late paster uv the Church uv the New Dispensation." Replete with poor grammar and misspellings, Nasby on the surface appeared to be sympathetic to the South, but his wry wit and humor actually poked fun at the Confederates.

Nasby was the creation of David Ross Locke, a New York newspaperman who moved to Ohio and eventually became editor of the *Toledo Blade*. Along the way, this itinerant printer/journalist/editor worked at the *Plymouth Advertiser*, *Bucyrus Journal*, *Mansfield Herald*, *Bellefontaine Republican*, and *Findlay Jeffersonian*. While at Findlay, Locke developed the character of Nasby, a whiskey-drinking, pro-slavery, illiterate politician who wanted to be postmaster. In one of his first communications, Nasby declared that his town of "Wingert's Corners" was seceding from Ohio: "It (Ohio) refoosed to locate the State Capitol at the Corners, to the great detriment uv our patriotic owners uv reel estate. It refoosed to locate the Penitentiary at the Corners, not-withstandin we do more towards fillin it than any town in the State. It refoosed to locate the State Fair at the Corners, blastin the hopes uv our patriotic groserys... Therefore, not bein in humor to longer endoor sich outrages, we declare ourselves free and independent uv the State, and will maintain our position with arms, if need be..."

Locke's political satires under Nasby's name were tremendously popular, and were read from the White House to Union campfires. So powerful were they in keeping public opinion supportive of the war that, after the war, the Union forces' success was attributed to three things: "the army, the navy, and the Nasby letters."

Point Pleasant

BIRTHPLACE OF
GEN. ULYSSES S. GRANT
18th President
Of The
United States

POINT PLEASANT *(Clermont County)*

Ulysses S. Grant, the 18th president of the United States, was born on April 27, 1822 in a small frame house at Point Pleasant, Ohio, an Ohio River village upriver from Cincinnati. His father, Jesse, a tanner by trade, and mother, Hannah Simpson, had been married the previous June. When Dr. Rogers delivered the small baby who would become the great Civil War general, he cautioned the parents that they "had better be especially careful of that little fellow. He's not so strong but what you may not bring him up if you're not careful." The Grants were to remain in Point Pleasant just a year before they moved on to Georgetown, Ohio (see Georgetown).

The birthplace of Grant in Point Pleasant was to later make some journeys of its own, and it became known as the most traveled three-room cottage in America. After Grant became a national hero, the house was removed from its original foundation and placed on exhibition all over Ohio. It even made its way onto a barge and was floated down the Ohio River to show Grant's humble beginnings. In the 1880's, Henry Chittendon bought the house and put it on display at the Ohio State Fairgrounds in Columbus. In 1927, the cottage was sent back to Point Pleasant, where it was stored in sections in a barn until 1936, when it was put back in its original place. Flood waters would reach its roof the same year, but the contents of the house had been moved to a church on higher ground.

The Ohio Historical Society restored the house to its original condition, and today Grant's birthplace, open to visitors, is operated by the Clermont County Convention and Visitor's Bureau.

Poland

**SITE OF
TOWN ONE, RANGE ONE
IN THE
WESTERN
RESERVE**

POLAND (Mahoning County)

Colonial Connecticut had claimed all the land lying within her extended borders from "sea to shining sea," and northern Ohio fell within that claim. After the Revolutionary War, she gave up her claims to most of the western land to the federal government. She did keep for herself the area of northeast Ohio called the Western Reserve, and in 1796 sent a party to survey the land.

The task of the first surveyors was an extremely rigorous one, involving dragging chains through dense brush, cutting trees down to get a straight sight-line, and slogging through marshy wetlands. Disease and hunger plagued the early crews, yet they persisted until the Reserve was surveyed. The boundaries of the Reserve were the western border of Pennsylvania, extending west for 120 miles between 41 degrees latitude on the south and 42 degrees plus two minutes on the north. The surveyors were to lay out townships five miles square.

The line marking the Pennsylvania border was still discernible ten years after it had first been marked, and the stone posts with the letter P carved in their tops were soon located. Seth Pease found a post at the 42nd parallel, and headed south to locate the southeast corner of the Reserve sixty-seven miles away. "We run about two miles south and encamped by a pond in a swamp. Plenty of gnats and mosquitos; poor water," he wrote on July 7. In spite of extreme hardships, the surveyors reached the corner on July 21. After taking observations by the sun and stars, "Mr. Porter set a chestnut post, sixteen inches by twelve." With the corner established, range lines were run at five mile intervals from the east. The townships were numbered at five mile intervals from south to north. Thus was the southeast corner of the Reserve designated Town One, Range One of the Western Reserve, the present location of Poland township.

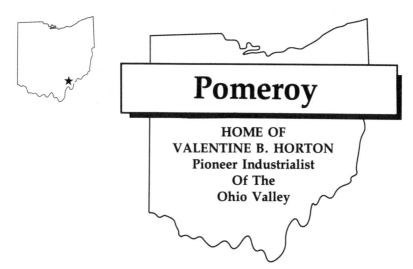

Pomeroy

HOME OF
VALENTINE B. HORTON
Pioneer Industrialist
Of The
Ohio Valley

POMEROY (Meigs County)

The Ohio River town of Pomeroy is named for Samuel Wyllys Pomeroy, who came to the area from Boston to inspect his coal interests in 1830. He was pleased with what he saw, and deemed it "a good and healthy place to live, and with proper management a bright industrial future." He sent his son-in-law, Valentine B. Horton, to further assess the area's potential and develop the salt and coal industry here.

Horton developed the mines at Pomeroy, attracting labor from the ranks of Germans, Irish and Welsh immigrants. He was responsible for developing river transportation of the coal, and built the first coal barges, including the *Condor,* which was fired by coal instead of wood.

The salt industry was another important industry in pioneer Ohio, and Horton used his coal to fire the furnaces of his Excelsior Salt Co. When two partners who had leased land from Horton for salt-making were unsuccessful using their horse-drawn power, one of them demanded a release from the agreement. Horton reluctantly obliged, then put steam-power to work at the site, creating a profitable salt business. After the death of one of the unsuccessful lessees, Horton paid back all the man's expenses to the widow, plus interest.

Horton brought about the incorporation of Pomeroy in 1841. An astute politician as well as able industrialist, he was instrumental in having the county seat moved to Pomeroy from Chester that same year. He went on to serve several terms in Congress, commencing in 1855, and served on the Board of Trustees of The Ohio State University from 1848 until his death at Pomeroy on January 14, 1888.

Port Clinton

NEAR HERE
OLIVER H. PERRY
CAPTURED BRITISH FLEET
BATTLE OF LAKE ERIE
1813

PORT CLINTON *(Ottawa County)*

September 10, 1813 dawned a beautiful day on Lake Erie. Gentle breezes were blowing from the southwest, and the sky was a beautiful blue. Against this backdrop sailed six magnificent orange and black British ships, their sails billowing against the azure sky. Out to meet this powerful British navy came the green, inexperienced American fleet of a twenty-eight year old commander named Oliver Hazard Perry. The peace of the day was shattered when a British shot tore through the side of Perry's flagship, the *Lawrence.* Within two hours, the *Lawrence* was out of action. Perry, clutching under his arm a blue flag with the words "Don't Give Up The Ship," made his way to the *Niagara,* and within minutes pressed her toward the powerful British ship *Detroit,* itself a floating wreck by now. Drawing alongside, Perry delivered a devastating broadside fire, and the sharpshooters on her deck, ordered aboard by Gen. William Henry Harrison shortly before the battle, began raking the decks of the enemy ship. The British gave up ten minutes later, the first time an entire British fleet had been forced to surrender.

"We have met the enemy, and they are ours," wrote the young Perry to Gen. Harrison. The lake belonged to the Americans, and soon Harrison would pursue the fleeing British troops to the Battle of the Thames in Ontario, where his victory would bring to an end the western portion of the War of 1812.

A century after the war, the United States erected the Perry's Victory and International Peace Memorial, the largest Doric column in the world, at Put-in-Bay. Visitors to the top of the 352 foot high monument have a spectacular view of Lake Erie, overlooking the site of one of the most famous battle scenes in American history.

Portsmouth

**CHILDHOOD
HOME OF
JULIA MARLOWE
Shakespearean
Actress**

PORTSMOUTH *(Scioto County)*

Sarah Frances Frost was born in England on August 17, 1870, and at the age of five moved with her family to America. Her father died when she was still young, and following her mother's remarriage, the family moved to Portsmouth, where Sarah was raised on Front Street. Perhaps it was her English background tinted with the pain of her father's loss that helped her evolve into one of the world's greatest Shakespearean actresses. She showed this ability to communicate with an audience from an early age. She was but twelve years old when she began her theatrical career in a juvenile comic opera company, and within a few years she was off to the east coast to make her debut as a star.

On April 25, 1887, Sarah appeared in New London, Connecticut, where she assumed for the first time her stage name of Julia Marlowe, a name she later adopted legally. She gained additional celebrity in a series of Shakespearean plays with the renowned Edward H. Sothern. In 1904, the two were paired for the first time on stage as "Romeo and Juliet," and life imitated art in 1911 when the couple was married. The couple appeared in *Much Ado About Nothing, Taming of the Shrew, Macbeth,* and many other Shakespearean productions, and continued performing together until their retirement.

Port Washington

**1836 BIRTHPLACE
OF ALEXANDER
HELWIG WYANT
Landscape
Artist**

PORT WASHINGTON (Tuscarawas County)

With Ohio's rugged beauty and unbroken wilderness dominating her natural heritage, it is not surprising that nineteenth century Ohioans were especially fond of paintings of landscapes and epic scenes of the type that drew the first settlers to the Ohio Country. It was the natural beauty of Ohio that awakened in Alexander Wyant a sympathy with nature that found its way onto the canvasses that he so beautifully painted.

Alexander Helwig Wyant was born in Port Washington on January 11, 1836. He was determined even as a youth to be an artist, and was completely disinterested in the business of harness making to which he had been apprenticed after high school. Hearing of a distinguished artist named Inness, he set off for New York City to visit him and show him his work. There he received his hoped-for encouragement. Wyant returned to Cincinnati, where he joined the ranks of several artists under the patronage of Nicholas Longworth. The year 1863 found him studying the beauty of the Ohio Valley, but soon he was off to New York, England, and Ireland for further study.

After his return to America, he set about again capturing her natural beauty on canvas. However, he was beset with health problems. Hoping to recover his strength and vigor, he joined an expedition to Arizona and New Mexico, but his treatment on the expedition and the conditions he lived under were too much for him. He suffered from exposure, and lost the use of his right hand. The determined young artist persevered, and, learning to paint with his left hand, created his best works.

Among his paintings are *The Storm* (1861), *Pool on the Ausable* (1871), *Sunset in the Woods, Driving Mists,* and *Cloudy Day, Keene Valley* (1892). One critic wrote, "He loved the gray sky and sombre tints of November, the subtle mystery of twilight and the fading glory of the sunset." Alexander Wyant died in 1892 at the age of fifty-six.

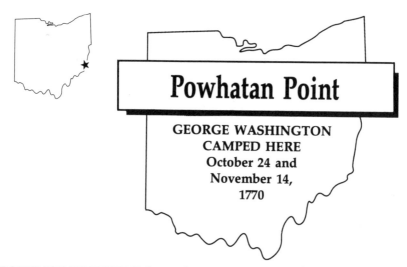

Powhatan Point

**GEORGE WASHINGTON
CAMPED HERE
October 24 and
November 14,
1770**

POWHATAN POINT (Belmont County)

George Washington was continuing his journey down the Ohio River in that autumn of 1770 (see Mingo Junction), locating bounty lands for the soldiers of the Virginia Regiment. At times encountering swift water, at other times confronting rumors of hostile Indians, Washington on this morning was just happy to see the foul weather that had plagued the party for almost a week finally clear, if only for a short while. "Clear & pleasant morning but cloudy and cold afterwards," he wrote in his diary for October 24, 1770. "We reached the Mouth of a Creek called Fox Grape Vine Creek abt. 3 o'clock in the afternoon - distant from our last camp abt. 26 miles."

The journey to this spot was one filled with tension, for the rumor heard at Mingo Junction was that two traders had been killed by Indians downstream at this spot. "This is the place where it was said the Traders lived, & the one was killed. Finding no body there, we agreed to Camp; that Nicholson and one of the Indians (accompanying Washington's party) might go up to the Town, & enquire into the truth of the report concerning the Murder," wrote Washington.

Nicholson and the Indian returned about seven o'clock the next day, and reported finding two "Old Indian Women" at the town. The women told them that the trader was not killed, but had drowned trying to ford the Ohio River at the mouth of the creek. Satisfied, Washington and his party continued their journey down the Ohio.

Today, Fox Grape Vine Creek is known as Captina Creek, and at its mouth, where Washington made camp, is the community of Powhatan Point, Ohio.

Proctorville

**THE ROME BEAUTY
APPLE
FIRST GROWN HERE
IN 1816**

PROCTORVILLE (Lawrence County)

"Here, son, set out this young democrat," Joel Gillett told his teenaged boy Alanson, referring to an apple seedling that was quite different from the others that he had obtained at the Rufus Putnam Nursery in Marietta. The year was 1816, and the Gilletts were just starting a new orchard on their farm in Rome Township, taking advantage of the superb fruit growing conditions along the Ohio River in Lawrence County, Ohio. Alanson did his father's bidding, and planted the seemingly worthless twig near the river bank away from the main orchard.

Several years passed, and the senior Gillett's orchard was now established and producing quite well. Remembering the lonesome twig planted by the river, Alanson set out to see if by some chance it had also survived. When he reached the spot where he had planted it, he found a tree loaded with beautiful bright red apples, "clustered as thick as grapes."

The apple that Alanson grew was named Rome after the township in Lawrence County where it was first grown. The Rome Beauty is a hearty late ripening apple that keeps well and is good for baking, cooking, and eating fresh. From its humble origin as a near outcast in Rome Township, it rose to great popularity throughout the country and abroad, becoming a standard product in many orchards.

Alanson Gillett went on to become a carpenter and steamboat builder as well as a farmer, and lived to a ripe old age in Lawrence County, Ohio.

Quaker City

HOME OF
THE OHIO HILLS
FOLK FESTIVAL
SINCE 1904

QUAKER CITY (Guernsey County)

The Ohio Hills Folk Festival, considered one of the finest such events in Ohio, had as its origin a fair organized in 1871 at Quaker City. As with other fairs of the day, prizes were awarded in a number of categories, as these prizes were inducements to share with others some of the best farm methods and products in the area. The early fair at Quaker City offered prizes for the best grain cradle, best oxcart, best horseshoe, best team of oxen, best wine, best melodeon, best boots, and best cheese.

That early forerunner of the Folk Festival vanished after several years when the fairgrounds fell victim to an expanding community, but was resurrected in 1904 under the name "Fall Entertainment." Later known as "Homecoming," the three day event featured coon hunting, baseball, professional aerial acts, and a parade that offered as prizes a pair of pants for Best Comic; a box of candy for Best Patriotic; and $2 for the automobile from the most distant state.

The modern day Ohio Hills Folk Festival, winner of the 1969 "Festival of the Year" award, features barbecue chicken, soap making, steam engines, old farm implements, the 1821 Quaker Meeting House, and other exhibits that recapture the heritage of this Quaker community.

Ravenna

SETTLED 1799 BY
BENJAMIN TAPPAN.
An Early
Glassmaking
Center

RAVENNA (Portage County)

Ravenna was settled in 1799 by Benjamin Tappan, Jr., acting as agent for his father, who was the principal proprietor. The younger Tappan, traveling from New England in the company of David Hudson, who would found Hudson, Ohio, entered the Western Reserve when the Reserve was almost totally wilderness. Moses Cleaveland, the surveyor, had set foot in New Connecticut only three years earlier, and his Cleveland was still a town of one cabin.

A series of misfortunes beset Tappan when he was building a path from the Cuyahoga River to Ravenna. After having many of his possessions taken from his camp at what is now Boston, Ohio by Indians, he attempted to remove the rest of his goods to Ravenna with a yoke of oxen that had been driven from the Connecticut River. Unfortunately, one of the oxen overheated and died, leaving him without a team and without money. Tappan and the future settlement of Ravenna were saved when Col. Hillman at ''Youngstown'' sold him an ox on credit. Intent on spending the winter at his settlement, Tappan and a man named Bixby passed the cold nights in a tent before moving into a log-cabin on January 1, 1800. Bixby was awarded 100 acres of land for settling at Ravenna.

Benjamin Tappan went on to become U.S. Senator from Ohio, and his settlement at Ravenna, which he laid out in 1808, prospered with the arrival in 1840 of the Pennsylvania & Ohio Canal, a branch of the Ohio & Erie. Pioneer glass factories and carriage works were among the notable manufactures of the town, as was a tannery owned by Jesse Grant, father of the future president.

**HOME OF
RIO GRANDE
COLLEGE
Founded 1876**

RIO GRANDE (Gallia County)

Nehemiah Atwood served as an officer under Gen. William Henry Harrison during the War of 1812. While in the service, he passed through this area of southern Ohio and took a genuine liking to it. After marrying his wife Parmelia, the couple returned to the area and spent the rest of their lives here. The Atwoods opened a small tavern on the stage route between Gallipolis and Chillicothe, an extremely profitable venture that allowed them to amass a small fortune. It was this fortune that decades later brought about Rio Grande College.

The couple had no children, and had spent many years discussing how best their money might be put to the use of the community. Mr. Atwood died in 1869, before the plans had matured. As members of the Freewill Baptist Church, the Atwoods had decided to aid in the building of a college for the church, and Mrs. Atwood persevered after her husband's death in seeing that Rio Grande College became a reality. She provided nearly $80,000 to endow the school, which opened in 1876, and upon her death in 1885 the entire estate passed to the college.

Today, Rio Grande College is part of a unique marriage between public and private education. The original Rio Grande College and the newer Rio Grande Community College share a campus, staff, and facilities, and the nearly 2,000 students take course work in either of the schools. The schools have separate Boards of Trustees, but share a president who reports to both boards. The name of the institution is the Rio Grande College and Community College.

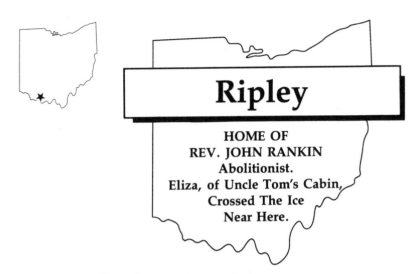

Ripley

HOME OF
REV. JOHN RANKIN
Abolitionist.
Eliza, of Uncle Tom's Cabin,
Crossed The Ice
Near Here.

RIPLEY (Brown County)

Fugitive slaves seeking to escape from the long, dark night of slavery could see a lantern light burning in a window in the house on top of the hill as they neared the Ohio River and freedom. Liberty Hill, they called it, and after crossing the river, only the steep climb up the long stone stairway to freedom separated the slave from sanctuary in the home of Rev. John Rankin.

Rev. Rankin was a Presbyterian minister and educator who dedicated himself to the antislavery movement, and in 1834 founded the Ohio Anti-Slavery Society. He and his wife, Jean, sheltered more than 2,000 fugitives in their home on the hill, which came to be called Station No. 1 on the Underground Railroad. Runaway slaves would pass through the home and onto the wagons of the Rankin sons and neighbors to continue their freedom trek north, endangered and threatened by slave catchers from the south intent on their capture and return.

One of the slaves who made it to the Rankin home with her child had made a desperate dash across the ice-choked Ohio River, risking her life for the liberty of her child and herself. Her story was told by Rev. Rankin to Harriet Beecher Stowe, and became the basis for the character of Eliza in *Uncle Tom's Cabin.* Eliza's story was read by millions, and Abraham Lincoln, upon meeting the celebrated author during the Civil War, said to her "so this is the little woman who made this big war."

The Rankin home is now a state historical site, and visitors may climb the reconstructed "stairway to liberty." Rev. and Mrs. Rankin are buried in the Ripley Cemetery beneath a monument that bears the inscription "Freedom's Heroes."

Rockford

**FOUNDED 1820
AS SHANESVILLE AT
HISTORIC ST. MARYS
RIVER CROSSING.
EARLY TRADING
POST**

ROCKFORD *(Mercer County)*

The community of Rockford is located on the south bank of the St. Mary's River near the site of the former Indian village of Old Town. Trails along the banks of the river here were heavily traveled, and a trading post was erected at this spot where the trail crossed the river to the north side. The army of Gen. Anthony Wayne crossed near here in 1795, and Gen. William Henry Harrison's troops camped here during the War of 1812. Anthony Shane, a French-Indian trader who lived here in a double-log cabin with his wife, had a trading post on the south side of the river, from which came the name Shane's Crossing.

The United States government granted a reservation to Shane, who had served as a scout for the army of Gen. Wayne, and he laid out his town here on June 23, 1820, the first town in Mercer County. It was recorded as Shanesville, the name it retained until 1866, when it was incorporated under its original name of Shane's Crossing. Shane himself, as a very old man, had left the area around 1832 to accompany the Shawnees to Kansas as a government agent.

The town was called Shane's Crossing until 1890, when it again underwent a name change. According to the Rockford Sesquicentennial Booklet, the townspeople wanted to adopt a historically significant name and chose Lacine, "but while the matter was pending the Post Office Department took it upon itself and designated it Rockford. No one knows where this idea was hatched."

Roseville

**FOUNDED 1813
AS NEW MILFORD.
William Lenhart
Founded A Pottery
Here In 1838**

ROSEVILLE *(Muskingum/Perry County)*

Settlement at Roseville dates back to 1814, when Ezekiel Rose built the first log cabin. Two years earlier, Mr. Rose had platted a village here and named it New Milford, but in 1830, when a new post office was established, the name was changed to Roseville by the postmaster. The town, straddling the Perry and Muskingum County lines, lay atop vast deposits of potter's clay, and it was these deposits that put Roseville on the nation's industrial map as one of the top producers of pottery and brick in the United States.

William Lenhart founded the pottery industry in Roseville when he made the first pottery from local clay in 1838. A number of small "blue bird" potteries sprung up in the area, these being small shed-type buildings found near many farmers' homes. In these small potteries necessary household items such as fruit jars, cream jars, bowls and baking dishes were made by hand on a potter's wheel. When large pottery plants joined these small producers, Roseville ascended to national prominence. In 1901, four brothers founded the Ransbottom Brothers Pottery Company, which became the leading pottery of Roseville and one of the nation's top producers, manufacturing 12,000 gallons of stoneware jars per day by 1906. Along with this general household ware, art and antique patterns graced the beautiful umbrella stands, cuspidors, and flower pots that issued from Roseville. With the success of the pottery industry came superb schools, wide streets, and beautiful residences to the prospering town.

Roseville today continues to be a pottery center, with a number of area shops, including the Robinson-Ransbottom Pottery, offering tours to the public. The communities of Roseville and Crooksville host an annual Pottery Festival in July, and the Ohio Historical Center operates the Ohio Ceramic Center between Roseville and Crooksville. At the museum a resident potter can be seen during the season manufacturing pottery pieces.

202

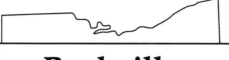

BIRTHPLACE OF
BENJAMIN R. HANBY
Composer Of
"Darling
Nelly Gray"

RUSHVILLE *(Fairfield County)*

(Please see Westerville.)

Russellville

**NEAR BIRTHPLACE OF
JAMES L. REID
Breeder Of
Yellow Dent Corn,
Popular 1900-1930**

RUSSELLVILLE (Brown County)

James L. Reid was born near Russellville on December 26, 1844, and when but two years old left Brown County with his family for Tazewell County, Illinois. It was in Illinois that the Ohio native developed his world-famous variety of corn known as Reid's Yellow Dent.

The Reids had taken with them from Ohio some of their own seed corn, a Brown County variety called "Gordon Hopkins Corn." This was a yellow corn, but had a reddish appearance that made it look highly mixed. The elder Mr. Reid prepared a seedbed very late in the spring of 1846, and planted the corn. The late planting resulted in the corn being harvested before it was completely matured, and the seed from this corn yielded a poor stand the following year. It was time to find new seed.

The farmers of the area were familiar with a "Little Yellow" that they believed to be derived from the original stock raised by the Indians. Cross-pollination resulting from these two varieties marked the beginning of the development of a new variety of corn that would sweep the world. James Reid spent his life perfecting his "Yellow Dent" through natural selection, and even furnished his neighbors with all of their seed corn to avoid undesirable cross-pollination with his own stock. After his corn won the gold medal at the Columbian Exposition in Chicago in 1893, agriculturists from around the world sought his corn. Reid's "Yellow Dent" became known throughout North America, Mexico, Central America, Russia, and Europe, and it is said that most of the hybrid corn of today is derived from Yellow Dent.

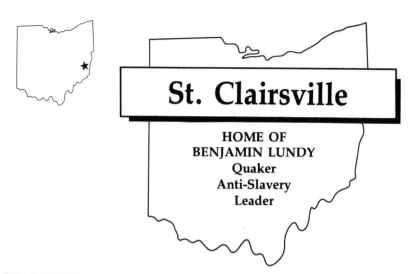

St. Clairsville

**HOME OF
BENJAMIN LUNDY
Quaker
Anti-Slavery
Leader**

ST. CLAIRSVILLE (Belmont County)

"I heard the wail of the captive; I felt his pang of distress, and the iron entered my soul," wrote the nineteen year old saddler apprentice after witnessing a gang of slaves being driven in chains through the streets of Wheeling. The impression recorded on the soul of Benjamin Lundy in that year of 1808 would forever change him, and set in motion the forces that would eventually topple the institution of slavery in the United States. Lundy left Wheeling, married and settled in St. Clairsville, where he founded the "Union Humane Society," the first western antislavery society. He wrote articles for Quaker Charles Osborne's *The Philanthropist*, one of the first antislavery newspapers, before establishing his own paper, *The Genius of Universal Emancipation.*

The diminutive Lundy walked thousands of miles spreading his message and planting the seeds that would grow into antislavery societies. He was attacked and nearly killed in Baltimore by a slave-dealer, and his property was burned by a pro-slavery mob in Philadelphia in 1838. Yet this quiet, demure man pressed on, publishing graphic accounts of the inhumanity suffered by the slaves. The small man with a big heart died in 1839, and of him it was written by William Lloyd Garrison, "Never was moral sublimity of character better illustrated. He has begun a work, the completion of which will be the salvation of his country."

St. Marys

**NEAR OHIO'S LARGEST
INTERIOR LAKE
Created As Reservoir
For Miami-Erie Canal,
1845**

ST. MARY'S *(Auglaize County)*

St. Mary's and Celina both proudly claim a relation to Grand Lake St. Mary's, the summit reservoir for the Miami & Erie Canal, a happenstance created by their strategic location on the Great Lakes - Ohio River watershed. Situated at the north end of Pioneer Portage, St. Mary's, known originally as Girty's town, has long been a key site, serving as an important supply fort during the Indian Wars of the 1790's.

Before the coming of the canal in the 1840's, boatloads of produce from the north would be offloaded onto wagons at St. Mary's and carted overland fourteen miles to Fort Loramie, where they would again be loaded onto boats to continue their voyage by water to the Ohio River. In 1845, Grand Lake St. Mary's, the largest man-made lake in the world, was completed. It fed the Miami and Erie Canal, and in turn, the canal fed the economy of St. Mary's. The town became a center for the shipment of grains, pork, and timber, and the canal supplied water power for the operation of mills. Although the canal died at the turn of the century, the lake became a popular fishing and tourist spot and continued to provide life for St. Mary's.

Today, Grand Lake St. Mary's State Park remains a popular recreational spot.

(For more information about Grand Lake St. Mary's, please see Celina.)

St. Paris

"PONY WAGON TOWN"
Once A Center
Of Manufacture
Of These Colorful
Carts

ST. PARIS (Champaign County)

Will Walborn and Freeman Riker, partners in the St. Paris carriage business that bore their names, had a problem. The 1887 Champaign County Fair was approaching, and the pair knew from experience that the fair was one of their most important opportunities to display their horse drawn carriages. Although the Walborn & Riker Co. had a reputation for fine workmanship since its inception six years earlier, they were still just one of a number of manufacturers that crowded the fairs, and in spite of their gaily painted carts and buggies, it was difficult to get noticed among the competition.

Walborn and Riker struck upon the idea of setting out a half-size model of their buggy, built to scale, in front of their space, with the big buggies grouped around it, as a lure to their display. Word spread around the fair that there was a "cute" exhibit down at the end of the line, and soon the display piece had performed its task - all the buggies were once again sold. But when a doctor from Urbana proposed to buy the little display buggy for his daughter, as it fit her pony perfectly, a new industry was born.

Ponies are not little horses, and the few "pony" wagons up to that time were merely horse carriages on smaller wheels, ungainly and unattractive. Walborn and Riker set about building carts and wagons of new dimensions to be in harmony and balance with the Shetland ponies that were just becoming popular in this country. When the partners displayed their new line of genuine pony carts at the 1893 World's Fair in Chicago, they walked off with blue ribbons and a world-wide reputation as the builders of the finest pony carts in the world. The catalogs of the Walborn & Riker Co. would soon show over 70 models of the colorful little carts, and orders came in to the little village of St. Paris from all over the world. The company prospered until 1909, when, facing stiff competition from the new automobile industry, the firm went out of business.

Today, St. Paris, proud of its colorful past, hosts the annual Pony Wagon Festival each September.

Salem

FOUNDED 1806
First Woman's Rights
Convention
Held In
1850

SALEM (Columbiana County)

Salem was founded as a Quaker settlement in 1806 by Zadock Street, John Strong, and Samuel Davis, all members of the Society of Friends. With its Quaker background, Salem's residents were keen to the ideals of human freedom, and a long list of notables passed through the village speaking out for personal liberty and equality. Horace Mann, Frederick Douglass, Sojourner Truth, James A. Garfield, Joshua Giddings, Susan B. Anthony, and Ralph Waldo Emerson were but a few of the great men and women who traveled to Salem to address the important issues of the day.

While antislavery issues and groups dominated the speaker's platforms in the mid-1800's, another issue was just emerging: women's rights. On April 19, 1850, the Second Baptist Church in Salem was the site where dedicated Ohio feminists came together for their first meeting. *The American Women's Gazetteer* reported that this was a unique convention, for "it was officered entirely by women; women officiated at all levels and no men were allowed to sit on the platform, to speak or vote... Never did men so suffer. They implored just to say a word; but no, the President, Betsy Cowles, was inflexible - no man should be heard. If one meekly arose to make a suggestion, he was at once ruled out of order. For the first time in the world's history, men learned how it felt to sit in silence when questions in which they were interested were under discussion."

The Second Baptist Church that hosted that first women's rights conference is no longer standing, its place having been taken by a supermarket.

Sandusky

WILLIAM HENRY HARRISON DEDICATED FIRST OHIO RAILROAD IN 1835

SANDUSKY (Erie County)

In 1822, the state of Ohio hired an engineer to survey possible routes for a canal that was to open the markets of the world to Ohio farmers and businessmen. It was widely assumed that the route would pass through the center of the state, in a north-south direction, and that Sandusky would likely be the terminus on Lake Erie. To the dismay of Sanduskians, it was determined that there was inadequate water supply on the divide separating the Scioto and Sandusky Rivers, and Sandusky was left out of the coming canal boom.

A decade later, local businessmen, still smarting from the canal debacle, urged the state to build a railroad to serve the city. In 1832, the General Assembly granted a special charter to construct the Mad River and Lake Erie Railroad from Sandusky to Dayton, a route that, ironically, would compete with the Miami & Erie Canal. The "line of iron rails" was commenced on September 7, 1835. When the first locomotive, *The Sandusky,* arrived, there were as yet no rails down, so the tracks were laid to fit the engine. The legislature then passed a law making that gauge standard for the state.

By 1840, the line stretched southward from Sandusky for 30 miles. In 1846, the line from Sandusky to Bellevue was joined with the Little Miami Railroad to Cincinnati, completing the first through line in Ohio. By the time of the Civil War, Ohio led the nation in miles of railroad track. The shrill whistle of the locomotive in Ohio sounded the death knell for the canals, which began a long decline to virtual extinction by the end of the century.

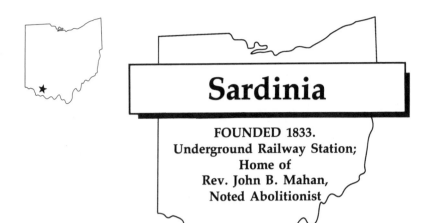

Sardinia

FOUNDED 1833.
Underground Railway Station;
Home of
Rev. John B. Mahan,
Noted Abolitionist

SARDINIA (Brown County)

Sardinia was one of several key stops on the Underground Railroad in Brown County, sheltering fugitives who had already passed through Ripley and Russellville on their way to Quaker settlements in Clinton County. With Brown County located just across the Ohio River from slave-state Kentucky, considerable animosity existed between the people along both sides of the river. The bitterness of pro-slavery Kentuckians toward the abolitionists of Brown County was manifested in the offering of rewards of up to $2,500 for the kidnapping or assassination of abolitionist Rev. John B. Mahan of Sardinia.

Such a contract abduction was never realized, but a legal one that stirred the ire of Buckeyes was carried out in the year 1838. Rev. Mahan, who operated a temperance tavern, was charged in absentia in Mason County, Kentucky with "aiding and assisting certain slaves, the property of William Greathouse, to make their escape out of and beyond the state of Kentucky." Ohio Governor Vance issued a warrant for the arrest of Mahan, and had him delivered to the sheriff of Mason County. Mahan was held ten weeks awaiting trial, but was acquitted by a jury that followed the judge's instructions that the court had no jurisdiction over a citizen of Ohio who had not been in Kentucky until brought there by the legal process. The case became a cause celebre for abolitionist forces, and Governor Vance drew the censure of many Ohioans for his conduct. Rev. Mahan wrote after the trial, "It ought not be concealed that a very great majority of Northern people are not capable of violating their natures by driving away from their doors the unsheltered, unprotected stranger, or send away unfed, unclothed, unprovided for the outcasts or wandering poor."

Seville

HOME AND RESTING PLACE OF CAPTAIN M. V. BATES' FAMILY
Famed Ohio Giants

SEVILLE *(Medina County)*

Martin Van Buren Bates was born in Kentucky on November 9, 1845, and joined the Fifth Kentucky Infantry of the Confederate Army upon the outbreak of the Civil War. He went on to earn several promotions, ultimately earning a captaincy. While increasing in rank, Captain Bates continued to increase in size, eventually achieving a height of seven feet eight inches and weight of 470 pounds. As with most larger than life figures, myth and fact have become blurred, but one story indicates that the Union Army arrested him at his home in Kentucky and transported him back to camp where word of "The Kentucky Giant" soon spread. Enterprising soldiers confined him to a tent and charged admission to see him, thereby beginning Capt. Bates' show business career.

While Capt. Bates was under the management of promoter Judge Ingalls, P. T. Barnum had convinced a teenaged girl from Nova Scotia named Anna Swan to join the Barnum show. Anna, called the "tallest girl in the world," stood seven feet eleven and weighed 413 pounds. Noted for her intelligence as well as her size, Barnum had promised her family that he would provide her with a tutor, music instruction, and fine clothes if she would be permitted to work for him. While a guest at the home of Gen. Winfield Scott, Anna was introduced to Capt. Bates, and the following year the couple was married. Capt. and Mrs. Bates did not participate in Barnum's tent shows, but rather mingled with guests at receptions, including those of Queen Victoria.

The couple eventually settled in Seville, Ohio, where they built a house with fourteen foot ceilings and similarly large furniture. Mrs. Bates gave birth to a twenty-three pound baby, called "the largest baby ever born," but it did not survive. Mrs. Bates died in 1889, and her husband passed away in 1901. The family is buried in Seville's Mound Hill Cemetery beneath an impressive statue of a young woman that Capt. Bates had erected upon Anna's death.

211

Shaker Heights

HOME OF NORTH UNION
SHAKERS, 1822-1889.
Erected In Memory Of
William J. Vanaken,
Mayor, 1916-1950

SHAKER HEIGHTS *(Cuyahoga County)*

Shaker Heights takes its name from the Shakers (The United Society of Believers in Christ's Second Appearing) who established the community of North Union here in 1822. The Shakers, so called because of their peculiar shuffling dance, originated in England in the mid-1700's as a spin-off of the Quakers. Ann Lee, the illiterate daughter of a blacksmith, believed that she was the second manifestation of the coming of Christ, and in 1774 she led eight followers to America, where they founded the first Shaker colony in New York. The first colony prospered, and soon several of its members headed to Ohio to establish new colonies.

Upon entering the society, members were required to turn over all property and make confession to two members of their own sex. The Shakers practiced celibacy, and lived in family groups where men and women were equal, but lived on separate floors. Each man was assigned a "sister" to look out for his household needs, but men and women were never permitted to meet alone. Household ornamentation was forbidden, giving rise to the simplistic yet beautiful furniture that is prized to this day. Outstanding farmers and carpenters, the Shakers are also credited with inventing the clothespin, flat-sided broom, and circular saw.

The Shakers took in orphans to keep the Society prospering, but after the Civil War, orphanages were organized into religious denominations, depriving the Society of a key source of membership. By the end of the century, with the old members dying off and the number of converts dropping drastically, these productive people had largely disappeared from Ohio.

Shawnee

1870-1880
CAPITAL OF THE
KNIGHTS OF LABOR
UNION MOVEMENT

SHAWNEE (Perry County)

The Knights of Labor was organized as a secret society of garment cutters in 1869 in a Philadelphia tailor shop. Within four years it had grown to 80 assemblies, as men in the national unions sought refuge from attacks by anti-union employers. In Shawnee, the history of the town was just beginning with the arrival of the great coal and iron companies in 1871, and these forces would combine to make Shawnee the capital of the Knights of Labor movement.

The area around Shawnee, located amid the great coal fields of the Hocking Valley, saw an influx of miners and businessmen, and on March 6, 1876 the town of Shawnee was platted. The population was primarily Welsh, Irish, German, Scotch and English, and was not without a rougher element found in many mining towns of the time. Big strikes in the 1870's were marred by violence, but the town continued to grow, as did the Knights of Labor. The Knights gave up their secrecy, and opened their doors to blacks and whites, skilled and unskilled - in fact, they welcomed everyone "except whiskey sellers, gamblers, lawyers and bankers."

The Knights' dream of uniting all workers into one big union faded when unrest cropped up within the union and independent trade unions were alienated. In December, 1886, the dissidents held an assembly in Columbus, forming the American Federation of Labor (AFL) under cigar-maker Samuel Gompers. The AFL model proved to be more attractive than the Knights, and soon the Knights of Labor was extinct.

Shawnee reached a peak population of about 4,000, but it too has seen a drastic decline. Today, the occasional photographer or painter wanders the nearly empty sidewalks of Shawnee, admiring the old buildings that have placed much of downtown Shawnee on the National Register of Historic Places.

Shelby

BIRTHPLACE 1890
OF THE
SEAMLESS TUBE
INDUSTRY
IN AMERICA

SHELBY *(Richland County)*

"You'll look sweet upon the seat, of a bicycle built for two" went the popular song about Daisy, and for Daisy and millions of others, the bicycle upon which they rode was probably made of seamless tube steel made in Shelby, Ohio. The bicycling fad was sweeping the country in the closing decades of the nineteenth century, with young and old alike pedaling their way along the streets of America. It was a good time for bicycle manufacturers, too, but American manufacturers, including Henry Lozier and Joseph Yost of Toledo, were confronted with a serious problem. There was no supply of domestic steel tubing for the frames, forcing them to import expensive steel tubing from England. The enterprising Lozier and Yost paid a visit to a seamless steel mill in Birmingham, England, and observed the manufacturing process. When they returned to Toledo, they conceived a plan to make their own tubing.

One of Lozier and Yost's employees was Jonas Feighner, and when he learned of the plan, he pressed to have the plant built in his hometown of Shelby. Lozier and Yost were not so inclined, but after the determined Feighner raised sufficient funds, the pair changed their minds. In 1891, ground was broken for The Shelby Steel Tube Co., known simply as "the Tuby."

Business boomed as orders from other American bicycle makers poured in. New uses were being discovered, and soon two of these bicycle makers were using the tubing in a new kind of craft that could fly - the airplane, built by Orville and Wilbur Wright. In 1900, the Tuby was the world's leading manufacturer of steel tubing, but disaster struck in 1908 when the mill burned to the ground. U.S. Steel Co., then Tuby's parent company, refused to rebuild, but the community rallied to buy the site, and soon they were back in business as The Ohio Seamless Tube Co.

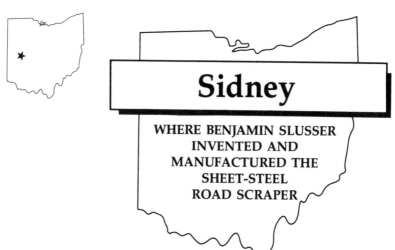

Sidney

**WHERE BENJAMIN SLUSSER
INVENTED AND
MANUFACTURED THE
SHEET-STEEL
ROAD SCRAPER**

SIDNEY *(Shelby County)*

Sidney was laid out in 1819 on the farm of Charles Starrett and named for Sir Philip Sidney, the sixteenth century British poet dubbed "the great light of chivalry." Mr. Starrett was alarmed at the news that circuit judges were about to hold court in a cabin at the new town of Hardin, thereby giving that town the inside track for being named county seat. Starrett offered the commissioners fifty acres of land, free of charge, if they would move the seat to his land. His chivalrous act was accepted, and Sidney became the county seat in 1820. The post office was moved from Hardin to Sidney, and construction of the first frame court-house and log jail was completed in that same year.

Sidney began attracting new settlers, including the Slusser family, who located themselves on a farm a few miles north of Sidney. On June 28, 1828, Benjamin Slusser was born on his parents' farm, and worked there until he was sixteen years old. He attended a simple country school, his interest in mechanics augmented by the experience of solving the unending stream of problems encountered on a farm. He received advanced training in Philadelphia in applied mechanics, and returned to Sidney at the age of twenty-one to begin his career as an inventor and manufacturer.

The self-loading excavator was Slusser's first practical invention and found immediate popularity in road-improvement operations, including those of Brigham Young and the Mormons in Utah. Slusser followed this invention with his steel road scraper, which he manufactured in Sidney in 1876. The Slusser & McLean Scraper Company, with its large blacksmith shop, emery wheelhouse, and fuel and storage sheds, was the largest scraper works in the United States in the 1880's. By the time of Benjamin Slusser's death in 1899, three Sidney companies were manufacturing the steel road scraper, an invention that put Sidney on the world's industrial map.

Somerset

**HOME OF
PHIL SHERIDAN
Civil War
General**

SOMERSET *(Perry County)*

"Up from the South at break of day, Bringing to Winchester fresh dismay" began the popular poem about the Union's greatest cavalry leader, Phil Sheridan. The diminutive leader was dubbed "Little Phil" by his admiring troops, who were impressed and inspired by his courage. Sheridan preferred to lead the cavalry charges from the front rather than push his men from the rear, and it was said of Sheridan that "he saw the backs of more rebels than any other federal General."

Phil Sheridan was born to Irish laboring parents in New York on March 6, 1831, and the family came to Somerset when Phil was yet an infant. His father labored on the National Road, and Phil later clerked in various stores in Somerset. When but a nine year-old boy, he must have been awed when Gen. William Henry Harrison gave a campaign speech beneath a tree in Phil's yard.

Sheridan went on to West Point, where he did not shine as a student, but nevertheless graduated. He rose through the ranks to eventually attain the rank of general. In 1865, he made a daring dash through the Shenandoah Valley, hot on the heels of the retreating forces of Robert E. Lee. Seeing the true condition of the Confederate forces, he sent a dispatch to Grant that read, "Hurry up the troops; Lee must surrender if closely pressed, I am sure of it." Grant hurried up the troops, and the war was over.

Phil Sheridan died August 5, 1888 in Nonquitt, Massachusetts, and is buried in Arlington National Cemetery.

Drawn by Henry Howe in 1886.

PORTRAIT AND BOYHOOD HOME OF GENERAL SHERIDAN.

South Point

MOST SOUTHERLY POINT OF OHIO OVERLOOKING THREE STATES, TWO RIVERS

SOUTH POINT *(Lawrence County)*

On November 6, 1985, a report was presented to the commissioners of Lawrence County in an effort to have an official county seal adopted. The proposed seal displayed within a circle an illustration of an iron furnace (see Ironton), a Rome Beauty apple (see Proctorville), and a steamboat. The steamboat illustration depicted South Point's contribution to shipping on the Mississippi and Ohio Rivers, and while South Point itself was not a major steamboat center, the town's native sons played a major role in the river trade of the American interior. According to the report, "between 1860-1880 men born in Lawrence County, Ohio controlled approximately 75% of the packet boat trade on the Ohio and Mississippi Rivers. Mr. W. F. Davidson, from South Point, Ohio, was the largest single owner of boats in his day, owning more than 40. Records show that Lawrence County, Ohio men at one time controlled more steamboat property than any other County on inland rivers; and some of the best pilots, masters, and engineers came from Lawrence County, Ohio..." The proposal was accepted, and the commissioners approved the attractive Lawrence County seal.

South Point is proud not only of the river boat men born in the community, but also takes pride in its special geography. South Point derives its name from its location as the most southerly point in Ohio, and its view of Kentucky, West Virginia, and Ohio at the confluence of the Big Sandy and Ohio Rivers has made it the subject of numerous scenic post cards.

Spencerville

**FOUNDED 1844
AT THIS SITE
BECAUSE OF ABUNDANT
WATER POWER
FROM THE CANAL**

SPENCERVILLE *(Allen County)*

Spencerville had its beginnings in 1844 as the village of Acadia, laid out by three Dayton men named Tyler, McConnell, and Conover. The town was located along the course of the Miami & Erie Canal, and when the canal opened in 1844, the three Dayton men built their first mill at the lower lock to harness the water power there. The name of the village was changed to Spencerville in honor of Col. William Spencer of Newark, a member of the State Board of Public Works in 1848 and enthusiastic supporter of canal projects.

One of the most spectacular engineering features of the entire canal is located just south of Spencerville, and was designed to solve the problem of getting the canal to cross the divide that separates the St. Mary's watershed from that of the Auglaize River. Lock building was a costly enterprise, and with the Spencerville area located on the highest plateau along the canal's course, water supply for the locks would be difficult to come by. It was decided to literally cut through the hard blue clay that separated the watersheds, so a force of 500 laborers spent four years digging a ditch 6,600 feet long and up to fifty feet deep. When it was completed, it came to be known simply as Deep Cut.

Deep Cut became a gathering spot for the rugged and brawling canal workers and builders, where it was said that there were frequent fights and whiskey flowed like water. A monument a few miles south of Deep Cut memorializes "Bloody Bridge," where Bill Jones killed Jack Billings over the love of Minnie Warren back in the 1850's. Deep Cut has earned a place on the National Register of Historic Places, and today serves as a memorial to the perseverance and industriousness of the early builders of Ohio.

Springfield

**4-H CLUBS OF AMERICA
FOUNDED HERE
IN 1902
BY
A. B. GRAHAM**

SPRINGFIELD *(Clark County)*

Please see Lena, Ohio.

Steubenville

**HOME OF
EDWIN M. STANTON
Lincoln's Secretary of War.
Fort Steuben Established
1787**

STEUBENVILLE *(Jefferson County)*

The city of Steubenville has its origin as the old Fort Steuben, built in 1787 and named for Baron Frederick William von Steuben, a Prussian drillmaster who aided the colonies in the Revolutionary War. The fort was erected to protect a party of surveyors from Indian depredations after an earlier surveying party was forced to return to New York. The garrison at the fort was withdrawn in 1787, and after a fire partially destroyed the fort, it was completely dismantled in 1794. Four stone posts were later erected to mark the site of Fort Steuben. A small community named LaBelle sprang up around the fort, and continued to exist after the fort was gone. Eventually, the town became Steubenville.

On December 19, 1814, Edwin McMasters Stanton was born in Steubenville, and he would later rise to the position of secretary of war under Abraham Lincoln. Stanton attended Kenyon College, and was appointed U.S. attorney general in the closing days of the Buchanan administration. He was a foe of incoming President Lincoln, yet Lincoln asked the abrasive Stanton to take the war department post. Stanton's tenure in the post was marked by distinction, and of him it was said, "He was like the Giant of the Great War, who more than any other trampled out the rebellion."

Stanton stayed on after Lincoln's assassination, but in 1867, President Johnson suspended him from office. Contending Johnson's action was illegal, Stanton refused to go, precipitating a national crisis which led to impeachment charges against the president. The Senate failed by one vote to convict President Johnson, and Stanton was forced to resign. President Grant was later to appoint Stanton to the Supreme Court, but Stanton died four days after his Senate confirmation.

Strongsville

BIRTHPLACE OF
DAYTON C. MILLER
WHO TOOK FIRST
SURGICAL X-RAY
1896

STRONGSVILLE *(Cuyahoga County)*

Dayton C. Miller was born in Strongsville on March 13, 1866. His father, Charles, was the organizer and president of the first suburban electric car line out of Cleveland. Dayton graduated from Baldwin University (now Baldwin-Wallace College) in 1889, and went on to obtain a doctorate in science from Princeton the following year. He served on the faculties of Baldwin University and Case School of Applied Science (now Case Western Reserve), and was a member of the National Research Council in Washington from 1927-30.

Dr. Miller's studies in physics included not only surgical X-rays, but also the velocity of light in a magnetic field, expansion of gases, the relative motion of earth and space, and the efficiency of incandescent gas light. He was also an accomplished flute player, and his studies relating to musical sounds occupied more than a score of his years. He designed an instrument called the phonodeik to photographically record the sound waves of musical instruments, and using this information he was able to design the acoustics for a number of public auditoriums in the United States.

Dr. Miller was noted for his magnificent flute collection, which was reputed to be the world's largest. Among his more than 1,000 flutes were nasal flutes, Chinese flutes of jade and ivory, walking stick flutes, a flute made from a human shin bone, and a flute he had constructed of 22 karat gold. This golden flute was said to have a "peculiarly rich tone."

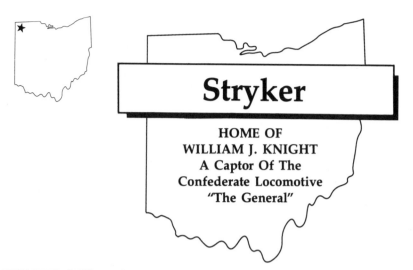

Stryker

**HOME OF
WILLIAM J. KNIGHT
A Captor Of The
Confederate Locomotive
"The General"**

STRYKER *(Williams County)*

Stryker is one of three Ohio communities that honors on its historical marker a participant in the famous Andrews Raid during the Civil War. Stryker proudly claims William J. Knight, who now rests in Oakwood Cemetery. On his tombstone is found the inscription "Engineer of Andrews Raid in Georgia, Apr. 12, 1862."

For details of the Andrews Raid, please see McComb.

Thompson

BIRTHPLACE OF
CHARLES M. HALL
Developer Of
Modern
Aluminum

THOMPSON *(Geauga County)*

For much of the nineteenth century, American scientists had been trying to discover a cheap way to manufacture aluminum. There was practically no pure metal manufactured in this country, and the aluminum imported to the United States cost about $5.00 per pound. While the laboratory scientists were intent on solving this scientific and economic problem, a high school student named Charles Martin Hall was busy working on the problem in an old woodshed.

Charles M. Hall was born in Thompson on December 6, 1863, and raised in Oberlin. The boy wizard went on to his hometown school of Oberlin College, where he continued his earlier experiments of attempting to develop pure aluminum in the improved facilities that Oberlin had to offer. He graduated in 1885, and within eight months the twenty-two year old Hall had succeeded in using electrolysis to extract the metal from its compounds, a process that would allow the metal to fulfill its long-known potential.

Hall's next task was to extract capital from cautious investors, a task made even more difficult by his young age. To complicate matters, a scientist in France was claiming to have invented the same process. In 1889, the U.S. patent office decided in Hall's favor and granted him the patent. Andrew Mellon decided that Hall was worth investing in, and provided capital for a company that was ultimately to become the American Aluminum Company. Shortly, the commercial production of aluminum began, with the company placing the metal on the market at the astoundingly low price of fifty cents per pound, about a tenth of the imported price.

Hall was to become a millionaire from his process, and a benefactor of his alma mater. He died in 1914, leaving much of his estate to Oberlin College and other educational institutions.

Tiffin

SITE OF
FORT BALL
War Of 1812
Post

TIFFIN (Seneca County)

Fort Ball was constructed on the west bank of the Sandusky River during the War of 1812 by Col. James V. Ball. A large spring of excellent cold water found flowing here induced the colonel to select this site for his fort. The fort, covering only about a third of an acre, was built as a temporary stockade to be used in case of emergency and as a supply for ammunition. The palisades consisted of one-foot thick stakes, pierced horizontally near their tops by old bayonets. Outside the walls the fort was surrounded by a ditch, and inside the fort 500 men could be quartered. The fort saw little activity, however, and was not involved in direct hostilities.

In the fall of 1817, Mr. Erastus Bowe, a soldier during the War of 1812, returned to build a log house on the site of the old fort, at the time still marked by a few remaining stakes, and opened the Pan Yan Tavern. Two years later the town of Oakley, including the land that the tavern stood on, was platted. The town went by that name until 1824, when Jesse Spencer laid out the town of Fort Ball, encompassing Oakley. While all this activity was taking place on the west side of the river, Josiah Hedges was laying out the town of Tiffin on the opposite bank, setting the stage for more conflict than the old fort had witnessed during the war. Fort Ball and Tiffin became intense rivals for county seat, and when Tiffin, a village of six cabins, was selected in 1822, Spencer urged Fort Ballites to boycott Hedge's mill on the Tiffin side of the river. When Hedges threatened to shut down the mill in retaliation, thereby forcing the residents to travel as far as Monroeville for milling, the boycott was broken. The victorious Hedges went on to buy Fort Ball, bringing peace to the border, and in 1850 the two towns merged as Tiffin.

The site of Fort Ball is now marked by a statue of an Indian maiden upon which is found the inscription, "This Indian maid keeps ceaseless watch where red men and sturdy pioneers drank from a spring whose sparkling waters flowed within the stockade of old Fort Ball."

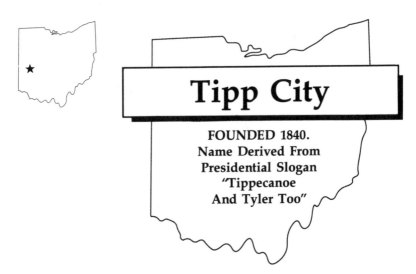

Tipp City

**FOUNDED 1840.
Name Derived From
Presidential Slogan
"Tippecanoe
And Tyler Too"**

TIPP CITY (Miami County)

It was well before dawn on November 7, 1811, and thirty-eight year old Gen. William Henry Harrison was dressing. He and his men had a practice of arising well before sunrise in the event of an Indian attack before first light. Tecumseh and his brother, the Prophet, had been organizing the Indian tribes in one last gallant effort to push the whites back to the eastern sea, and in the predawn hours of this November morning, near Tippecanoe, Indiana, the first attack came. The Indians fought with an uncharacteristic abandon: the Prophet had told them that the bullets fired from the guns of the soldiers would bounce off of them, and that the soldiers would be fighting as if in darkness, while the Indians would see as at noonday. Dawn showed the errors of the Prophet's predictions, alarming the Indians into a retreat. Although one-hundred fifty soldiers lay dead on the battlefield, and only thirty-eight Indians had been killed, the Battle of Tippecanoe was a victory for the army.

Twenty-nine years later, William Henry Harrison was his party's candidate for president of the United States. In the remarkable campaign of 1840, Harrison, known as "Old Tippecanoe," had as his running mate John Tyler, and the campaign slogan of "Tippecanoe and Tyler, too!" rang throughout the country. A.C. Ross of Zanesville wrote a popular campaign song of the same name, which he sang to a tumultuous reception at a political meeting in New York City. After his rendition, Ross took his seat "amid thundering applause and three times three for the Buckeye State." Soon, in the saloons, streets, and elsewhere, people were singing "Tippecanoe and Tyler, too," a tune that helped carry William Henry Harrison to the White House.

Toledo

GLASS CENTER
OF
THE WORLD

TOLEDO *(Lucas County)*

The discovery of natural gas in northwest Ohio in the 1880's brought with it an explosion in industrial growth in the Maumee Valley, and Toledo rode the crest to become the "Glass Center of the World" by century's end. Toledo's advantageous position on Lake Erie, its high silica-content sandstone, and abundant fuel supply were touted by the Toledo Business Men's Committee to lure several glass makers from the east, chief among them Edward Libbey, who on February 6, 1888 agreed to move his New England Glass Company with 100 craftsmen to the area. On August 17, 1888, the workers' train was met at the station by a crowd of citizens and the band of the Grand Army of the Republic, and the workers were escorted to the new factory amid much pomp and celebration.

The Libbey plant struggled in its first years, but prosperity arrived with the firm's entry into the light bulb field. Playing no small part in this success was a genius from Wheeling named Michael Owens. Owens invented the semi-automatic bulb making machine, and followed this with other machines that introduced mass production to glass making. Libbey and Owens were later joined in Toledo by Edward Ford, who had earlier organized the Pittsburgh Plate Glass Company. Ford built an entirely mechanized factory across the Maumee River, and established the model industrial town of Rossford to house his work force. Under the guidance of these three men, the Toledo glass industry thrived, and in 1930 the three men merged their operations into the Libbey-Owens-Ford Glass Company, one of the largest glass producers in the world. The company continued to grow when Prohibition ended, filling the demand for more bottles.

In 1951, the Libbey-Owens-Ford plant received the Declaration of Independence to be sealed in "Thermopane" glass, but England won out in 1986 when a British firm purchased the company's glass operations for $353 million.

Troy

HOME OF
OVERFIELD LOG TAVERN
Meeting Place Of
County Court
In 1808

TROY (Miami County)

The town of Troy was laid out in 1807, and the following year Benjamin Overfield built a two-story double-log house, the first house in Troy. Overfield, a man without pomposity yet determined to rise with the town, took out a license as a tavern keeper, and hung out the shingle of the "Overfield Tavern." He had competition from the start, as a Mr. Trader had also opened similar quarters.

Overfield showed himself to be a shrewd competitor. From the Commissioners records of December 16, 1808, we learn that "it was ordered that the court to be held in Miami County shall be held in the house of Benjamin Overfield in Troy until a courthouse is built; he has agreed to furnish a room for the court to sit in, gratis, during the time aforesaid." Everyone who had to journey to the court became well acquainted with the amenities offered alongside justice at Overfield's place.

The practice of dispensing justice and grog under the same roof was not without its problems, but Judge Dunlavy was determined to maintain order. When George Kerr, a wealthy Miami County farmer, and ex-Governor Arthur St. Clair, who sometimes practiced in both the courtroom and barroom, became overly intense in the latter, the Judge summoned them to come into the court room to answer to him. He fined Kerr $10, to which Kerr retorted, "Judge Dunlavy, I knew you when you were so poor you had to lie in bed while your wife washed your breeches."

The Court was moved to a new log courthouse in 1811, and in 1828 a new jail was constructed that did not allow the inmates the easy comings and goings of the original. In 1831, Benjamin Overfield passed away. "The citizens of this place have lost a worthy citizen. He made little display - tended to his own business, and to none else; and thus secured the good will of all and the enmity of none," read his obituary in the Troy paper.

The Overfield Tavern still stands in Troy, one of only two surviving log buildings in Ohio that served as original temporary courthouses.

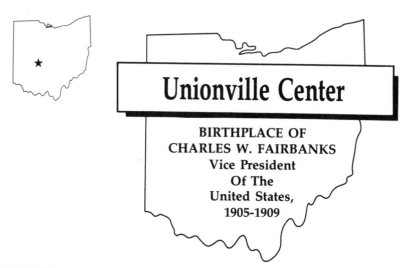

Unionville Center

BIRTHPLACE OF
CHARLES W. FAIRBANKS
Vice President
Of The
United States,
1905-1909

UNIONVILLE CENTER (Union County)

Charles Warren Fairbanks was born at Unionville Center on May 11, 1852, the son of a farmer and wagonmaker. After attending local schools, he went to Delaware, Ohio to study at Ohio Wesleyan University, from which he graduated in 1872. He was admitted to the Ohio bar in 1874, having completed his preparations at the Cleveland Law School. He soon moved to Indianapolis, where he established the law office that he would maintain for twenty-three years.

Charles Fairbanks entered Republican politics on a national level when he managed the unsuccessful presidential campaign of Walter Q. Gresham in 1888. He served as the chairman of the Indiana delegation at that and nearly all other Republican conventions in his lifetime, and at the 1896 convention, which saw William McKinley win the nomination, he rose to national prominence with a fiery keynote address. The following year, he became a member of the U.S. Senate, and was reelected in 1903.

Theodore Roosevelt chose Fairbanks as his running mate in the 1904 election, and Fairbanks took the oath of office of the vice-presidency on March 4, 1905. Fairbanks himself received forty first ballot votes for the Republican nomination for president in 1908, and twice that number in 1916. When Theodore Roosevelt came out of retirement in 1912 to again seek the presidency, Fairbanks supported William Howard Taft, who lost to Woodrow Wilson in the three way race. In 1916, Fairbanks was again on the Republican ticket as the vice-presidential candidate, this time in the unsuccessful bid of Charles Evans Hughes.

Charles Fairbanks died in Indianapolis on June 4, 1918.

Upper Sandusky

SITE OF LAST
WYANDOT INDIAN
RESERVATION
IN
OHIO

UPPER SANDUSKY (Wyandot County)

Tarhe the Crane, chief of the Wyandots, was facing pressure from Tecumseh to join in the great uprising of 1811, the last hope of the Indians to push the white settlers back to the eastern sea. Tarhe was no stranger to battle with the Americans, but after agreeing to the terms of peace at Greenville (see Greenville), he "still held high the wide white wampum of peace" and resisted Tecumseh's pleas. Two years later, Gen. William Henry Harrison appealed for help from the neutral tribes to fight the British and Tecumseh, and Tarhe responded, "We have been waiting many moons for an invitation to fight for the Americans. I speak on behalf of all the tribes present when I profess our friendship. We have agreed, without any dissension, to join you." The Wyandots fought bravely, and earned the respect of Gen. Harrison, who wrote, "With all other tribes but the Wyandots, flight in battle brought no disgrace. With them, it was otherwise."

After the war, the Wyandots were granted a reservation of twelve square miles centering around Upper Sandusky. In return for their loyalty to the Americans during the war, they were also presented with a mill along the banks of the Sandusky River. Here the Wyandots would remain until 1842, when by treaty they were forced to move west. Charles Dickens was making his celebrated trip through America in 1842, and passed through Upper Sandusky. "It is a settlement of Wyandot Indians who inhabit this place," he wrote in American Notes. "The Indians had just concluded a treaty by which they bound themselves to remove next year to land west of the Mississippi. (Col. Johnston) gave me a moving account of their strong attachment to the familiar scenes of their infancy, and in particular to the burial places of their kindred, and of their great reluctance to leave them." But leave they did, the last Indian tribe to leave Ohio. Especially wrenching was leaving behind the grave of Tarhe. Today, just north of town, is a simple marker that reads, "Distinguished Wyandot Chief and Loyal American, Tarhe, died here in Cranetown in 1818."

229

Urbana

HOME OF
BRAND WHITLOCK
Author, Statesman,
First Ambassador
To Belgium

URBANA *(Champaign County)*

The late 1800's were a time of monopolies, corruption and bossism in both Ohio and the nation, and the dawning of the twentieth century brought with it the hope of political reform. The Progressive Movement sought to restore economic competition, widen participation in government, and eliminate favoritism for monopolies. In Ohio, the Progressives had the greatest impact in municipal government, and Toledo, with Sam "Golden Rule" Jones and Brand Whitlock, his successor, paved the way for reform in Ohio.

Whitlock (1869-1934), an Urbana native, served as Toledo's mayor from 1904 to 1913, and was elected four times. The independent-minded Whitlock helped secure passage of a state law requiring the election of judges on a nonpartisan ballot and oversaw the development of municipally-owned utilities. He went on to become ambassador to Belgium during World War I, but in spite of all his political accomplishments, he saw himself first and foremost as a writer.

Whitlock started his career as a political writer on the *Chicago Herald,* and later wrote popular novels about political and social injustice, including *The 13th District* (1902) and *The Turn of the Balance* (1907). Perhaps his best known work is *J. Hardin and Son* (1923), a realistic picture of Ohio small-town life. Among his nonfiction works are *Belgium: A Personal Narrative* (1919) and *Forty Years of It* (1914), an autobiography. For Brand Whitlock, his career was truly a case of life imitating art.

Utica

SETTLED 1810.
Center Of Hand-Made
Window Glass
Industry
1903-1929

UTICA (Licking County)

The history of glassmaking in the United States dates back to colonial days, when Capt. John Smith started a glassworks at Jamestown, Virginia in 1608. It took more than a century for commercial glassmaking to take root in North America, and even into the 1800's wealthy Americans continued to import their fine glassware from Europe. The domestic industry that was born in New England moved to the Wheeling-Pittsburgh area at about the time of the Civil War, then skipped to Indiana before heading eastward again to Ohio, making the Buckeye State the center of the American glassmaking industry at the turn of the century.

In the glassmaking industry, the availability of fuel supply determines location. Before 1900, the gas fields of Indiana drew the blowers away from Pittsburgh, and when new gas fields were discovered in Ohio, glassmakers fired up their furnaces in Ohio. Near Utica, rich wells described as "the greatest in the country" attracted five glass companies to start up production at the Licking County village.

The first of the companies was The Utica Glass Company, organized in 1903 as a cooperative venture of the workmen. Thomas Blackstone was the blower who mixed the first batch, and he would later become president of the company. In 1909, the Utica works burned down after a tank burst, nearly engulfing the workers in a flood of molten glass. After rebuilding, the company was said to produce more window glass per man than any other plant in the nation. In addition to window glass, Utica companies produced cathedral glass and heavy white opal glass used in refrigerators.

Automation eventually killed the handblown glass factories. By 1914, the percentage of hand-made window glass fell from 100% to 40%, and the outbreak of the Depression in 1929 brought the end of glassmaking in Utica.

Vandalia

**HEADQUARTERS
SINCE 1924 OF THE
AMATEUR
TRAPSHOOTING
ASSOCIATION**

VANDALIA (*Montgomery County*)

On June 12-15, 1900, the first four-day shooting event that would become the Grand American Handicap was held at the Interstate Park on Long Island. There were 74 gunners in the field, shooting at a total of 100 targets from handicap distances of 14 to 25 yards. The winner of that first event was a Dayton man by the name of Rollo "Pop" Heikes, who hit 91 of the 100 targets and walked away with the top prize of $130.25. It was fitting that a Dayton man should win that event, for Vandalia, located just north of Dayton, was to become the home of the Amateur Trapshooting Association and the Grand American Handicap event.

The targets in the early days of the trapshooting event were live birds, but after the 1902 event at Kansas City, glass ball and clay targets were substituted. Feathers were sometimes placed in the glass targets to simulate a live target before the sport went to clay "pigeons". Prior to 1924, the event roamed from city to city, but when the amateurs took control from the American Trapshooting Association, their dream of a permanent home for the event was rekindled. Dayton's offer of a tract of land at Vandalia was accepted, and Vandalia became home of the Amateur Trapshooting Association and "The Grand." The roster of men who helped bring the ATA to Vandalia includes Charles Kettering (see Loudonville), James M. Cox (see Kettering), and F.B. Patterson of the National Cash Register Company.

Today, Vandalia is headquarters of the 100,000 member association, as well as the home of the Trapshooting Hall of Fame and Museum. Among those enshrined in the Hall is Annie Oakley, who hunted in the fields here with her husband in the last year of her life. The "Grand" has continued to grow, with over 5,000 participants lining up each August on the mile and a half trapline, the world's longest. And while the 1900 total purse was $714, 1989 saw a purse of $150,000.

Van Wert

NAMED FOR A CAPTOR OF MAJOR ANDRE BRITISH SPY

VAN WERT (Van Wert County)

Van Wert County, with the town of Van Wert as county seat, was named after Isaac Van Wart, a farmer in West Chester County, New York. Van Wart was born in Greenburg in 1760, and died May 23, 1828, at the age of sixty-eight. He was a soldier of the Revolution, and an episode in New York during the war led to his having a county in Ohio named after him in 1820.

John Paulding, David Williams, and Isaac Van Wart were three militiamen who captured Major John Andre, Benedict Arnold's contact in treason, on September 23, 1780. The three young men, the oldest being only twenty-three, had been playing cards among some bushes by the roadside when they heard a galloping horse approach. Aiming their muskets at the rider, they stopped him for questioning.

The three militiamen searched their captive, and found in one of his boots some papers marked "Contents, West Point." A similar package was found in the other boot, and the three young men realized that the rider was a spy named Major Andre. Andre offered the three young men his horse, equipage, and money in exchange for his freedom, but they resisted and delivered him to the nearest military station at Newcastle.

Williams, Paulding, and Van Wart were all present in the ring when Andre was hung. In return for their deed, Congress awarded each of Andre's captors a farm in West Chester County, N.Y., a life pension, and a silver medal. On one side of the medal was engraved "Fidelity," and on the other side "Amo patrice vincit," "The love of country conquers." Years later, an additional honor was bestowed upon them when all three men had counties in northwest Ohio named in their honor. A clerical error in transcribing the county's name onto state records resulted in Van Wart's county becoming Van Wert.

Vermilion

**NAMED FOR
ITS RED CLAY
USED BY INDIANS
TO MAKE PAINT**

VERMILION (Erie County)

For several centuries before Columbus' arrival in the New World, the Erie tribe of Indians inhabited the land south of Lake Erie. Called the "Cat People," or the "People of the Panther," the Eries lived along the banks of a river that they called "Oulanie Thepy," which is translated to Vermilion Creek. The river derives its name from the red clay found along the stream, clay that was used for pottery, medicines, and paint. The Eries lived here for several centuries, but unlike other later tribes forced out by white encroachment, the Eries met their demise at the hands of other Indians.

No tribes were more powerful, or more feared, than the fierce confederation of Iroquois tribes known as the Five Nations. Strategically located astride the St. Lawrence River trade route to the interior and the Ohio Country, the earliest settlers in the New World knew they had to deal with these Iroquois people. It was not an easy task, for the shrewd and mighty Iroquois had a reputation for belligerence and torture unsurpassed by any other tribe. And it was not just to other tribes and Europeans that the Five Nations were hostile, but prior to their confederation they were hostile even among themselves. The Eries, an Iroquois tribe not aligned with the Five Nations, lived just to the southwest of the Five Nations, and after witnessing the Five Nations vanquish its other neighbors in the mid-1600's, the Eries launched an offensive of their own in 1653. After two years of fierce fighting, the outnumbered Iroquois of the Five Nations vanquished the Eries, who all but disappeared from the region.

Among the few traces now remaining of the Cat Nation are the name they gave to Vermilion, and some nearly obliterated pictographs carved into Inscription Rock on nearby Kelley's Island.

Wapakoneta

HOME OF
NEIL A. ARMSTRONG
First Man
On The Moon

WAPAKONETA *(Auglaize County)*

The historical markers that stand at the edge of Ohio's towns generally bear witness to great feats of another day, celebrating the pioneers who crossed the Atlantic and moved on to the western frontier called Ohio, the heroes who crossed the Ohio River into forbidding Indian territory searching for adventure, or the compassionate people in the days of slavery who sheltered freedom-seeking people escaping from the torment on the other side of this nation's "Jordan River." Other towns proclaim pioneers in medicine, law, art and music, automobiles and electricity. Ohioans have from the time the first frontiersmen crossed the Appalachian Mountains been on the cutting edge of an ever renewing world - and beyond. When the bonds of the earth were first broken, it was the Wright Brothers of Dayton who broke them. When the confines of gravity were eclipsed, it was John Glenn, Jr. of New Concord who transcended them. And on July 20, 1969, it was an Ohioan from Wapakoneta named Neil Armstrong who crossed the great river of space to land on another terrestrial body, sending back to a stunned world the chilling words, "Houston, Houston...The Eagle has landed."

Neil Armstrong, born in Wapakoneta in 1930, graduated from Purdue University and served as a combat pilot in the Korean War and a top test pilot before joining the space program. The flight of Apollo XI culminated a crash program to beat the Soviet Union to the moon, and met a challenge issued by President Kennedy in 1962 to put an American on the moon before the end of the decade. And while it took years for the world to know about the Wright Brothers flight at Kitty Hawk, untold millions of people watched Armstrong descend the ladder from the "Eagle" and utter those immortal words, "That's one small step for man, one giant leap for mankind."

Wapakoneta is now home to the Armstrong Air and Space Museum that features exhibits of Ohio's pioneers of flight.

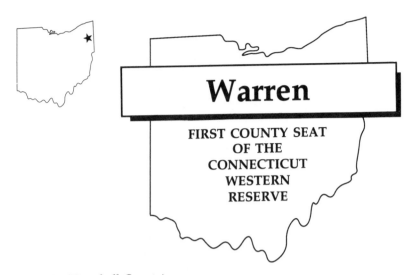

Warren

**FIRST COUNTY SEAT
OF THE
CONNECTICUT
WESTERN
RESERVE**

WARREN (Trumbull County)

Settlement in Ohio typically occurred first along principal water routes such as the Ohio River, with the population in a given area concentrating itself in a central community, sometimes within the shadow of a protecting fort. The advantages of this pattern allowed for early commerce and cooperation, as well as a social life that helped conquer fear and boredom. The desire for fairness and equity in distributing the land in Connecticut's Western Reserve (see Poland) worked against this pattern, however, and ultimately created hardships for the settlers. Those who owned shares in the Connecticut Land Company drew their land by lot, balancing the fertile land along Lake Erie with the less desirable land away from the lake that contained bogs, marshes, or steep hillsides. Solitary families and small groups then entered the Reserve and followed the township lines to their allotted spot. There, alone in the forbidding wilderness, they would attempt to carve out a life in the dense forest. The nearest neighbor might be fifteen or twenty miles away, laboring at the same lonely task.

In 1799, Capt. Ephraim Quinby came to the Reserve and built a cabin at Warren. Quinby's cabin, in addition to having three apartments and a bedroom, contained a little-used jail. A plat of Warren at the beginning of 1800 showed two log cabins, but by the end of the year Warren's population had grown to sixteen settlers, earning it the designation as the seat of the Western Reserve. By comparison, a survey that same year showed one family at Vienna, three at Hartford, and five each at Poland, Deerfield, and Boardman. Cleveland boasted seven residents.

In 1800, Connecticut relinquished control of the Reserve, and it became part of the Northwest Territory. Trumbull County was formed by proclamation of Gov. St. Clair on July 10, 1800, encompassing all of the Western Reserve, and Warren was made the county seat.

EMIGRATING TO NEW CONNECTICUT, 1817–1818.

From an engraving in Peter Parley's Recollections.

**SETTLED BY
VIRGINIA VETERANS
OF THE
AMERICAN REVOLUTION**

WASHINGTON C.H. *(Fayette County)*

Four of the original thirteen states along the eastern seaboard claimed part of the Old Northwest Territory, including the Ohio Country, in 1787. In order for the new United States to grow and develop westward, the states of New York, Massachusetts, Connecticut, and Virginia would have to relinquish their claims to their Ohio lands. Virginia had the most valid claim to the entire territory, as she had been active in the region from the time George Washington traveled to the Ohio Valley to protest the French presence in 1754. When Congress accepted Virginia's lands "lying northwest of the river Ohio" in 1784, it agreed that she could retain the land lying between the Scioto and Little Miami Rivers for the purpose of paying her citizens who had served in the military during the Revolutionary War. That portion of Ohio thence became known as the Virginia Military District. The irregularly shaped townships of the counties in this area clearly distinguish the Virginia method of survey, using metes and bounds, from the neat right angles generally found in the rest of Ohio.

After 1790, Virginia veterans of the Revolution began arriving in Ohio to claim their land. The amount of land they could claim depended on their rank and length of service, so after selecting a site, the settler would hire a surveyor. The surveyor was often paid with a portion of the lot surveyed, and many surveyors acquired a good deal of land and influence as a result. One of the early surveyors in Fayette County was Jesse Milliken, who settled in Washington and built several of the town's first homes. He also served as the town's first postmaster and clerk of the common pleas court. It was by virtue of the first session of the court being held here in the log cabin of John Devault in 1810 that Washington added Court House to its name, an appendage commonly used in the settlers' old home state of Virginia.

Waterville

**SITE OF 1818
INDIAN TRADING POST
AND 1828
COLUMBIAN INN,
STAGE STOP**

WATERVILLE (Lucas County)

John Pray came to this area from Rhode Island in 1817, and the following year began constructing an inn on the old Detroit-Defiance stage coach route. Pray did not intend for his inn to be just another rough and crude tavern where travelers would climb a ladder into a loft for a night's sleep. Rather, he envisioned a hostelry that would become the social and commercial center of the town that he planned to lay out here. His plans came to fruition with the completion of the Columbian Inn in 1828 and his founding of Waterville three years later.

The Columbian Inn became known as one of the most superb examples of colonial architecture in the Midwest. The inn has three stories, originally housing a barroom and storerooms on the first floor, sleeping quarters on the second, and a grand ballroom on the third. Fireplaces were built at either end of all three floors. The building was constructed of hand-hewn fourteen inch beams held by wooden pegs, and the woodwork in the twenty-three rooms is of black walnut. The solid walnut doors that swing on wrought iron hinges are paneled with the "witchcraft cross," a device borrowed from Salem, Massachusetts to ward off evil spirits.

Notwithstanding the witchcraft crosses, there have been a number of ghost stories swirling around the old inn. One night in the early 1800's, a weary guest retired to his room, never to be seen again. Shuffling noises and the sounds of footsteps, attributed to the vanished boarder, unnerved guests for many years. Thirty years later, a dying farmer made a death bed confession that he had murdered the man, and authorities uncovered a skeleton right where the farmer said it would be.

The Columbian House still stands in Waterville, and is on the National Register of Historic Places.

Wauseon

**HOME OF
WAUSEON
Chief of
The Ottawas**

WAUSEON *(Fulton County)*

Wauseon, Chief of the Ottawas, was one of four notable half-brothers, all the sons of Ottawa Chief O-to-sah. Wauseon and his half-brother Autokee (see Oregon, Ohio) were among the last of the Indians to live in northwest Ohio, being forced to move westward by the government in the spring of 1838. Within a few years, the displaced chief, unable to adapt to his new reservation, was dead, a young man of only forty-five winters. Ironically, Wauseon's name translated into English means "far away," and serves as a fitting epitaph to the long, hard journey forced upon the Indians of northwest Ohio.

A decade after Wauseon's death in Kansas, Nat Leggett, W. Hall, E.L. Barber and J.H. Sargent purchased 160 acres of land at the future site of the town of Wauseon. The owner of the land, Thomas Bayes, must have thought that the four men had little knowledge of land values, as they paid the high price of $16.00 per acre - five times the going price for nearby land. Barber and Sargent were railway surveyors, however, and knew that a depot was to be built along the right of way west of Delta somewhere in the vicinity of their newly purchased land. Like other railway surveyors in advance of lines coming through Ohio, they saw an opportunity to take advantage of their knowledge by becoming landholders. When the railroad reached the area in 1854, they recorded their plat and named their town Wauseon in honor of the Ottawa chief.

Wauseon was platted with wide, spacious streets and sidewalks, the main street being 100 feet wide and the sidewalks eight feet across. The east-west streets were named after species of trees, with the intersecting north-south streets named for famous people. The town was incorporated in 1857, and became the county seat in 1870. A courthouse was duly erected the following year, and in 1973, a century after it was built, the Fulton County Courthouse earned a listing on the National Register of Historic Places.

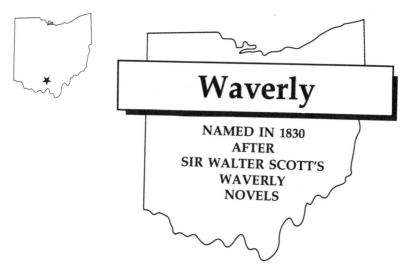

Waverly

NAMED IN 1830
AFTER
SIR WALTER SCOTT'S
WAVERLY
NOVELS

WAVERLY *(Pike County)*

Located in Pee Pee township, the town of Waverly was founded by James Emmitt, and was originally called Uniontown. Emmitt was born in Pennsylvania in 1806, and came to Ohio as a boy. He worked as a farm laborer, blacksmith, woodchopper, and teamster before engaging in a partnership in a small grocery business. Through his industriousness, and in spite of limited educational opportunities, he went on to own a bank, store, distillery, furniture factory, lumber yard, saw and grist-mills.

In 1830, the citizens attempted to establish a post office in Uniontown. It was learned at that time that a Uniontown already existed in northern Ohio. Capt. Francis Cleveland, an engineer on the Ohio Canal that passed through Uniontown, was deeply engrossed in Sir Walter Scott's Waverly novels, and suggested the name of Waverly for the town. The idea was accepted, and Uniontown became Waverly.

In 1831, Emmitt was appointed postmaster, and in 1861 he was largely responsible for the county seat being removed from Piketon to Waverly. He went on to serve two years in the Ohio Senate. And as for Capt. Cleveland, who gave the town of Waverly its name, he saw his nephew, Grover, go on to become president of the United States.

Wellington

**"THE SPIRIT OF 76"
PAINTED BY
ARCHIBALD M. WILLARD
WHO LIVED HERE**

WELLINGTON (Lorain County)

Archibald MacNeal Willard was born in Bedford, Ohio on August 26, 1836. As a youth, his paintings attracted the attention of the residents of his community, and, as was the case in many professions, he received some training from an itinerant artist passing through the area. In order to support himself as an artist, Willard took a position at a carriage factory in Wellington, where he was able to use his talents in the decorating and painting of carriages. His employment at the carriage factory was interrupted by his service in the Civil War, where he painted several pictures of the countryside through which his company was marching.

After the war, Willard sold his first paintings that were widely known by the public, two comic drawings entitled *Pluck.* He then moved on to Cleveland, where he painted the most widely reproduced canvas in America, *The Spirit of '76.* The painting depicted an aged drummer with a fifer on one side and a boy drummer on the other, marching at the head of a column of Revolutionary War soldiers. The model for the aged drummer is said to have been Willard's father, and the fifer Hugh Mosier. The painting was a sensation at the nation's centennial celebration in Philadelphia, and Willard went on to paint several variations on the theme. In 1912, at the age of 76, he painted a reproduction of the piece for the Cleveland Municipal Building.

Archibald Willard died in Cleveland on October 11, 1918. He is buried in Greenwood Cemetery in his hometown of Wellington. The town remembers him with the Archibald Willard Monument on the town square, and the Spirit of '76 Museum that houses over a dozen of his original works.

Wellston

**FOUNDED 1873
AS AN
IRON AND COAL
PRODUCING
CENTER**

WELLSTON *(Jackson County)*

In the mid-1800's, Ohio led the nation in the production of iron for implements and weapons, with the production being centered chiefly in the six-county area of southern Ohio known as the Hanging Rock Region. Forty-six charcoal iron furnaces burned in this area, converting thousands of acres of woodland into iron products. In 1869, seemingly inexhaustible beds of a superior quality coal were discovered at a location in Jackson County, attracting capital and people. In November of 1873, the town of Wellston was laid out on a farm and named in honor of its founder, Harvey Wells. Contracts were let out three months later for the construction of the first iron furnace, a "double blast," for the Wellston Coal and Iron Company, and within a decade, the town had grown to more than 5,000 people.

Wellston's leading role as a coal and iron producing center was described in an article in the *Wellston Argus* of April 30, 1887: "No mineral region in the United States can bear comparison with Wellston and its surroundings, whether we consider the extent and quality of the mineral treasures or the unparalleled development of the coal and iron industries. The quality of the coal has become so fully established that there is no longer dispute as to its rank. It stands at the head of the bituminous coals of the United States. The Hanging Rock iron is known all over the Untied States for its superior quality for the manufacture of car-wheels, ordnance, and other castings which require to be made out of unusually tough and strong iron."

Although the iron furnaces of Hanging Rock no longer issue forth their clouds of charcoal smoke, some of the stone structures can still be seen in isolated areas of southern Ohio, standing silently as monuments to another time.

242

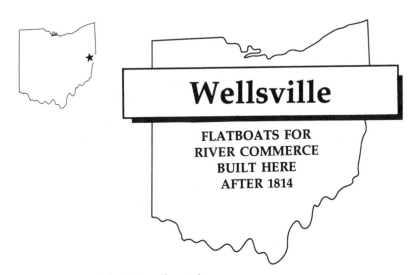

Wellsville

**FLATBOATS FOR
RIVER COMMERCE
BUILT HERE
AFTER 1814**

WELLSVILLE *(Columbiana County)*

George Clarke was squatting on the land now occupied by Wellsville in 1796, while to the north at Lake Erie Moses Cleaveland was surveying a town at the mouth of the Cuyahoga River. In less than two decades, these two sites would emerge from the wilderness to become Wellsville and Cleveland, linked by commerce and natural happenstance.

The shortest line between Lake Erie and the Ohio River has at its ends Cleveland and Wellsville, the latter being located at the northernmost bend in the Ohio. Prior to any road opening from Wellsville into the interior of the state, flour was being flat-boated from a mill on Yellow Creek down the Ohio to New Orleans. In 1814 a mud road was built to New Lisbon, and "Well's Landing" became a shipping point for goods headed inland. Daniel Skillenger was building flat boats for river traffic here at the time, and in 1818 he built the hull for the steamboat *Robert Thompson,* a portent of Wellsville's future as a steamship port. William Wells recorded the town of Wellsville in 1823, and when a road from Wellsville to Cleveland was built two years later, the town's property values doubled.

Wellsville's landing was considered one of the best on the Ohio, and it became an important center for the shipment of goods up and down the river and overland to the lake. Warehouses and hotels sprang up, and by 1850 it was not unusual to see upwards of 150 teams arrive and depart daily. Wellsville controlled the river shipment of goods for fifteen Ohio counties. A line of daily steamboats to Pittsburgh was established, and in 1834 a stage route was opened to Fairport on Lake Erie which did a thriving passenger business. By the end of the nineteenth century, Wellsville's population was poised on the verge of 5,000, about where it stands a century later.

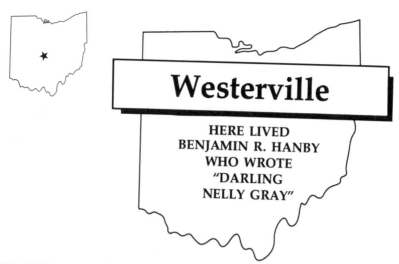

Westerville

HERE LIVED
BENJAMIN R. HANBY
WHO WROTE
"DARLING
NELLY GRAY"

WESTERVILLE *(Franklin County)*

Benjamin Russell Hanby, born in Rushville in 1833, was attending Otterbein College in 1856 when he wrote *Darling Nelly Gray*, a poignant song of love and tragedy based on an earlier experience at his family home in Rushville. Joe Selby, a fugitive slave, was on his way to Canada to purchase freedom for his Georgia sweetheart, Nelly Gray. Mr. Selby's desperate flight across Ohio to secure the freedom of his Nelly ended in tragedy when he died at the home of the Hanby family in Rushville. On his deathbed, he spoke of his darling, Nelly Gray. The song inspired by this event stirred the emotions of the country, and was sung around Union campfires during the Civil War. Its appeal spread to the south, where it enticed many slaves to flee to the north.

Ben Hanby died at the early age of 34 in 1867, and is buried in Otterbein Cemetery in Westerville. He never received the monetary fruits of *Darling Nelly Gray,* being informed by his publisher that *"Nelly Gray* is sung on both sides of the Atlantic. We have made the money and you the fame - that balances the account." Time, however, has tipped the balance in the songwriter's favor: three communities claim him on their historical markers. (New Paris, where he wrote the Christmas favorite *Up on the Housetop,* and Rushville, his birthplace, are the others.) The Hanby House in Westerville is now a state historical site and museum, administered by the Ohio Historical Society. Joe Selby, the slave who inspired the song, is buried in the Rushville Cemetery.

West Union

DESIGNATED
ADAMS COUNTY SEAT
BY LEGISLATURE
IN 1803

WEST UNION (*Adams County*)

West Union was designated the Adams County seat in 1803, and remains the seat of justice, but it was a convoluted path that Adams County followed in securing a permanent seat of government.

The game of musical chairs for county seat began on September 12, 1797 when Manchester (see Manchester) was the scene of the first session of court in the county, but by December 12, 1797 the court was being convened in Adamsville. With the opening of that session, agitation began immediately to again move the seat. Among the players were Nathaniel Massie, who offered one acre in Manchester to have the seat returned there; John Wills, who offered one acre in Adamsville to retain it; John Belli, who offered 50 acres at Turkey Creek; James Collins, one acre at Adamsburgh; and Noble Grimes, two acres at the mouth of Ohio Brush Creek. When court adjourned on September 11, 1798, Massie had won and the court was to reconvene in Manchester in December. However, Massie's opponents had the order revoked, and the court held its next session on December 11, 1798 in the town of Washington, laid out by Noble Grimes at the mouth of Ohio Brush Creek. Construction for a new courthouse had apparently begun, for in the June, 1798 session, none other than Noble Grimes was charged by the grand jury with "felonously and forcibly taking from the court house at Adamsville, a quantity of plank, the property of the county." A court house in Washington was never completed, but a jail was.

By 1803, the county seat was again on the move. The Ohio legislature designated West Union to be the county seat on April 13, 1803, and almost a year later a site one-half mile south of Zane's Trace was selected. Here in the new town of West Union the seat of justice has rested, but not always peaceably. In 1870, Manchester made yet another bid to retrieve the seat, but the voters of the county decided to keep it at West Union - at least for the time being!

Williamsburg

FOUNDED 1796
Oldest Town And
First County Seat
Of Clermont
County

WILLIAMSBURG *(Clermont County)*

Settlement at what is now Williamsburg dates back to 1796, when James Kain came from Pennsylvania to build a cabin and clear a tract of land for Gen. William Lytle, who in 1795 had platted a town to be established here. Lytle, of Lexington, Kentucky, had been a land surveyor in the region, locating military land warrants in the area. Anticipating the formation of the new county of Clermont in 1800, he laid out his town in the belief that it would become the county seat.

The plat of Lytlestown, as the village was first called, included 500 in-lots "6 poles by 12"; 140 out-lots of 4 acres each; and a public square embracing 12 lots and located on a beautiful elevation. The square was to be used for the county buildings that would accompany the town's designation as the seat of justice for Clermont County. Apparently there was some squabbling concerning the original plat, for in 1815 it was refiled with these words: "That the plat of the town has before been recorded in due season and agreeable to law, but it having been suggested by some meddling person that the first record was vague and unsatisfactory, the above is placed on record to remove all doubt or ambiguity."

Gen. Lytle himself moved to Williamsburg in the summer of 1800, residing on a farm adjacent to the village. Soon, other settlers followed, and in 1801 the village became the county seat. It attracted so many notable men that the distinguished Thomas Morris (see Bethel), a one-time resident of Williamsburg, left for Bethel in 1804, explaining, "I would rather be a king among fools than a fool among kings." Gen. Lytle moved to Cincinnati in 1810, where he lived until his death in 1831. The county seat was moved from Williamsburg to Batavia in 1824.

Willshire

**FOUNDED 1822 BY
CAPTAIN JAMES W. RILEY
Pioneer Surveyor
Of The St. Marys And
Maumee Valleys**

WILLSHIRE *(Van Wert County)*

Capt. James Riley must surely be considered one of the more colorful characters in Ohio's history, although the incidents that first brought him to the attention of the American public occurred not in Ohio, but in the faraway deserts of Morocco. Riley, a seafaring New Englander, set sail from Connecticut in 1815 on a trading voyage across the Atlantic, but was shipwrecked on the African mainland in a land barren of vegetation, food and water. Captured by a band of nomadic Arabs, Riley and the other sailors were stripped and marched off into the burning desert as slaves. The British consul in Morocco, William Willshire, eventually ransomed Riley and the others, saving the emaciated men from certain death. When Riley returned to the United States, he wrote an account of his adventure entitled *Authentic Narrative,* which became a best seller here and abroad. Part of the book's interest was that it demonstrated that whites as well as blacks could be seen as ''particularly suited'' to slavery by their captors.

In 1818, Riley secured a position as a surveyor of lands in northwest Ohio, where he saw great promise in the unbroken wilderness. In 1822 he laid out a tract and named it Willshire in honor of the man who saved his life in Africa. He and his family braved wolves, illness and other hardships while establishing the community, and built a mill that made Willshire a center for pioneers weary of grinding their own meal. In 1823, Riley was elected to the state legislature. But while the community was growing, Riley was plagued by illness and debt, and eventually left Ohio to resume a seafaring life. In March of 1840, Capt. James Riley, three days out of New York on a voyage to the West Indies, died at sea and was consigned to the waters forever.

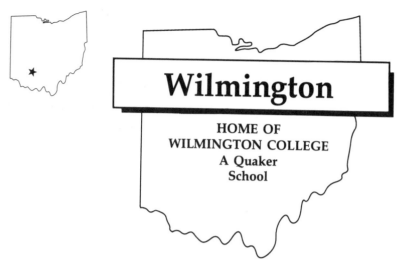

Wilmington

**HOME OF
WILMINGTON COLLEGE
A Quaker
School**

WILMINGTON (Clinton County)

Wilmington, the county seat of Clinton County, is home of Wilmington College, a four year private liberal arts school of about 800 full time undergraduate students. The college had its beginnings on the site of the old Franklin College, established in 1866, but that school went out of existence in 1869. Franklin's building, College Hall, was sold to the Quakers in 1870, marking the birth of Wilmington College, one of about a dozen Quaker colleges in the United States. Today, the members of the Board of Trustees are still approved by the Wilmington Yearly Meeting of the Religious Society of Friends (Quakers), and the Yearly Meeting offices are found on campus.

Quakerism has historically been concerned with the end of war and the establishment of world peace. Wilmington College offers a Peace Studies program, and its peace resource center draws visitors and scholars from around the world. The Center's Hiroshima-Nagasaki collection of materials related to the atomic bombings of those cities is the only such collection outside of Japan. Included in Wilmington's academic programs are inter-disciplinary courses of study in the Philosophies of Self Reliance, the works of 18th century Quaker John Woolman, and Mohandas Ghandi.

The red-brick buildings of Wilmington College range from the early College Hall of 1866 to modern student and athletic buildings. The library, which houses 100,000 volumes, is also home to the Quaker Room, a small museum dedicated to Quakerism.

Woodsfield

**PLATTED 1814 BY
ARCHIBALD WOODS
AS
MONROE COUNTY
SEAT**

WOODSFIELD (Monroe County)

Rivalries among communities for the honor of being the county seat are legendary among Ohio towns, but in 1814 the honor of Monroe County seat was granted to Woodsfield, a town that did not even exist. Selected in part because of its central location, the town was laid out in unbroken wilderness by Archibald Woods of Wheeling. The task of establishing a community in a forest is a sizeable one, calling for ingenuity as well as perseverance. Legend has it that, facing the job of clearing the forest from the streets, Woods "got a keg of brandy and invited all the men and boys within a circuit of five miles to come into the place on a certain Saturday, have a grand frolic and clear out Main Street." This was done and the first trees felled.

By 1820, Woodsfield had grown to a hamlet of six log houses and twelve log cabins, and boasted a combination log court-house and jail. Prior to that time, court was held in the home of Levin Okey. The lock-up was apparently little used, for Henry Howe, Ohio historian, noted in 1889 that "the behavior of the people was such that the jailer's office was of little account." Woodsfield was incorporated in 1834, and the outside world eventually arrived at this secluded village via the Bellaire, Zanesville, and Cincinnati ("Bent, Zigzag, and Crooked") Railway that wound its way into the hills of Monroe County.

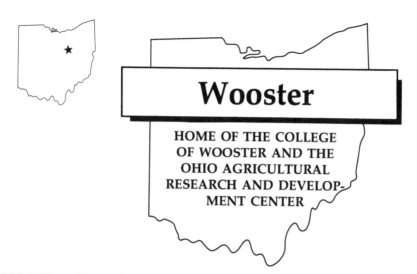

Wooster

**HOME OF THE COLLEGE
OF WOOSTER AND THE
OHIO AGRICULTURAL
RESEARCH AND DEVELOP-
MENT CENTER**

WOOSTER *(Wayne County)*

Wooster, the seat of Wayne county in the heart of Ohio's dairyland, is home to the College of Wooster and the Ohio State University's Ohio Agricultural Experiment Station, now called the Ohio Agricultural Research and Development Center.

The College of Wooster had its beginnings in the vision of Rev. James Reed, a Presbyterian minister who believed the oak-covered knoll overlooking the Killbuck Valley was the perfect place for a college. The reverend persuaded Ephraim Quinby, the land's owner, to donate 22 acres on the hill, and in 1866 the College of Wooster was founded by the Presbyterians to do "their proper part in the great work of educating those who are to mold society and give shape to all its institutions." On September 8, 1870, the College opened its doors to its faculty of five and student body of 30. A fire in 1901 destroyed the main building, but it was replaced by several others. The College of Wooster today is a four-year private liberal arts college with a full time student population of about 1,900. It was one of the first institutions in the country to offer a pre-medical course.

While the College of Wooster lends a cultural air to the community, Wooster is also home of advanced scientific work at the Ohio Agricultural Research and Development Center. Established in the early years of The Ohio State University, the experiment station was partly a response to criticism that the university was not meeting the needs of the agricultural community. Moved from Columbus to Wooster in 1891, the station continues to seek improvements in farm methods and products.

Worthington

**NAMED FOR
THOMAS WORTHINGTON
"Father Of
Ohio Statehood"**

WORTHINGTON (Franklin County)

As Thomas Worthington rode along the twisting and treacherous mountain trails on his way to Washington from Chillicothe, he must have been reminded of the winding and tortuous path to statehood Ohio had been following for the past fifteen years. From the creation of the Northwest Territory in 1787, the future state of Ohio had gone through three stages to statehood decreed by Congress: first, the territory was under the rule of a territorial governor and three judges appointed by Congress; second, when the territory reached "5,000 free male inhabitants of full age," a territorial legislature was elected by the people; and third, when this easternmost of the three proposed state areas within the territory reached 60,000 inhabitants, statehood could be achieved. With Worthington on his way to deliver the new state constitution to Congress, Ohio was about to be admitted to the Union as the seventeenth state.

Worthington and his supporters had been fighting for statehood against Arthur St. Clair, the aristocratic governor of the territory who did not believe the people were ready for the responsibility of statehood. St. Clair's attempt to have the boundary lines of the state redrawn to prevent achieving the necessary number of inhabitants failed, and on November 29, 1802, the constitutional convention approved a state constitution. On February 19, 1803, President Jefferson signed into law an act stating "the people had formed a constitution and state government, and did give to the said State the name of the 'State of Ohio'." With this, Ohio "had become one of the United States of America," and Thomas Worthington would become one of Ohio's first senators.

In that same year of 1803, James Kilbourne founded the town that he called Worthington, and in 1810 offered to donate land and buildings to have the state capital located there. In spite of his town's name and the generous offer, the legislature selected Columbus to be the capital.

Xenia

HOME OF
WHITELAW REID
Diplomat-Historian
Journalist
1837-1912

XENIA *(Greene County)*

Whitelaw Reid, the grandson of one of Xenia's founders, was born near Xenia on October 27, 1837. His grandfather had emigrated from Scotland to Kentucky, and moved into Ohio in 1800. After finding that the deed for the land he purchased at Cincinnati required him to operate a ferry across the Ohio River seven days a week, including the Sabbath, the strict old Covenanter sold his land and headed for Greene County, where he established his family.

Whitelaw Reid graduated from Miami University in 1856, and soon became editor of *The Xenia News*. When the Civil War broke out, he went to Washington as a correspondent for *The Cincinnati Gazette,* where his letters under the name "Agate" gained much attention. His experience in the field as aide-de-camp to Gen. William Rosecrans, a fellow Ohioan, and his presence at the Battles of Gettysburg and Shiloh, undoubtedly served him well in the writing of his most famous book, *Ohio in the War,* published at Cincinnati in 1868. The book was called by some "the most important of all the State histories of the Civil War".

After moving to New York, Mr. Reid became editor and principal owner of *The New York Tribune* upon the death of Horace Greeley, and he actively served Republican causes. In addition to serving as President Benjamin Harrison's running mate in the unsuccessful campaign of 1892, Reid's political career also included ambassadorships to France and England.

When The Ohio State University established the Journalism Hall of Fame in 1928, Whitelaw Reid was one of those distinguished Ohio newspapermen included among the ranks of the state's greatest journalists.

Yellow Springs

**HOME OF
ANTIOCH COLLEGE
Founded 1853.
Horace Mann Was Its
First President**

YELLOW SPRINGS (Greene County)

"Be afraid to die until you have won some victory for humanity" was the motto of Horace Mann, and years after his death these words grace his monument on the campus of his beloved Antioch College. The famed educator, only six years after leaving Massachusetts for Ohio, died while serving at Antioch, his death literally coming from overwork in the service of his fellow man.

The middle years of the nineteenth century were difficult ones for higher education. It seemed that every religious denomination sought to have its own college, and the narrow sectarian nature of many of these institutions did little to enhance their educational reputations. Horace Mann, the college's first president, sought to establish Antioch free from sectarian influences. For Mann, the goal of the college was more than simple instruction, but the development of a complete personality. Antioch was one of the first colleges in the country to admit women and blacks, the latter being done in 1856-57 by Mann over the objections of the college's board of trustees and in the face of several white students leaving the school.

The financial problems that plagued many Ohio colleges at that time also plagued Antioch. Pledges were not honored, faculty members, their salaries unpaid, often resigned, and Mann had to resort to using his personal funds in some cases. In the face of sectarian opposition, financial difficulties, and the heat of racial politics, Horace Mann died in 1859 at the age of fifty-three, having expended all of his energies in his service to Antioch and its students.

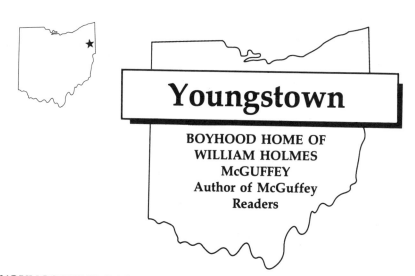

Youngstown

BOYHOOD HOME OF
WILLIAM HOLMES
McGUFFEY
Author of McGuffey
Readers

YOUNGSTOWN (Mahoning County)

William Holmes McGuffey, who had lived as a child in Youngstown, graduated from Washington College in Pennsylvania. After his graduation, the young westerner presented himself to the board of Warren Academy, seeking a position as a teacher, but the board, upon which sat two graduates from Yale, refused him a position. Such was the inauspicious beginning of the career of the author of the famed McGuffey *Readers.*

The Ohio schoolchildren of the early nineteenth century had to suffer through schoolbooks that had little relation to their lives. Stilted prose with themes of pessimism and death, rooted in the Pilgrim heritage of New England, did little to inspire children of the Ohio frontier growing up in a land of promise and possibility. McGuffey, a native of the region, saw a need for books that stressed the rewards of hard work and industry, using examples that would inspire the students. In 1834, while teaching at Miami University in Oxford, McGuffey began writing his series of *Readers* that would shape generations to come. "A is for Adam (in Adam's fall, we sinned all") was replaced with "A is for Ax," a symbol of individualism and hard work. The *Readers* introduced pupils to excerpts from great literature, and in many homes of rural Ohio, the McGuffey *Reader* and the *Bible* were the only books to be found.

More than 122 million copies of the Readers were sold, and although they netted their author less than $1,000, they earned for William Holmes McGuffey the lasting title of "schoolmaster of the nation."

Zanesville

SECOND CAPITAL
OF OHIO
1810-1812

ZANESVILLE (Muskingum County)

Ohio has had three capitals since it became a state in 1803. Chillicothe, the first capital, served as the seat of government until 1810, when the capital was moved to Zanesville. It returned to Chillicothe in 1812, and finally moved to Columbus in 1816.

Chillicothe had been made the capital on a temporary basis, and other Ohio communities were hopeful that the capital prize might be theirs. Chief among them was Zanesville, being more favorably located toward the center of the state than Chillicothe. In 1809, Zanesville erected a handsome brick building, complete with cupola, that could be used by the legislature as a capitol (or, failing that, as a courthouse by the county). In 1810, with the new building beckoning, the legislature passed a resolution moving the capital to Zanesville. It was not all good news for Zanesville, however, as the day after this action, the legislature resolved that the permanent capital would be located "not more than forty miles from what shall be deemed to be the common center of the state." Zanesville was located just outside this radius.

The building which served as the state capitol in Zanesville for two legislative sessions was to become known as Old 1809. Part of the inducement to move the capital to Zanesville had been the erection of the state buildings at no cost to the legislature. Muskingum County was unable to bear this burden alone, and a few individuals stepped forward to get the construction underway. Eventually, the county incurred a heavy debt that took several years to redeem, long after the capital had been removed from Zanesville back to Chillicothe.

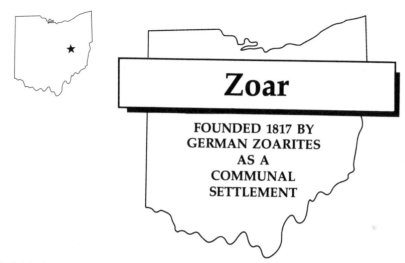

Zoar

**FOUNDED 1817 BY
GERMAN ZOARITES
AS A
COMMUNAL
SETTLEMENT**

ZOAR (Tuscarawas County)

Pioneer Ohio, unburdened by tradition, was an open society, and this openness proved to be a magnet for a number of "utopian societies". Many of these utopian societies, comprised of groups of people who wished to separate themselves from a culture which they perceived as corrupt, originated in Europe, including a group of German separatists who came from Wurtemberg, Germany. Led by Joseph Bimeler, this group of farmers, bakers, carpenters, and other industrious people bought 5,000 acres of rich bottomland in the Tuscarawas River Valley in 1817, eventually contracting to build portions of the Ohio & Erie Canal to pay for the land. They named their new community Zoar, after the biblical name of the town to which Lot fled after escaping Sodom.

Among this group of 250 people were a number of elderly people needing care, leading to a decision in 1819 to form a communal corporation that became The Separatist Society of Zoar. The Society prospered, increasing to over 300 members owning 7,000 acres of land in Ohio and Iowa, employing 50 nonmembers, and holding property valued at over $1,000,000. The members of the community could be distinguished from visitors and employees by the distinctive red, blue and yellow star on their shoulder.

Following Bimeler's death in 1853, the Society went into a long decline. Ironically, it was the canal the separatists' helped build that brought an end to their isolation. The younger generation, seeing the lifestyles of the travelers along the canal, grew restless, seeking more personal freedom and private ownership of property. In 1898 the Separatist Society of Zoar divided its property among the members and disbanded. Today, many of the structures remain, and are under the auspices of the Ohio Historical Society.

Bibliography

The following bibliography represents some of the sources used in compiling this book. In addition, there were other newspaper articles, pamphlets, brochures, college bulletins, and other material too numerous to list here. Of special note is the work of Henry Howe, the pioneer historian who traveled throughout Ohio in the 1840's compiling his first edition of *Historical Collections of Ohio.* He followed up some forty years later with another tour of the state that resulted in an updated and expanded version of his earlier work. Howe's style, phrasing, and descriptions of early Ohio capture the spirit of Ohio's pioneer days, and the author has quoted him liberally.

Anthony Wayne *Standard.* July 8, 1960.

Arthur, T.S. *Grappling with the Monster.* Philadelphia: Cottage Library, 1892.

Barnes, J.D. *Memoirs of the Miami Valley.* 1919.

Before the Memory Fades, 1795-1950. Wellsville Historical Society.

Belmont County Museum Gay '90's Mansion brochure. Barnesville, Ohio: Belmont County Historical Society.

Bennett, Henry Holcomb (ed.). *The County of Ross.* Madison, Wisconsin: Selwyn Brant, 1902.

Betts, George Herbert and Otis Earle Hall. *Better Rural Schools.* Indianapolis: Bobbs-Merrill, 1914.

Biographical and Historical Memoirs of Muskingum County, Ohio. Chicago: Goodspeed Publishing, 1892.

Bloom, Mary Jane. *From Triumph to Tragedy: A History of the Easter Seal Society.* Elyria: The Easter Seal Society of Lorain and Huron Counties.

Brandon, William. *The American Heritage Book of Indians.* New York: American Heritage, 1961.

Brief History of Van Wert County, Ohio. Van Wert County Historical Society.

Bryan Times. September 20, 1988.

Burns, James J. *Educational History of Ohio.* Columbus: Historical Publishing Co., 1905.

Calvin, Marguerite. People and Places: *Putnam County, Ohio 1800-1900.*

Carriage Journal. Autumn 1979, vol. 17, no. 2. The Carriage Association of America, 1979.

Cavin, Lee. *There Were Giants on the Earth.* Loudonville, Ohio: Hanover Publishing, 1959.

Civil War Letters of Petroleum V. Nasby. Columbus: The Ohio State University for the Ohio Historical Society, 1962.

Columbian House. Anthony Wayne Business and Professional Women's Club, Waterville Business and Professional Men's Club.

Commager, Henry Steele (ed.). *Documents of American History.* New York: Appleton-Century-Crofts, 1963.

Cox, James M. *Journey Through My Years.* New York: Simon and Schuster, 1946.

Coyle, William (ed.). *Ohio Authors and Their Books.* Cleveland: World, 1962.

Crawford County 1826-1976. Bicentennial Edition.

Crestline Historical Society Bulletin. vol. 10, no.1 Crestline: Crestline HIstorical Society, March, 1969.

—————————————————————. vol. 2, no. 1. Crestline: Crestline Historical Society, January, 1951.

Delphos Vicenqui-Bicentennial Historical Book. 1976.

Diamond Jubilee of the Immaculate Conception Parish, Ottoville, Ohio: 1848-1923. Ottoville, Ohio. (1923).

Dickens, Charles. *American Notes.* London: Chapman & Hall, 1842.

Douglas, George William. *The American Book of Days.* New York: H.W. Wilson, 1937.

Eckert, Allan W. *The Frontiersmen.* Boston: Little, Brown, 1967.

—————————————. *Wilderness Empire.* Boston: Little, Brown, 1969.

Eldridge, Mabel. *Franklin in the Great Miami Valley.* 1982.

Ellis, William Donohue. *The Cuyahoga.* Dayton: Landfall Press, 1966.

Elwer, Imogene. *Historical Fort Jennings 1812-1976.* Fort Jennings Bicentennial Committee, 1976.

Evans, Lyle S. *A Standard History of Ross County, Ohio.* Baltimore: Gateway Press for Ross County Genealogical Society, 1987 (reprint of 1917 edition).

Evans, Nelson W. and Emmons B. Stivers. *A History of Adams County, Ohio.* West Union, Ohio: E. B. Stivers, 1900.

Fairport Harbor Bicentennial Committee. *A History of Fairport Harbor.* Fairport Harbor, Ohio: Fairport Harbor Bicentennial Committee, 1976.

Farmland News. September 2, 1986.

Fisk, William L. *A History of Muskingum College.* New Concord, Ohio: Muskingum College, 1978.

Friends Meeting House State Memorial: Mount Pleasant brochure. Ohio Historical Society.

Founding of Plain City, Ohio.

Fowkes, Gerard. *Archaelogical History of Ohio.* Columbus: Ohio State Archaelogical and Historical Society, 1902.

Frankel, Stanley. *The Real Story of Rodger Young.* Coronet Magazine, 1950. Reprint.

Fulton County Historical Society. *Fulton County, Ohio.* Wauseon, Ohio: Fulton County Historical Society, 1976.

Gerber, David A. *Black Ohio and the Color Line 1860-1915.* Urbana: University of Illinois, 1976.

Gibson, R.M. *History of Shawnee.* Columbus.

Gieck, Jack. *A Photo Album of Ohio's Canal Era, 1825-1913.* Kent: Kent State University Press, 1988.

Golden Jubilee of First Concrete Pavement in America. Bellefontaine, Ohio. 1941.

Gordon, Francis M. *Hocking County Sesquicentennial: 1818-1968.* Hocking County Historical Society, 1968.

Goulder, Grace. *This is Ohio.* Cleveland: World, 1965.

Governors of Ohio. Columbus: The Ohio Historical Society, 1969.

Hanging Rock Iron Region of Ohio. vol. 1. Lewis Publishing Co., 1916.

Hart, Val. *The Story of American Roads.* New York: William Sloane Associates, 1950.

Hassett, Mary. *Historical Souvenir of Franklin, 1796-1913.* 1913.

Hatcher, Harlan (state director). *The Ohio Guide.* New York: For Work Projects Administration by Oxford University Press, 1940.

_____. *The Western Reserve.* Indianapolis: Bobbs-Merrill, 1949.

_____. *Lake Erie.* Indianapolis: Bobbs-Merrill, 1945.

Heald, Edward Thornton. *The Stark County Story.* Canton: The Stark County Historical Society, 1949.

Hickok, Ralph. *Who Was Who in American Sports.* New York: Hawthorn, 1971.

Historic Antwerp.

Historical Hand-Atlas (Lawrence County, Ohio). H.H. Hardesty & Co., 1882.

History of Allen County, Ohio. Warner, Beers & Co. 1885.

History of Brown County, Ohio. Chicago: W.H. Beers & Co., 1883.

History of Clermont County, Ohio. Philadelphia: Louis H. Everts, 1880.

History of Crooksville. Crooksville Lions Club.

History of Fayette County, Ohio 1984. Fayette County Genealogical Society, 1984.

History of Medina County. Chicago: Baskin and Battey, 1881.

History of Mercer and Van Wert Counties. 1882.

History of Ottawa County, Ohio and Its Families. Ottawa County Genealogical Society, 1985.

History of Perry County. Perry County Historical Society, 1980.

History of Portage County, Ohio. Chicago: Warner, Beers & Co., 1885.

History of Ross and Highland Counties, Ohio. Cleveland: Williams Brothers, 1880.

History of Van Wert County, Ohio. Van Wert, Ohio: Van Wert County Historical Society, 1981.

Hitchcock, A.B.C. *History of Shelby County, Ohio.* Chicago: Richmond-Arnold Publishing, 1973 (reprint edition).

Hoot: The Otto E. Ehrhart-Paulding County Historical Society Newsletter. Antwerp, Ohio.

Howe, Henry. *Historical Collections of Ohio.* Cincinnati: Derby, Bradley, and Co., 1847.

_____. *Historical Collections of Ohio in Two Volumes.* Cincinnati: C.J. Krehbiel, 1888.

Hutslar, Donald A. *The Architecture of Migration.* Athens: Ohio University Press, 1986.

Iman, C.E. *The Heritage of Our Home Town* (Crestline). Crestline: Crestline Public Schools, 1967.

Jackson, Donald (ed.). *The Diaries of George Washington, Vol. II, 1766-70.* Charlottesville: University Press of Virginia, 1976.

Jordan, Philip D. *The National Road.* Indianapolis: Bobbs-Merill, 1948.

Journal-Gazette. p. 10, January 13, 1985.

Kinder, George D. *History of Putnam County, Ohio.* Indianapolis: B.F. Bowen & Co., 1915.

Knepper, George W. *An Ohio Portrait.* Columbus: Ohio Historical Society, 1976.

_____. *Ohio and Its People.* Kent: Kent State University Press, 1989.

Lafferty, Michael B. (ed.) *Ohio's Natural Heritage.* Columbus: The Ohio Academy of Science, 1979.

Lang, W. *History of Seneca County.* Springfield, Ohio: Transcript Printing, 1880.

Large, Moina. *A History of Ashtabula County.*

Lochary, Clara. *Pomeroy.* (article). (1979).

Louisville, Ohio Sesquicentennial 1834-1984 Souvenir Pictorial. (1984).

Marks, Geoffrey and William Beatty. *Epidemics.* New York: Charles Scribner's Sons, 1976.

Martzolff, Clement L. *History of Perry County, Ohio.* New Lexington, Ohio: Ward & Weiland, 1902.

Martin, William T. *History of Franklin County.* Columbus: Follett, Foster, & Co., 1858.

McCord, William B. (ed.) *History of Columbiana County, Ohio and Representative Citizens.* Chicago: Biographical Publishing, 1905.

McMurray, William (ed.). *The History of Auglaize County, Ohio.* Indianapolis: Historical Publishing, 1923.

Mercer County, Ohio History. 1978.

Moritz, Charles (ed.) *Current Biography Yearbook 1974.* New York: H.W. Wilson, 1974.

National Cyclopedia of American Biography. New York: James T. White, 1898.

Newark *Advocate.* Sept. 30, 1984 and July 2, 1988.

Ninety Degrees South: The Story of the American South Pole Conquest. New York: G.P. Putnam's Sons.

North Olmsted Community Day Brochure. 1947.

North Olmsted *Westlife.* March 4, 1981. _____. July 16, 1969.

North Olmsted Municipal Bus Line 1931-1981. (Olmsted Historical Society).

Our Bicentennial Salute to Liberty Township and Ohio City. 1976.

Our Yesterdays. vol II. Quaker City, Ohio: Home Towner Printing, 1975.

Overfield Tavern brochure. Troy Historical Society.

Perrysburg *Messenger.* March 1939.

Porter, Tana Mosier. *Toledo Profile: A Sesquicentennial History.* Toledo, Ohio: Toledo Sesquicentennial Commission, 1987.

Putnam County Heritage Newsletter No. 23. Kalida, Ohio: Putnam County Historical Society, 1985.

Putnam County Pioneer Association Centennial History, 1873-1973. Columbus Grove, Ohio: Heffner Printing, 1973.

Quarterly Bulletin "The Window Glass Industry of Utica, Ohio". Cincinnati: Historical and Philosophical Society of Ohio, July 1954.

Raimo, John W. (ed.) *Biographical Directory of the Governors of the United States 1978-1983.* Westport, CT: Meckler, 1985.

Riker, Ben. *Pony Wagon Town.* Indianapolis: Bobbs-Merrill, 1948.

Roberts, Robert B. *Encyclopedia of Historic Forts: The Military, Pioneer, and Trading Posts of the United States.* New York: Macmillan, 1988.

Rockford *Sesquicentennial Booklet.* Rockford: 1970.

Roseboom, Eugene Holloway and Francis Weisenberger. *A History of Ohio.* New York: Prentice-Hall, 1934.

Rusler, William (ed.) *A Standard History of Allen County, Ohio.* vol. I of 2, 1921.

Schneider, Norris F. *Y Bridge City.* World Publishing Co., 1950.

Shankle, George Earlie. *State Names, Flags, Seals, Songs, Birds, Flowers and Other Symbols.* New York: H.W. Wilson, 1941.

Sherr, Lynn and Jurate Kazickas. *The American Women's Gazetteer.* New York: Bantam, 1976.

Story of the Glorious Past One-Hundred Years. Ironton Centennial Commission, 1949.

Sword, Elmer B. *Scioto County Photo History.* Portsmouth, Ohio: Knauff Graphics for Portsmouth Area Community Exhibits, 1987.

Tartikow, Jackson, M.D. and John H. Vorperian. *Foodborne and Waterborne Diseases.* Westport, Ct.: AVI Publishing, 1981.

These Things Stay By You (Clyde Sesquicentennial 1816-1966). Whirlpool Corporation.

Thompson, Carl N. *Historical Collections of Brown County, Ohio.* 1969.

Thornton, Francis Beauchesne. *Catholic Shrines in the United States and Canada.* New York: Wilfred Funk, 1954.

Trapshooting Hall of Fame brochure. Vandalia, Ohio: The American Trapshooting Association.

Traylor, Jeff and Nadean. *Life in the Slow Lane: Fifty Backroad Tours of Ohio.* Columbus: Backroad Chronicles, 1989.

Tullis, John. *Overfield Tavern* (collection of articles from Troy *Times* 1868). The Historical Society of Troy.

Van Gundy, Paul. *Stories of the Fountain City 1840-1900.* Bryan: Bryan Area Foundation.

Vastine, Roy E. *Scioto, A County History.* Portsmouth, Ohio: Knauff Graphics, 1986.

Wagnalls Memorial Scholarship Fund (brochure). Lithopolis, Ohio: Wagnalls Memorial.

Wagnalls Memorial (brochure). Lithopolis, Ohio: Wagnalls Memorial.

Washington C.H. *Record-Herald.* p. 18C September 18, 1976.

Wellsville Union 1885.

What's What in Shelby, Ohio. Shelby, Ohio: Ohio Steel Tube, 1921.

Williams County, Ohio vol.II. Williams County Historical Society, 1978.

Wilkinson, Raymond. *The Story of Early Shelby.* Miamisburg, Ohio: Miamisburg News, 1962.

Wittke, Carl (ed.) *The History of the State of Ohio in Six Volumes.* Columbus: The Ohio State Archaeological and Historical Society, 1941.

World Almanac 1990. New York: Pharos, 1990.

Yesterday and Today in Guernsey County, Ohio. Guernsey County Genealogical Society, 1979.

Index

Index of cities, counties, and proper names found on Ohio historic corporate limit markers.